ALI
THE IMMORTAL

Published by:
Bridge of Intersection
P.O.Box 4275
West Hills, CA 91308-4275
USA

www.bridgeofintersection.org

Website: www.alitheimmortalbook.com

ISBN-13:978-0-9985631-1-4
ISBN-10:0-9985631-1-0

Author's note: The Scripture verses and passages in this book were not taken from any one version or translation of the Bible. Unless otherwise noted, combined portions of various translations were used to more accurately portray or expand on the intended meaning. All biblical quotations, however, were taken from recognized, authentic, and published Bible translations.

The Spirit of the Lord is upon me, because the He has anointed me to proclaim good new̱ ᴄo the poor. He has sent me to heal the brokenhearted, to proclaim freedom for the captives and the opening of the prison to those who are bound, to proclaim the year of the Lord's favor and the day of vengeance of our God, to comfort all who mourn, and provide for those who grieve in Zion — to give them a crown of beauty instead of ashes, the oil of joy instead of mourning, and a garment of praise instead of a spirit of despair. They will be called trees of righteousness, a planting of the Lord that He may be glorified.

Isaiah 61:1-3

Table of Contents

A Warrior for Islam

I took my life into my own hands at the age of 15. It weighed as heavy as an AK-47[1]. Once you had an AK-47, the teachers stopped dealing harshly with you. In fact, they stopped dealing with you entirely. On the other hand, I learned quickly that a machine gun and the school simply interfered with one another. I mastered the disassembly and assembly of the AK-47 with impressive swiftness and even learned how to perform the same blindfolded. I challenged my peersin shooting competitions, but no one could match me. The exhilaration of handling this powerful weapon made school feel like a waste of my time. I dropped out, eager to volunteer in the revolutionary Islamic militia. I felt ready. Not that it was important – as long as you were physically fit to carry a machine gun, you were given one. The mosques were full of weapons. We had transported so many of them there from the military warehouses.

In particular, my neighborhood was full of warehouses stocked with weapons. It was the suburb of the Afsarie (the Officers' suburb) where enormous military units of both the air and the ground forces were a common sight. It seemed then that it was not very long ago when my friends and I would run through the streets, hurriedly climbing trees to get a good look at the soldiers marching by. In their beautiful uniforms, and with their polished black weapons, they carried out the commands of the officers.

We all dreamed of becoming soldiers one day, and that day came much quicker than we had anticipated. We, the neighborhoodlads, were now the ones walking around in the plaza in our uniforms. We went to the warehouses along with the older guys to help them carry the guns outside and felt so proud. How nice it was to suddenly feel like a grown-

---

[1] AK-47 a.k.aKalashnikov is a Russian Assault Rifle

up! Those of us raised in this particular part of Tehran felt superior to our peers from the other parts of the city. Situated in the outskirts, on a road that provided an easy escape into the mountains, this suburbanarea had become saturated with violent gang activity. The pulse of the Islamic Revolution[2] ran through my veins. Nothing could hold my interest more than an AK-47. Learning to fire an Uzi, the automatic Israeli sub-machine gun, was another thing that brought me great satisfaction. Not to mention the Iranian G3, an automatic rifle made after an English patent. My weapon of choice, however, remained the Kalashnikov – the weapon that transformed me into a grown up.

As kids, my friends and I would jump up and down to count the passing cars on the street. At that time, my friends and I were pulling over any cars that appeared suspicious to us. We pointed our guns at the people inside and checked their papers and their trunks. It was required because during those first few months of the Revolution, all kinds of criminals had begun to appear – burglars, alcohol smugglers, drug dealers, you name it. As my brother Daud used to say, many are the enemies of Revolution. He was always deeply convinced that, despite everything, the Revolution would eventually persevere. He spent his time eagerly reading the works of Marx, Engels, Lenin, and Stalin. To an extent, Daud's belief turned out to be correct. The Revolution was successful, but it was not a proletarian one, as he had hoped. Instead, soon after the Revolution drove out the Shah, it became clear that it was a Revolution in the name of Islam. Nonetheless, this didn't discourage Daud as he continued to read on diligently. He believed that the proletarian Revolution was inevitable, and that it was only a matter of time. Daud felt that the new Islamic authority was an enemy of the proletarian Revolution.

I didn't understand why Daud wanted another Revolution after we had just had one, but I didn't care enough to give this stance of his any thought. It was all too complicatedto my restless young mind any-

---

[2] The Islamic Revolution a.k.a. the Iranian Revolution or the 1979 Revolution.

way! After all, I had dropped out of school to get away from the whole 'thinking' business. None of it made sense to me and I didn't have to think when I had a Kalashnikov in my hands.

Everything was twisted and bent regardless of what I thought. In the beginning, everyone had participated in the Revolution against the Shah, and everyone was pleased when he was forced to flee the country. Yet, these very same people had different expectations for the time that was to follow. Many republicans wanted a secular republic, while others wanted a socialistic one; a third group wanted an Islamic republic, whereas a fourth group wanted an Islamic one, albeit in a different way. Those who had fought as allies against the Shah not very long ago suddenly became fierce enemies.

The most dangerous enemies of the new order established under Ayatollah Khomeini were the Mojahedins; and this came as no surprise because they were equipped with the best weaponry. What I didn't understand was that both Khomeini and the Mojahedins claimed that they were fighting for the one true faith in the name of Allah. Having already become an adult man, I decided that I already knew as much as I needed to know. I found no use in complicating life when I was getting by just fine. Most important to me was that the new order in Iran was no longer the one dictated by Shah Reza Pahlavi and his clergy, but that of Ayatollah Khomeini and his clergy. "Neither with the East, nor with the West – we are an Islamic Republic!" opined Khomeini, and the people liked that. From that moment onwards, we Iranians, the one-true-faith Muslims, were going to handle our business ourselves and on our own terms. We needed neither the Americans nor the Russians. We were taking our fate into our own hands. All we needed to do then was to pass the Islamic laws under the purview of the Iranian legal system, and Allah would take supreme reign over Iran. Of course, Iran, under the Ayatollahs belonged to Allah, not Marx and not Lenin. It made some sense, although Daud didn't want to hear that.

Marx vs. Allah

Communist ideas rose in popularity during the Shah's reign.Many young Iranians were carried away by them, including my brother Daud, who was fired up in favor of the class struggle movement. In fact, a sports club called *Kaveh the Blacksmith*, named after one of the heroes of the resistance movement, was set up where free style wrestling could be practiced. The boys wore uniforms, and there was even a flag that depicted a scruffy man with huge arms and a hammer in one hand. The new clubs were, however, only a cover for a platform where lectures about the class struggle would be delivered, aimed at converting the young. There were similar clubs in other parts of the country as well, and the Shah's secret service was well aware of the intentions of those clubs. Communists and Mojahedins were the biggest enemies of the monarchy.

Possessing communist literature was dangerous in itself, and our basement was brimming with it. The basement was Daud's secret reading room where he would bring books after books penned by his idols, Marx, Engels, and Lenin. Hidden in that tiny basement, he would read for hours, underlining certain passages, and daydreaming of how wonderful life would be when communism would finally take over. This persisted until a family friend came over one day to warn my father that the Shah's secret police was on the move and was likely to start arresting anyone found to be affiliated with the sports clubs. This was indeed a terrifying piece of information because political opponents of the regime were gruesomely persecuted by the all-powerful secret police, the SAVAK, generating panic and fear throughout the country. An infinite number of stories began being circulated, full of blood-curdling details about the heinousabuse that arrestees endured and the dreadful methods of torture. During the Shah's reign, there was no room for mercy for communists – a tradition that was continued under the Ayatollahs' rule as well.

When my father heard the news, he called Daud and immediately uprooted the library in our basement. Our family secretly packed away all the books into cardboard boxes, and under the cover of darkness, we dumped them into a nearby river that very night. My brother moved in with some relatives and stayed there for some time before returning home. When the danger had diffused, he never asked about his basement library books again, though he mourned them quietly. He kept his disappointment to himself, as he understood he had put our entire family in danger.

By a good twist of fate, it was almost the beginning of a new school year, and the time had come for Daud to depart for his boarding house at the Tehran University. There, he could share his ideas with other like-minded students without directly threatening his relatives' safety.

It was clear that the majority of the people were inspired not by the communist ideas but by the *Sharia Law*. Everybody was talking about the Islamic Revolution with Ruhollah Khomeini as the leader of this brewing rebellion. Right after his return following the Shah's escape, Khomeini gained power, persecuting the supporters of all other political parties and ideologies. He purged the disloyal officers from high military ranks. The generals, who remained faithful to their oath under the Shah were sentenced to death and executed. Only military officers who were completely devoted to Ayatollah were appointed. The Islamic Revolutionary Guards, more formally known as the *Sepah-e Pasdaran-e Enqelab-e Eslami*, or *The Army of the Guardians of the Islamic Revolution*, was put in force. Among the people, it became known as the Pasdaran. The Pasdaranbegan to cement their dominionthroughout the country. Everybody was supposed to return their firearms to the military storehouses, but most mosques still stashed arms. Moreover, additional quantities of weapons were transported towards mosques because it was the mosques themselves that were now taking charge. Combat troops that controlled the streets were positioned at the headquarters in the mosques. With all this happening, I could not even bear the thought of attending school. In my mind, it was simply out of the question. The Revolution, to me, was infinitely more interesting than going to class. School had always been boring, even before the Revolution began, let alone now.

My mother's hopeless hopes

My mother sensed what was going on and she had no intentions of letting me give up on my education. My poor mother could always sense when something was wrong, the way mothers always can. She convinced my father to send me off to my brother Daud to board with him and to study at the nearby school under his care. What logic led my parents to believe that this would somehow hold me back was a mystery to me. However, this move devised by my parentssuited my unacademic pursuits quite well. Most likely, my mother hoped that the academic environment would have a positive impact on me and would somehow stir up within me a desire for learning. My poor mother's hopeless hopes! At that particular time, Tehran University had become a place driven by vigorous activities pertaining to the Revolution. It had turned into a battlefield peppered by political debates, secret meetings, and public demonstrations. Students were drunk on their newly acquired freedom of speech. They were not aware, however, that this new-found freedom would be short-lived. Every day, they protested, argued, and fought. It wasn't uncommon to hear shootings in the streets surrounding the university. Some students, the ones who attacked the American Embassy and arrested some of the diplomats, were regarded as heroes, whereasothers hoped for their own opportunity for heroism. One of them was my own brother. In the name of the proletarian revolution, he made me give a fake residential address to my new school. All letters regarding my absences were delivered there, andthat is how we protected our parents from trouble. Having a clear conscience following that arrangement, I could help Daud in the activities of his political party. We distributed leaflets and posted posters at night. There was no time to lose!It seemed to us that the bright future could not wait any longer. During our days off, Thursdays and Fridays, my brother took me on mountain hikes arranged by the communist group comprised by older students. We lit a fire, listened to political lectures, and sang songs about revolution and freedom. My best friends,Shiravan and Hassan, were always there with me. The three of us were inseparable when it came to troublemakingand always driven by the same mischievous ideas. We wreaked disaster for anyone around us. The more dangerous a deed seemed, the more we wanted to do it. That's what had attracted us to the communist rebellion to begin with. It had been forbidden during the Shah's rule, and it was forbidden even then.

But our motives were all different. I hung around Daud constantly because I was bored. I would not have been doing it if it were not for him. To me, the speeches and slogans were cheesy and always sounded far too utopianto be true. I found their philosophies unrealistic and ungrounded. All that wasn't for me, but I enjoyed the thrill and didn't have anything better to do. Hassan was completely consumed by the idea of being a part of something big,something that would eventually rule all of Iran, and maybe, even the world in the future. He was eager for the Communist Party to come into power in Iran and to spread into the region so that he could invest himself into what he believed an honorable cause. Unlike Hassan or myself, Shiravan was a true follower of Marx, Engels, and Lenin. He was a fanatic and a dreamer, completely possessed with the spirit of the communism. The future, however, did not turn out how he had hoped it would. Friction developed within our inseparable trio. Shiravan spoke openly against the new rule of Khomeini. Hassan, on the other hand, was in opposition. Hassan was convinced that as long as the battle was to put power into the hands of the people, it counted as a revolution. He insisted that, Communist or Islamic, the revolution would bring down tyranny, and the people would be the ones in power at the end. As for me, I was irritated by their bickering. I hated the thought that such a stupid issue could cause a fissions in our friendship. How could we fight over some dumb political matter? Were we not friends? Nonetheless, our friendship was coming to an end. Not too long after, Hassan told us that he had joined the Pasdaran. In addition to a gun and a uniform, he was promised a motorcycle on the condition that he would stop meeting with the communists. He told us that the communists and the followers of Islam were enemies, and before long, communists would be condemned for their faulty ideologies and actions. Shiravan became enraged at this and proceeded to fight him. I could hardly wring the two apart, yelling "What's going on, what's happening!" When they finally let go of each other, Hassan took off, and then there were just two, Shiravan and I. For what it is worth, I would have chosen him anyway,if I indeed had to make a choice. I liked him because he was the craziest among the three of us. He stood his ground and spoke assertively about Lenin and against Khomeini. He was always in the first rows of the communist meetings and demonstrations. He didn't care about anything; he was ready to die for the cause. Although, I doubt whether at that time, he had any idea what dying for a cause entailed. Shiravan had always been a dreamer, unlike the practical Hassan. Hassan eventually came to see me one day,riding his Honda 125, a motorcycle given to the Pasdaran guardians. He pulled over, showing off his new uniform and said, "Stop hanging out with the communists, and tell Shiravan as well. It is dangerous; I am not warning you anymore." "Why are you warning us even now?" I retorted, picking on him. I was upset that he had ruined our magnificent trio. "Because no matter what you think, I am your friend; and if tomorrow I saw you on the streets while I am with the other guardians, I would have to tell them that you are communists, and they would have to arrest you." Shortly after, the enemies of the Islamic Revolution began to get arrested and persecuted. Not surprisingly, communists were the first on the list. My brother had the prudence to safeguard himself, and very quickly, he cut himself off from all activities that could be deemed illicit. I followed suit of course, and without any complaints, I stopped working for the communist resistance. Despite all the warnings, Shiravan remained faithful to his cause – a lost cause, a *causa perduta*. If a single communist was left in Iran, it would be Shiravan. In a million years, I could not have imagined that Shiravan would ever give up, or that we might go separate ways. But he had to leave one day, and I never saw him again. Later I heard that he was arrested and hung after being heinously tortured. I was mortified and cried my eyes out. I loved him so dearly despite his ideology,as if he were my own brother.

Communist ideas could never take a deep hold over me. Communism actually irritated me with its insistence upon atheism. If I had to choose between communism and Islam, I would choose the latter. Within my heart,I searched for a higher authority and Darwinism didn't do it for me. I liked Islam because it gave me a God to believe in. This was important to me. There were quite a few good things about the Islamic Revolution. All universities were shut down because a lot of support was being garnered for the political opposition from the students. Daud was very disappointed but I didn't care. With great pleasure, I went back to my native neighborhood and joined the volunteer troops of the newly formed Islamic militia called Sazman-e Basij-e Mostaz'afin(or *The Organization for Mobilization of the Oppressed*). We were under the rule of the Pasdaran Islamic Revolutionary Guard, which directly fell under Khomeini's reign. The militia here had no say. Very little communication existed between the local militia and the army. Under the instruction of thePasdaran, which now occupied the mosque of every neighbor-hood, I began to get to know my new best friend, an AK-47.

What could my parents possibly say when every boy was doing the same thing at that time? My parents were always busy, work-ing hard from sunrise to sunset. They hardly had time to get into any of my business. My father, Ibrahim, left for work before the sun showed itself over the horizon and returned home long after dark. With six children to feed –three boys and three girls, my father didn't have time to catch a break. I remember him as a good man, dedicated to his wife and children, always in deep thought, tired and concerned. He would come home in the evening, and we would stand up to greet him with great respect. He withheld himself from us. Yet I do remember his fatherly embrace, warm, protective, and safe. His way of showing love for the family was through working hard. Every minute of every day, it was his way of saying, "I am do-ing all I can do, I care about you, I love you." No matter how a young Iranian had envisioned his life, once he had a family, he had to com-mit to it entirely.

To my biggest surprise, I discovered that the youth of my father had been quite rambunctious. I discovered this by chance when I was a grown man visiting his home town,Zandgan. A big burg situ-ated in the north-west, close to the border of Turkey, Zandgan was well-known for its skillful craftsmen of knives and daggers. This area was populated mainly by people from Azerbaijan, further con-tributing to its dissimilar identity and atmosphere. Every visitor was fascinated by Zandgan; let alone a curious boy visiting his fa-ther's hometown. Father never talked about his childhood or youth, he had always been private and contained. It was as if that part of his life had been lived by somebody else, a completely different per-son who had nothing in common with my father. That's why I was amused with his old friends' stories about the mischief they had gotten into together. My father even seemed to have been the leader of the whole bunch! "You remember what Ibrahim did then... How can I forget? And do you remember when Ibrahim ..." I could not believe my ears! My father had been a real prankster! Back home in Tehran, I picked a suitable moment, or at least I thought so, and I asked him about it all. He just looked at me sternly, gave a little smirk, and mumbled, "Don't listen to those blokes; they are making up stories." Even though it was the end of that conversation, not only did it confirm that all those stories had been true; but in addition, my imagination ran wild and my father won even more respect from me.

My mother,Mahbube, was an altogether different story: a humble and modest woman and a fervent Islam follower, she hosted religious meetings for women from the block twice a month at home. They would get together and talk, read the Quran, meditate over a certain *surah*, explaining different verses to one another. Of course, the conversations were not limited to religion only. They ranged from recipes to looking after children. The most important topic was disciplining the latter. That was my mother's expertise. She was the one who used to scold me the most, although there wasn't much time for discipline anymore. Times were different. Our country was in danger; the enemies of the Revolution kept sprouting in every corner. The foes could be found both within Iran and past its borders. Iraq, under the rule of Saddam Hussein, was our biggest concern. It was Hussein who finally decided to invade Iran.

Saddam and the horrid aggressors

The invasion happened overnight! Loud and violent! We, as a country, had done nothing to provoke it. Suddenly, the whole country was under fire. Previously, Iran was divided and torn by internal conflict, collisions of opposing political doctrines, and religious beliefs, but now, it was completely united against one external enemy, Iraq. There were no more divisions regarding the supreme authority of our country. Ayatollah Khomeini and all Iranians became united. It became clear that the real enemies of Iran and the Islamic Revolution were the threatening Iraqi Sunnis. This was not their first aggressive attack, neither was it their first daunting scheme. Iraq was attacking then because they believed that Iran was weak enough at that point to be overtaken. Sunnis were capable of such atrocities, and that Iranians were well aware of. History is full of devastating attacks by the Iraqi Sunnis, andworst of all, these people are unforgivable liars! Sunnis reckoned that they were the one –the true believers, whereas, we knew that we, the Muslim Shiites, were the true followers of the one true faith! Sunnis had twisted the meaning of one true faith in Allah and changed the inheritance left by the prophet – something we could never forget or forgive. They had killed Mohammed's son-in-law, Ali, and the first Imam who was to be the next leader of Islam. They even had the audacity to declare that Imam Ali was the illegal fourth *caliph*. Moreover, they accused Ali of killing the third *caliph*, Omar, in order to take his place;however, every person with common sense knew the truth. Ali was the true successor of Prophet Mohammed. It was actually the prophet himself who had proclaimed his son-in-law, Ali, the husband of his daughter, Fatimah, as his successor. Ali had been the first person to accept Islam; Omar was simply the successor of the tyrant, Abu Bakr, who had unlawfully tried to steal Ali's right to inherit his father-in-law's kingdom. All of this was crystal clear to us – the Shiites, the real fundamental believers. There was no doubt about it.

We were not open to settling! Sunnis usurpers had killed not only Ali but also his son, Hussein, who had rejected their requests to appoint their leader,Yazid I as the *caliph*. In addition to this blasphemy, they had killed him on the tenth day of *Ashura*, the month of *Muharram*, a month declared holy by the prophet himself. Heresy at its finest! Hussein and 72 of his followers murdered – it happened around 1,400 years ago, in a place close to Karbala, not that it actually mattered when it had happened. Since then, and to this very day, to us, the Shiites, Yazid I was a violent tyrant, an enemy of the one true faith, and his followers were just like him. Those events set the tradition of mourning over Hussein Ibn Ali, the son of Ali and the grandson of Prophet Mohammed. Ali and Hussein started this tradition of martyrdom that became very well-honored across Iran – to the extent that it has become a great part of our culture. *Behesht-e Zahra* (the *Paradise of Zahra*) is the biggest memorial in our tradition – our most prominent political and spiritual leaders and the bodies of all battle martyrs have been buried there.

The Iraqi Sunnis and their despised leader, Saddam Hussein – these unworthy and pathetic followers of liars and usurpers – were our enemy! Ayatollah Khomeini's most logical step was to declare this defensive war a holy war. War in the name of Iran! War in the name of Allah and the one true faith! War to protect the honor of the motherland! Faith and patriotism together, hand in hand! To Allah and Iran! It was well worth volunteering in the army, to give one's own life and become a martyr for this cause!

Inbetween army and love

Before turning 18, I joined the army as a volunteer, quite impatient to be trained for the battlefield so that I could fight the aggressors. I chose the air force unit located in our neighborhood. I was looking to enter the army in a couple of weeks. All preparation was going fine until Afsaneh came into the scene – a girl with dark blonde hair, green eyes, and the most charming smile in the world. A gorgeous and stunning girl! The time came for me to leave my country was counting on me. My mind was set on one path, my heart on another... It was a painful decision for me to make! Even before I was enlisted, I found myself contemplating how I could manage to leave more often to spend time with Afsaneh, just to look at one another and talk. I had never been the one for small talk,action is my strength. For a long time in our relationship, we did not touch each other. This was the norm in Iran. It was her eyes I looked into day and night. There was nothing strong enough to hold me inside the barracks. It was good that the barrack premises was huge, with so many departments and soldiers that my absence was hardly noticed. I made a deal with a sergeant that I would bring him hashish and opium whenever I was out, which worked very well for the both of us. However, I attended shooting practices regularly. After all, this was exactly what a soldier of Islam needed – to be able to aim and shoot and kill the enemy and not just know how to march. I found great pleasure in shooting, and I was good at it! Thanks to this, I was allowed a few days of leave. Either way, I had already arranged my little escapades to see Afsaneh myself, so it wasn't the biggest deal... I was also offered the privilege of being able to choose the base where I would continue observing my service after the first three months of preparation. Without a doubt, I wanted to remain in this unit, in my own neighborhood, close to home where I had secured myself the freedom to come and go, allowing me to see my Afsaneh. This was the deciding factor. All was going well, but when the time for the assignments came, my plans got screwed. The commander of the unit somehow found out that I had been allowed to come and go as I pleased through the preparation time, and he forbade me to leave the unit. His decision didn't bother me because assignment day was nearing, and I was going to exercise my right to choose this unit. I was to stay there until the end of my military service. Then, of course, I was going, as a volunteer, to join the soldiers at the battlefield!

At last, this long-awaited ritual began. Those who were excellent shooters were lined up on one side, and each stated out loud the unit where they wanted to serve. After being enrolled, they moved over to the other side. My turn came. Right before I opened my mouth, the officer cut me off, "You wait here. Whatever place is left after everyone is finished, that's where you are going." I was dumbstruck. Two other recruits stood there with me, watching, as our opportunities dwindled one by one right before our eyes. Finally, two units were left to choose from. Of course, both were the worst choices. The first one was the air force base close to the border of Pakistan; the second one, a very strict military headquarter in Tehran where soldiers were outnumbered by generals and officers. Notorious for its fierce discipline, order, and structure, it was the most terrifying place for a man with a character like mine. Soldiers kept watch every other day, losing their minds in doing so. No leaves. Strict order. I cringed at the thought of being sent there. I would have given anything to avoid it. It was in the middle of our town, which was the only good thing about it;however, thiswould make me feel even worse – just watching the people on the outside while being stuck inside, stripped of all my freedom. The air force base close to the border of Pakistan did not look so bad anymore. It was better to be in a remote area temporarily with hopes of being transferred than entering a prison and not being allowed to leave until the end of my service. If somebody had bothered asking me, I knew which one I was going to choose, but nobody did. The commander pointed at me and announced in front of everyone, "You are going to the headquarter to learn discipline." Right there, he became a part of the club of all those people in my life who unsuccessfully tried to teach me discipline. He too, would fail, but it didn't matter then. I was disappointed to the point of despair. I had honestly earned the right to choose, and I couldn't believe that it was taken away from me. Deep down, I knew the commander had a point; nevertheless, I was heartbroken. All my dreams, plans, and hopes were wiped out by the words of this hideous creature. I packed that night, and was noteven allowed to go out to tell Afsaneh goodbye. I lay in bed that evening and could not fall asleep. My whole childhood flashed before me. Playing marbles, Afsaneh, my friends… Afsaneh, stealing motorcycles, Afsaneh, Afsaneh… It was a very long night. The next day, early in the morning, I was on my way to this horrible place –my prison for the next twenty-one months. So close, yet so far away from my favorite neighborhood,Afsarie, and from my beloved,Afsaneh... I had told her that I would be staying locally for sure, and that even if I was not in our neighborhood, I would definitely be somewhere in Tehran. This is exactly what happened, but it was nothing like I had foreseen... I could picture her bright smile, her graceful dark green eyes, smiling whenever she saw me, Afsaneh – the most beautiful girl in the world. I was hurt and angry. Still, I knew I would make it. I had no idea how, but I knew I was going to make it. Then, for the first time, I felt a strong drive fueling me toconceive a plan, somehow... I could feel it throbbing within my bones. That is exactly what I repeated to myself as I stood there, while the heavy gates of this nightmare were being drawn open to engulf me: "I will make it; I will find a way." The reputation of the place was well-deserved. There was no space for messing around once inside, let alone outside. I was on watch every day. Every single day! Cleaning my weapon, getting ready for watch, checking my weapon, shift change; a 24-hour watch was followed by a 24-hour rest. Then it began all over again. First shift, second shift, third shift... The third shift was the worst. Time went by unbearably slowly. Anyone on such a watch schedule knows just how much rest it is possible to get during the 24-hour break. Hardly any! I was always so wound up from keeping watch for so long that I couldn't get my mind to be still when I was off it. On top of everything, I had to study theory. Is this what I had run away from school for?! The seams of day and night got knit closely together. I became disoriented, and it was impossible to get enough sleep. During the long hours of night watch, my thoughts wandered... during my breaks, as I would drift in and out of sleep, entertaining various options in my head, my thoughts wandered. Two months had passed. I was still thinking and thinking. It would be a thousand times better on the front lines. Once there, they got a 15-day leave after every 45 days on the battlefield. They could at least go home to spend time with their loved ones, to see their beloved girls, to feel free. There in that unit, it was worse than prison... or at least that's what I thought at the time.

Too much thinking was not good

It was around this time that my mind began to reach its overload limit. Exhausted with my thoughts, I decided that too much thinking was only a waste of my time. Action was needed, and the more I thought, the bigger my schemes became. From the very beginning, I knew that my only hope was to escape...and that's why, I finally did it.

I went back home to the surprise of my family, and openly told them of my escape strategy as well as about me having no intentions of going back. What had been done was done. They didn't make any comments, but I knew my mother well – she was not going to give up. I knew it was just a matter of time before she would come up with something, and she would use my uncle as an ally. I was positive about that. My uncle was a massive, sinewy, grumpy man, with bushy eyebrows and huge hands, the weight of which I had felt on many occasions. I loved him like a father and was more afraid of him than my own father. I knew something would be said or done about my escape, but whatever it was, I knew it would come whether I wasted time thinking about it or not. Meanwhile, I started working as a building all-rounder on construction sites around Tehran. I came across this really good welder who happened to be a good man as well, and I started helping him. He used to tell me, "You don't learn a skill, you steal it." What he meant was that it was very important to watch carefully and take heed of the details of how things were done. It wasn't difficult for me, not at all. Eventually I started working with a welding machine, became a pro at welding, and worked from sunup to sundown. Afsaneh constantly occupied my mind. We would meet, talk, and gaze at one another, because it was forbidden to show any public displays of affection under the new authority. One time, we touched each other's hands, as if it were by accident. Love can drive you absolutely insane! Her friends, who always accompanied her like chaperons during those dates, became quite startled. So we did not do it again for a very long time. Afsaneh was a brave girl. Once, she came to see me, wearing Kurdish folk clothes – those clothes were startling and beautiful on their own. What could I say... When I saw her dressed in those clothes, she looked like a doll! I was speechless. I lost my train of thought, and I couldn't budge, nor think of a single thing to say to her. She could tell I was awestruck, and she played on it a bit. She felt awkward, but good. Good more than awkward. Afsaneh was stunning, especially in those clothes that suited her so well – she looked like a beauty straight from a fairy tale. In our language, every name has a meaning. In Farsi, Afsaneh means a *fairy tale*, a beautiful fairy tale. Her parents couldn't have picked a better name for a girl who seemed to have walked right out of one. Oh, I wanted to marry her so badly! I did! But it was her parents' say before mine, and as I had predicted, they demanded that I return to the army and finish my business there first. They would not allow me to marry her otherwise. No real man escaped from the army! My parents agreed. I knew they were right, but it did not suit me at all. I didn't want to, and I wouldn't go back to that prison. Months passed by while I continued to work on construction sites during the day, after which I faced the tension at home, and, finally, in the evenings, I had my most precious moments with my beautiful fairy tale. It was a childish, pure love. At last, my parents won with the support of my uncle, who appeared on the scene at the right moment. My mother told me, "Go finish the army. Anyway, that's what you have to do!" My poor mother, her hope to discipline me never ceased. She hoped the army would do that job. She was right about one thing, however – I did have to finish the army, because otherwise it was going to be very difficult for me to find a job, or even to get married. As for me, I was so determined to marry Afsaneh that I eventually returned. I could not oppose my parents, no matter how stubborn I wanted to act. I had always honored their authority. Years later, my mother said to me, "I will always regret that your father and I put forth hindrances, and did not allow you to marry Afsaneh. If we had allowed you then, now you wouldn't be here stuck." The truth was, my mother did not appreciate the fact that Afsaneh and I had met on the street, just like that. During those times, one could not simply meet a girl on the street and decide to marry her, no matter how beautiful she was. It wasn't the way. I did everything possible for Afsaneh. I surrendered to my parents' command to return to that prison-like army unit,the one I had escaped from earlier. My peers were done with their time six months later. My service... I was not even half way through. Once again, the torture began!Being on watch every day, going crazy.Unbearable routines that werecompletely despairing. I had to figure a way out. I had no idea what, but I would figure it out. Then, a few months later my right leg started to swell. Upon looking closely, one could see varicose veins appearing. At last, there was some hope! I went for a check-up with the doctor who was already familiar with my case and my troubles from my previous visits to him. Needless to say, I didn't go empty-handed. The doctor did a thorough exam and was obviously concerned about the condition of my leg. In his conclusion, he stated that I was not to continue keeping watch, as the long hours of standing would lead to unpredictable complications with a high possibility of the need of a surgical intervention. The commanders had to take some adequate actions, and so, they pulled me out of the watch crew. They gave me various assignments outside of the headquarter, such as driving or delivery. I could see Afsaneh and the boys from the neighborhood. I didn't realize how quickly the time passed this time around.

Ready to sacrifice

Every time I was out in the town, I noticed more and more veterans with missing limbs, walking around, if they could, supporting their weight on crutches. The war was taking legs, arms, and life from some while delivering millions into the pockets of others.

In the neighborhoods, more and more of these fixtures, called hejleh, began to appear,elaborately decorated in the shape of the Shah's crown. Photos of all the martyrs were displayed on these structures, illuminated brightly by electrical lights. These crowns of sorrow were roughly seven-feet high, about a yard wide at the base, and two-feet wide at the top. They symbolized a place for public worship of the shahids who had died in service to Allah and our motherland. Before the war, they had been a very rare sight. There used to be one for a few neighborhoods. After the war began, one could see them in various places around Tehran, and as time went by, their numbers grew. Within a few years, there was a hejleh on every street. Then, there were two crowns of death on every street, with photos of the martyrs plastered across– the Iranian men who had died for the one true faith. Then, more photos, more dead people in every neighborhood, and then, on every street. The braver the citizens who lived there, the braver the sons they had raised for Allah and the one true faith.

Eventually, they could not continue to add more crowns, and every month, the photos of heroes began to change. More and more young men died and were turned into shahids – thus requiring more honor from the public.

Soon, they started changing the photos every week. Meanwhile, crippled men with no legs and arms became a very common sight on the streets of Tehran.

All of this impacted the people greatly. Everything around us and inside of us talked of the duty one had toward his motherland and faith. The whole atmosphere was soaked with the smell of war, blood, death, and sacrifice. It was considered holy duty to defend the motherland, horridly attacked by infidels. Our strong belief that Iran was right and needed to be defended, while Iraq was wrong and needed to be punished gave us great vantage. It did not matter that Saddam overpowered us with weapons. We were careless and filled with hatred. We overpowered our aggressors with our loyalty to the war and our faith in Allah, and we believed we were the followers of the one true faith. There was nothing that could stop us from pushing them back to the place where they had come from, but it was not all that we wanted. We wanted something else, we wanted to set the harbor of Basra free. It was situated in a very key location, and it was part of Iraq's territory, although it was completely populated by our Shiite brothers. Everybody in Iran knew that this mission would require sacrifices to be made. Every family had sent at least one soldier to the battlefield. Many families sent two, and even three soldiers. It was not a matter of choice, but a matter of duty. One could not hang back at home while everybody else was giving their lives to the war. When your neighbor, your cousin, your friend, your classmate, and everybody else was fighting, it was decided beyond questioning that you had to go too. There was no hiding while others were dying. You had to go to war for Allah, for the motherland, for the honor of your family, and for the honor of your relatives. This was a holy war, and you were a soldier of the Islamic Revolution. Were you going to be turned into a shahid? That was up to Allah. But, you were expected to be ready to give up your life.After all, you weremade to believe that you were a warrior of Islam.

To Kill and Die for Allah

To be a volunteer in the war against Iraq was considered a heroic act. Actually, it was the most heroic thing a person could do with their lives at that point. A holy war! Martyrdom! To die for one's own motherland! To die for Allah! Everybody was talking about the war – people on the streets, families at home, newspapers, and every television channel. Literally, war was all everybody could talk about. The atmosphere was electrifying, euphoric, and even hysteric at times. The unprovoked invasion of the Iraqi army on the territory of Iran had caused extreme fury and anger that overflowed through the streets. The special revolutionary Islamic services were looking for volunteers for the war. The army, of course, was doing the same. If one considered themselves a Muslim belonging to the one true faith, a real man, a devoted Iranian, a fiery patriot, nothing could stop him from going to war, from fighting with honor and dignity against the army of the wicked Saddam Hussein, the enemies of the one true faith, i.e. the Sunni, the aggressors.

On the battlefield, by facing the bullets, one could prove the kind of man they were, the kind of hero the one true faith asked for. We, the Shiites, who follow the one true faith and are fighting in the name of Allah, against the heretics, the Sunnis.It was absolutely legally, and under the blessingsof Allah, to shoot and kill those who did not bow to him. Could anything be more exciting for a Shiite boy? Killing was a good and noble service paid to Allah, for there would now be one less enemy in the world. Being killed was too, a good and noble service to Allah, one more shahid in the afterlife. Kill without fear, die without fear. This was the philosophy, and it was all in the name of Allah! Here I was, six months into my fight against the heretics in the southern province of Khuzestan. Our army was reaping success, the enemy was withdrawing, and the offence was strongerthan ever. It was time we bade farewell to Shalamcheh and left for Halabja. We were now invading the territory of Iraq. The aggressors were going to get what they had deserved all along.

We were on our way to the front lines on the day of our New Year's Eve. In Iran, we celebrate New Year's Eve in the spring, on March 21st, together with the spring solstice. Actually, New Year's Eve changes every year because it falls at a different time every year. Sometimes, it happens during the day, and sometimes, during the night. It is not like how it works in Europe and the way Christians do it either, always at 12:00 o'clock midnight. According to our tradition, the head of the family gives new clothes to the family members as a gift. At the banquet table, we have to have traditional vegetarian meals, and all of them start with the letter 'S'. Moreover, garlic and vinegar, wheat sprouts, and green leaves broth aremandatory. According to an ancient heathen tradition, people also light big fires on the street and have to jump over the fire to stay healthy. At the very moment when New Year's Eve begins, one holds a silver coin as a promise to never leave their family and birthplace. Ironically, I was going to spend this New Year far from my family and birthplace. Not a single silver coin in the whole world could help me. I welcomed 1988on my way to a town whose name was going to become a symbol of terror, genocide, and massacre.

The terror of Halabja

On March 22, 1988, we approached Halabja. Halabja was an Iraqi territory that was then under the attack of our army. We had taken by siege a part of it and had gained the complete support of the local Kurdish people. The region had become a battlefield in itself. The Kurdish soldiers, the Peshmerga, were fighting against Saddam Hussein's Sunni regime. For Iraq, this was a huge stab in its back because the Kurdish people were siding with Iran. I had no idea how long I was going to be fighting in this region. I was confident, being an experienced fighter of the front lines. With a license and without fear, I opted for driving an ambulance, an army job that theothers were not very keen on undertaking. Anything large, like an ambulance or a truck, made for a very easy target, both on ground and from above. There was always the risk of getting bombed while driving. It was a lot easier to be spotted and destroyed that way than it was when on foot. The same went for the big trucks that transported soldiers and ammunition to the first lines of the battlefield. Nearly every day, we'd hear of another ambulance being bombed. For obvious reasons, transportation vehicles were among the very first targets of the enemy. This only led me to believe that I was being that much more desirable in the eyes of Allah. I wanted to achieve the impossible; I wanted to be as useful as I could for the cause of my country, Iran, and the Revolution. There was nothing as important to me as this at that time, and that was the reason I was there. I needed to push everything as far as I could, just like everything else I had done in my life. I didn't care to do anything unless I was in it wholeheartedly. That's why, from the very moment that I had joined the front lines six months before, I had not wasted any time. I quickly adapted to the new military surroundings, Shalamcheh, Halabja, Sulaymaniyah, the Karun River... Just recently, all these names were nothing more than points on a map. But then, they were all known to me. I could navigate through them easily, their coordinates imprinted upon my mind. It was a world of daily air strikes and regular chemical attacks, a world of fear and terror, violence and blood. Being in Halabja was the same. This world 'welcomed' us with corpses and nightmares, emptiness and meaninglessness. It was a world of death, accompanied by thousands upon thousands of corpses. A few days after our arrival in Halabja, on March 16, 1988, a siren went off to signal an air attack. This sound was different than the one that sig-

naled a chemical attack, and the people in Halabja knew the difference. So, this time, just like all the other times, people rushed to hide
underground, in basements and tunnels, getting as low as they could
to get their lives spared and to save themselves from the dropping
bombs. Surrounded by thousands of corpses, and after hearing these
attacks daily, there were those who had grown so numb to what was
going on, that they did not even bother to take cover. Many had just
lost hope, giving up the fight to keep themselves alive. Those people
just stayed inside their homes, quietly surrendering themselves to
whatever the outcome there was to be. One could not escape his fate,
andthis had become a part of the general way of thinking. Not to
mention that fatalism and surrender to the will of Allah have been
character traitsof the Muslim way of thinking in general. There was
no way for the civilians to know that this time, the signaling was
staged. No one would have guessed that this attack was not just going to be limited to the military region but that the civilian regions
were also going to be targeted. And it was actually an attack of chemical gas! The horrid gas developed in Saddam's laboratories of hell
couldn't be escaped, no matter how far you went underground. In
fact, being heavier than air, the gas sank through cracks and crevices,
completely diffusing in the atmosphere by polluting the airflow.
Mercilessly,it killed every unprotected living creature. It consumed
anything alive. The gas worked so quickly that most people did not
even have the time to take stock of what was happening. A few days
later, we entered the outskirts of the city, now turned into a ghost
town. We walked the empty streets punctuated with cadavers of
shops that were once functional. We peeked into silent houses, and
everywhere, we saw the same sight of motionless people, almost as
if they had all fallen fast asleep with their faces frozen. They did not
wear the mask of death that I had seen on so many dead soldiers.
When gas went off in the military regions, the soldiers were generally aware of it. Their faces bore grimacinglooks of anguish, the fear

of losing their lives writ across. The dead soldiers I had seen over and over again were always covered by that same mask of death. But here, the civilians had not had time to realize that their death had come to nullify them. Those hideously grimaced faces had become my constant companion, but this time, I didn't see them. Instead, I saw a father with his child in his arms, collapsed at the front step of their house. Another man leaned against the open door of his car... also with a child in his arms...I saw a family sitting around a table, a man, leaning back on his chair, still, with a spoon in his hand; the plates still full of food, the whole family appeared as if they were asleep... Thatsight was haunting – all of these motionless people, frozen in time as they tended to their children and daily chores. Death looked terrifying... it was like a macabre painting on lifeless faces. As horrific as it was to witness hundreds of unburied corpses, one had no choice but to get used to the get used to the terrible scene of life stopped completely and abruptly in its tracks. No matter how badly you wanted to avoid looking at them, they were everywhere, and it was inescapable. Try as you may, you couldn't get rid of the constant feeling that they were looking straight at you, trying to make eye contact, trying to understand what happened to them, "Why did I die? Did I have to die?" But we didn't have an answer. Deep down, we knew that no possible meaning could ever be attributed to deaths. Soldiers came to fight knowing that there is death in war, yet the masks of death that covered their faces failed to justify their presence on the battlefield. Even the effort and determination with which the soldiers fought from the beginning to the very end was all rendered meaningless in their last moments. At least, however, these soldiers had come here to fight and had given this purpose their all. So did that mean any semblance of logic could be found in their death? Sure, they had come to fight, and in battle, people die. There was always the understanding that a soldier and a martyr were only divided by one final moment. Unfair, yes, but at least there was some sensethat could be attributed to a soldier's death. These fellow countrymen, brothers in arms – some of them my friends, had gone to the battlefield and had died; but there was no sign of pain on the faces of the civilians of Halabja. I did not see any. Peaceful, calm, and still as if they were simply asleep. As if they were resting, because the coming morrow, life would meet them with chores, problems, and dreams. As if they would wake up and get up any moment... Except that I knew they wouldn't. They were never going to wake up, and that was scary. Among such peace and silence, death was good at camouflaging itself as life. The scariest of all was the deadly peace amidst the military hell. Upon leaving, we took some eggs from a shop. The gas had poisoned all other food items, and as attractive as some goods seemed, we could not take the risk. We knew that, and so, we could at least save ourselves from death from poisoning. It was more difficult to protect our souls from the poison that was penetrating and gradually devouring our inherent human nature. Suffocating all that was good and human, and taking root deep within. That's how we left Halabja that day, with poisoned souls and with the memory of that merciless massacre. As if that were not terrible and ugly enough, in the outskirts of this ghost town, we came across a mooing calf, lying on the road. Where had this poor little creature come from in the midst of this ruin, how did it survive the poison, where did it hide to save itself the deadly gas? No explanation could be found. War created pictures, all devoid of sense, and there was no logic in this picture either. As we came closer, we saw that the calf was lying next to a dead cow. The mother was lying dead and the calf was mourning over her, with its head next to hers... mooing, sobbing... We continued forward toward our headquarter, but my eyes could still see those calm, innocent children's faces in Halabja. Frozen in stillness, faces of mothers and fathers and peaceful civilians. My ears could still hear the echo of that bellowing, desperate calf's cries.

I started crying...

Later on, I discovered that the attack had been organized by a relative of Saddam Hussein, a brother or cousin, Ali Hasan al-Majid. Due to this diabolical act, he was nicknamed the "Kurdish butcher" and the "Chemical Ali". For the attack against Halabja, they had used a chemical gas, a mixture of Sulphur mustard, Sarin, Tabun (a nerve agent), and VX. Some 5,000 Kurds died in this region, and since then, the peaceful victims of this atrocious genocide are commemorated on that same day every year.

Saddam gassed this area because we had invaded it. We believed that their chemical attacks were a violation of all international agreements, and it was indeed true. Iraq, however, kept claiming Iran was attacking them with gas and hence, the gas attack by them was actually a reaction, a counter-attack. I was always in this region where they were attacking us, but never in the place where they claimed we were gassing them. Later, I often asked myself what the truth was. I tried to find some meaning in thisgame of perpetrated lies. What was the point? But I had no time for such questions. There were a lot of things I did not know at that point. The only thing I knew was that I had to stay alive among all this poison and senselessness. We were given the following instructions: the moment one smelled onion (that was the smell of the gas that we called *mustard gas*) they had to run somewhere high. The higher, the better – tall buildings, hills, mountains... somewhere high. We, the Iranian soldiers, were given an antidote that I always carried with me wherever I went. During the first chemical attack, I had been driving the ambulance on my way to the front lines to collect the wounded and take them to the hospital. For the first time then, I felt the poisonous bitter-sweet smell sticking into my breath and stopping the oxygen flow to my chest. The moment I felt it, I drank the potion, and felt immediate relief. This magical liquid blocked the effect of the gas and relieved my breathing; my lungs filled with oxygen again. I stepped hard on the accelerator, and the ambulance, a big Toyota Land Cruiser, nearly flew towards the closest hill. I had to drive up that hill. I was driving like crazy, up and up, far from the stinging "mustard" death in the valley, up where the gas couldn't reach me. I saw other vehicles around me and other people running up that hill.

Yakub and the silver coin

The Land Cruiser was powerful and fast, but I wanted to drive a truck. That way I was going to be able to do more work and be more useful. They were powerful – the big trucks delivered straight to your sites from the roads of Iran. As the owners drove them, conducting their business, militants would pull them over, confiscate their trucks, and take them to the war zone. Every large vehicle had its own mobilization assignment, and in the times of war, the state could utilize them for any military duty. The truck they gave me was a military one, not one of the seized ones. So one day, I handed the ambulance over to another volunteer, a young man with a big smile. "I am Yakub," he said with a smile. "Why is this guy smiling? People don't smile here," I thought to myself and replied, "Yakub or Ali, who cares? What matters here is to remain alive. Listen to me carefully..." I looked into his eyes and gave him instructions about the vehicle. Then I handed him the keys. "Good luck with it, it is a good sled. The other day I put in some new curtains." He smiled again and showed me a chain around his neck with a silver coin attached to it. "This brings me luck. The silver coin will take me home. I am engaged to the most beautiful girl in the world. When I get back, we shall get married." "Send me an invitation," I said, giving him a smirk and thinking to myself, "He's talking nonsense! My girl is the most beautiful in the world." And there she was, Afsaneh, running through my mind again. One day, I too, would get married... to her, I thought, while getting on that big rig, a Mercedes 911, four-wheel drive. I would have a blast, I thought. Such a powerful rig! At first, they did not want to give it to me. "Show us your driver's license," they demanded. I did. They examined it and pointed at something, "See, you're not allowed to drive a truck, only a car." I did not need to see for I already knew that, but anyway, out of courtesy, I looked. "Give me the truck," I kept saying. "You don't know but my father has been driving a truck all his life. He's taught me, he's showed me, he's let me drive with him. I know all the gadgets in this machine. To me, it is like riding a bicycle." I continued to speak convincingly. As for my father, my poor father, he could not even ride a bicycle or a car, let alone a big truck. They did not know that, they could not have known that. It wouldn't have been much help even if they had known because somehow, nobody else wanted to drive the truck like I did, and nobody else had any class of a driver's license. And hence, they gave me the Mercedes, and I did a good job driving it. Man, how I liked it. It was a powerful, strong, and loyal lorry, with separate controls for every wheel. One could not have any trouble with such a grand vehicle. I could easily vamoose myself through the lousy places where I used to go. No shortage of lousy places during the war. The whole war was a lousy place in itself. I transported all kinds of things,driving the truck – bullets, weapons, food, people... Cluster bombs caused a lot of damage. These were usually used on people, and they caused damage of a very high intensity. This was because, first, they exploded in the air, and second, because they exploded again when they hit the ground. Very often, the whole bomb would not explode, and, this way, the targeted region would turn into a mine field waiting to explode. That's why the cluster bomb attacks were so dangerous. Lo and behold, who should they send during one of these attacks? Me. "Go, Ali, drive!" I was driving toward the place when yet another bomb attack began, but I continued to drive! There was nowhere for me to take shelter from the attacking air planes in the wide open field that I was in. So I drove hard and fast. Everything around me was crashing, my ears were ringing... violent roaring and rumbling surrounded me. I continued to drive through what became a thick cloud of smoke and fire, bombs falling everywhere around me, yet, somehow, not on me. This happened over and over again. Not just once. Soon, my comrades were able to ring me. We had these radios, walkie-talkies, and through them, they told me where to go. This time, they said, "Go, go, fast, there is an ambulance. We don't know if there are survivors." I drove; I got there and saw the ambulance completely smashed... The driver's body literally torn apart in pieces. You couldn't tell who the driver was,there were just pieces of flesh covered in blood. I looked around, and then inside again. The new curtains were splattered with blood. I could still recognize them. This was my ambulance. I was supposed to be in that front seat. The smiling boy whose body was now mincemeat was inside. Yakub. The silver coin had not been able to save him from death. His fiancée was never going to see him again. She was only going to receive the little metal identification tag every soldier had around his neck. In case of death, the tag was how they identified a person. The tag bore the person's name and his identification number. For the volunteers, there was no name, just a number. Both sides collected the tags from the dead, and if there were any that belonged to the enemy's camp, they would exchange them on a regular basis. Just the tags, though. Not the bodies. The latter never even got buried. Flesh rotted into exposed skeletons by the road, just like that... another common sight. At least their identification tags were taken and submitted. While driving the ambulance, I, myself, had collected hundreds of tags.

Please shoot me!

While I was still driving the ambulance, Mahmud, a friend of mine, had come to me. We knew each other from our neighborhood. Mahmud and I became even closer during the war. He pulled me to

the side, looked around and whispered, "I want you to do me a favor." "What?" I asked him, wondering why he kept looking around.
"I want you to shoot me," he told me in a commanding voice. "Have
you lost your mind?" I stepped back. "I have a wife and children. I
don't want to die. I don't want to be a martyr." He caught my upper
arm with his hand without letting go. I pulled myself away abruptly
and looked at him, fuming, "You must be out of your mind, you crazy
fool! You understand what you are risking if they find out it wasn't
an accident? What about me? Why did you pick me?" "Please, Ali, I
don't trust anybody else. You'll never give me away! You are a good
shooter. Shoot me in a watthat I stay alive and am not crippled." He
was begging like a little child. I kept looking at him, unable to believe that he was indeed serious. The number of shootings had been
on the rise, and they were investigating for self-inflicted wounds.
Despite all of these measures, the human nature of these soldiers
throbbed stronger than the patriotic and religious euphoria around.
But a friend asking me to shoot him? There was no way I was going
to do that. "No way!" I cut short the argument. He kept quiet for a second, then he looked straight at me, lowering his face, and he replied,
"Yes way." And he walked off. Then, every single day that followed,
he continued to beg me. I started trying to avoid him, but it didn't
help. Mahmud kept chasing after me with his crazy request. How
was I supposed to shoot him? There was no way. Period. I wasn't
giving in. I kept telling myself there was no way, furious with the
thought of shooting my friend, but his persistence eventually won.
One night, I was transporting a wounded soldier who had walked
over a mine and cut off both of his legs. Mahmud came to me in my
trench and pulled out a photo of his family, his wife and three children... "I don't want my children to be orphans, Ali. I do not!" I stood
up and said, "Are you ready?" "Whenever you are!" he replied, before I had even finished my question. "Now." I said abruptly. I had
to finish this nightmare. There were way too many nightmares to

think about, let alone another one of how this was supposed to play out. I wanted to get it over with. I couldn't stand his begging any longer. We got up and went out of the trench. Thick, black darkness surrounded us. It was pitch black, so dark that I could not even see Mahmud, my target... I could really mess this up. We went to the nearest shelter, so he could step on it. This way I could see his silhouette. He stood there and stretched his arms out to the side. I had his Kalashnikov in my hands. Carefully, I aimed at the chest area, to the right, close to his armpit. Bang! He gasped sharply and swayed to the side. I went close to him. He was panting and breathing very fast. I took the cartridge out of the gun and I put a bullet back into the mag. I had to make sure that they wouldn't accuse him of self-infliction. "Run to the med camp before it starts hurting real bad... before you lose too much blood," I whispered to him and put the gun strap over his head and across left shoulder. He proceeded forth toward the med camp. Meanwhile, I ran home to get in bed. My clothes were next to me, I was ready to get up and go. A minute later, one of the guys came calling after me for an emergency. A wounded soldier in the med camp needed to be taken to the field hospital. I rushed, "startled" by the news. As for Mahmud, he was already bandaged up, and ready to go to the hospital. I saw the bandages soaked with blood, his face – pale and distorted with pain. My heart filled with remorse. Why did I have to bring this upon him? Why did it have to be me? Why to him? I was driving to the hospital, and I couldn't stop asking myself these questions over and over... There, they took the bandages off and tried to stop the bleeding by stuffing the wound with Vaseline. The wax in the Vaseline helps the blood clot. But the blood kept gushing, it pushed the Vaseline out and popped like the cork of a champagne bottle. Champagne of blood! Tears were streaming down my face. Mahmud's face was getting paler. When they were finally able to stop the bleeding, they put more bandages on. I sat next him, my head leaning towards him and started crying out loud. "Brother, brother, why? Why did this happen? Why did it have to happen?" I could not say a word more. Everybody was listening. I was going to give myself away. They were all standing there, touched by my friendly concern because they had no idea what the real truth was. Mahmud whispered in my ear, "I'm okay, the wound is not that deep." As much as I wished to not believe that, as much as I hated myself and the whole world at that moment, he turned out to be right. He returned to Tehran to his family, and step-by-step, he recovered, and eventually, he was completely healed. One time, while I was on leave, he found out that I was home, and he came to see me with his wife and children, bringing me gifts. "Kiss his hand. He saved my life. You would have been orphans otherwise," he commanded the kids. His children and wife lined up before me, bowing down, thanking me for firing at him. Not knowing they were kissing the same hand that had pulled the trigger.

One would eventually get used to the horror of the war. Well, not exactly used to, but you would grow hardened to it. At one point, your mind and heart just refused to deal with it. They both became so full of tragedy that there was really no space left for new despair. They called us, the volunteers, men without any breaks, because it was our own choice, our own realized duty that moved us forward. We only thought of going forward. There was no space or time for looking back. Eventually, the new volunteers who were brought to the battlefield comprised only the weak-hearted. Traders, merchants, suppliers, drivers... They were brought here to fight, but they didn't even know where in the world they were. Their legs could hardly hold them as they walked, so horrified and full of fear they were. If they could, they would run away. But they couldn't. They were afraid of running too. Scared to die and scared to live! Their souls were completely paralyzed. At first, I would get angry with them, because theirheads couldn't wrap around what they had to do. They moped around, getting in my way. There was no time to mope around at the

time of war, you had to act, and you had to act fast and with preci-
sion. But this thumb rule didn't make it through their thick skulls. It
took one look in their direction, and they would shake like women.
Well, one night, along with the newly arrived volunteers possessed
by fear, we had to switch the front line shift. Soldiers would fight on
the front line for fifteen days, after which they would move to the
second line for the same term. The third 15-day shift was served at
the nearest base. In our case, it was located in the town of Ahvaz. At
the end of all three shifts, if you were still alive, you'd receive your
long-awaited 15-day leave. Our whole life was made up of 15 by 4.
For some of us, that would be the end of our life. Every second was
precious, especially for those on the front line. However, it was iron-
ical that when on the front line, you couldn't even muster mental
space to count the seconds, so alert one needed to be. The change of
the front line soldiers was always done during the night. It was the
least dangerous that way. There was no way we could do any shifting
during the day, since the enemy could see us. At night, we couldn't
use any lights either, since it would make us an easy target for the
enemy, not to mention that we would risk an air attack by night. So,
on one of these nights when shifts were changing, there were five
trucks lined up, with me leading in the first one. We started to move
through the dark field. Nobody wanted to go forward, but nobody
was asking to stop either. Had anyone asked, I guarantee those volunteers wouldn't have been there in the first place. So we moved forward in the pitch black night. There wasn't a single light that could
have given the soldiers away, not even the lit end of a cigarette. I
knew the road to the front line like the back of my hand. All the others
had to do was follow me. So, slowly, we crawled forward. We could
distinguish the lights of machine guns in the dark and could hear
the crackle of gunfire. We approached the Karun River, the water
divider between the front line and the second. We got to the hill that
served as a hiding place, and from there, we had to descend toward

the river. That's when I realized something was wrong. I stopped and looked behind me. No trucks. I got out and went backward to look for them. I could make out their black silhouettes, they had all pulled over. At that same moment, I collided into one of the drivers. He was trembling and crying, just like a woman. He fell on his knees before me. "What are you doing?" I hissed at him. "Get up now! Our men are waiting for us to pick them up." He began to beg, "Ali, I don't want to go down there. You are not scared. Everybody says you are bulletproof. I am not like you. I have a family, a wife, children, my parents are old... They are all waiting on me. If I am destined to die, you kill me, here and now, so I can get it over with! That way, at least I will know that I died by the hand of one of my own!" I felt so sorry for him. Pity tore at my heart. "Wait here. I will go to the front line to take the soldiers in my truck, and I will get the other ones from the river. You guys stay here, and don't you dare move!" He nodded with his head, sobbing, and proceeded to kiss my hands with gratitude. I got into my truck, and slowly and carefully, made five consecutive rounds in each direction. The change of the front line was completed that night. When all the trucks were loaded with soldiers, we took off back to our positions.

Piles of dolls

On another night, my truck was stocked full with ammunition – missiles, weapons, cartridges, you name it. It had been quite a difficult day. Not that there was ever an easy one. I wanted to get to the base as quickly as possible and get to bed. I could hardly keep my head on my shoulders. I delivered everything, and off I proceeded toward the base. As I was driving, a Kurdish man appeared standing on the road in front of me. He did not budge. He kept waving his hands, as if making some signs to me to stop, and then, he put his hands together in front of his chest, as if he was praying. A crazy man! During war, there was no shortage of craziness, you could stumble upon just about anything. I slowed down, stopped, opened the window, and shouted, "What are you doing, you crazy man? Move over!" He fell on his knees, shouting, "Please, for God's sake, please, take my wife and children, take them to Iran. Please save my family." I could not see anybody but him. My first thought was that they must be hiding somewhere off the road, in the bushes. The next thought that ran across my mind was that the whole thing could be a trap, and that, maybe, some bandits would jump out, shoot me, and take my truck. Anything was possible at war. My intuition, however, recognized the desperate, honest look in his eyes, and I had a feeling thatthe urgent plea wasn't a trap. He was truly looking for help. "They are right here," he said, running towards some bushes, calling to them. A woman and two children appeared out of the bushes; a young girl of about 17 or 18 years of age, and a younger boy who looked about ten. The woman held a small bundle in her arms, a baby wrapped up inside. They ran toward the truck, I opened the door and signaled to them to get in. The man helped the children climb in first, and the woman with the baby followed. Finally, the man jumped in and shut the door behind him. All of them were trembling, I could see their bodies shaking. They looked at me with their timid eyes, showing mixed feelings of gratitude and fear. We headed off. "Is this the meaning of war?" I thought to myself. Children trembling for their lives like frightened animals? Mothers with babies hiding in dark corners of the roads, pleading with strangers for help? Begging for mercy, hoping for a miracle that would save their lives? It was so ridiculous. It didn't make any sense at all. I wasn't being able to stand it much longer.

As I was driving them back to the Iranian territory, I saw a big pile on the road. It was about three meters high, a pile of figures that resembled dolls, like small mannequins. Piled on top of one another, the dolls were dressed in the traditional Kurdish folk costumes. Kurds have very beautiful attires, even their everyday clothing is beautiful. The outfits worn by these dolls were the same. They had the little puffy "wings" on the shoulders, as if they had come right out of a fairy tale. Whenever children wore these costumes, they looked just like fairy tale characters. Approaching closer and closer, we strained our eyes to see. Thosefigurines were indeed clad in Kurdish folk costumes. What were these dolls doing here? I stared at the Kurd in the truck. He was trying to tell me something, but his mouth was so dry I could hardly hear him. What was this man whispering? Then I heard him... They were children. "Children" the Kurd whispered, sobbing. These were not children! I insisted, "No, these are dolls! These are dolls!" But they weren't dolls... I saw them. They were children. Hundreds of murdered children.A whole pile of children's lifeless bodies.

"Children..." I muttered to myself... "These are children!" I was shouting now. "They've murdered the children!" Hollering like a mad man, my words were all distorted as they came forth from my throat. I felt like I was losing my mind. The kids in the cabin began to vomit inside. The woman started a painful wailing, and then, the baby woke up and started crying... "Drive, drive! For God's sake, drive!" the man screamed at me, and I pushed down on the accelerator. The machine roared, it strained forward, it shook, and the RPMs shot up. But still, there we were, with that pile of children right beside us. I accelerated again, this time with more power, but we couldn't escape the nightmare. It was like a picture, following us, plastered onto the window. For a moment, it was like this whole pile of small lifeless bodies was moving alongside us. I couldn't get away from the nightmare, a nightmare we were now a part of. "How fast do I have to drive to get out from this hell? How fast!?" I shouted frantically. "Slow down, slow down! You will tip us over! Slow down!" The Kurd screamed at me, grabbing my shoulder and pulling at me. The truck screeched... I wouldn't lift my foot off the accelerator. This was too much. I led the truck out into a field, anywhere to get thatblood-curdling thing behind us. I did not know where we were heading, but I called out to God, I prayed for the horrific scene to disappear behind us, disappear into the distance. I kept praying, but I didn't know who I was praying to anymore. I couldn't turn my head to look out the window, desperate and terrified that I would see that lifeless pile again. Kurdish children, dressed like dolls, thrown one on top of the other, like toys, motionless...void of life. The war had conspired with death to play its game with them, and when it was done with them, it had tossed them aside. When I took a second look, the pile was gone. At last, I couldn't see any of it. I was relieved, but only for a moment, because I knew, deep down, that those murdered little dolls would never be erased from my memory. Somewhere there, hidden in the depths of the hell that accompanied this war, in a mausoleum of horror, they would always be there. Just like little dolls... A pile of dead children.

Someplace, on the field of Iraqi Kurdistan, I turned the engine off and got out. The Kurd ran after me... "I will clean the cabin. I am sorry the children threw up." I put my hand on his shoulder, without even raising my eyes to meet his, and I said, "Go. Just go." I fell on my knees, clenched my fists and cried aloud, "Allah, Allah, is this what you want? The death of children? Is THIS what you want? War and blood? God does not want that! You are cruel, Allah, you are not God!" I bent my head down and dug my fists into the dirt. I knelt there, the turmoil of emotions consuming me, pouring out of me, until I was left speechless and motionless for some time.

I didn't know how long I had been standing there in the field of Halabja, in the cold spring wind of Kurdistan. When I stood up, I felt my heart all cold and hard, like it had had a burial somewhere in my chest. The list of things that could horrify me was growing shorter with every passing day. So was the list of the things that brought me joy. Not long after, I could face fear with a smile, whilst I responded to the smiles of others with total indifference. Fewer things could make me feel human again. My heart was turning stone cold. Yet, this war was still so terrifying that fear lurked, ubiquitous, in the shadows around me. This fear reminded me that I was still human; there was always a bit of room for fear that could creep into the marrow of my bones, making them as soft as cheese. I experienced that kind of fear just a month later, during that night when the attack against the enemy began. We had to overcome three consecutive defensive lines. The first was a minefield. The second was a water canal, about nine meters wide and six meters deep, full of barbed wire and cutting "stars" of sharp metal. The third defensive line was made of bunkers where the Iraqis hid as they shot at us. It was a defensive wall that couldn't be conquered. But we had to conquer it! We were the one true faith followers, not them. We had to conquer it in the name of Allah, no matter how many lives we were to lose in the process.

Death is their banner

The first to attack were from the air planes; then the infantry followed. During that most terrifying night, the volunteers ran through the minefield in rows of ten, holding onto one another, arm-in-arm. If one stepped over a mine, their body went flying into the air in pieces, and the rest would run. Another group of men were blown, the second group, and then, a third... Those who landed on mines instantly turned into flying pieces of flesh. A fourth and a fifth row... Pieces of flesh fell all around, leaving the souls of these boys suspended mid-air. All for the glory of Allah! A speedy making of shahids, martyrs for Allah, rushing off for paradise to enjoy their 40 virgins. This went on until the row of ten finally reached the end without any casualty. Only then could our military vehicles pass through the mine areas, by then swept safe by all those martyrs. The orderlies and janitors were the last ones running, listening for the moans and screams of survivors so that they could get them back to the infirmary. Hundreds of soldiers of the one true faith, advancing in attack, passed through the canal. Some fell, and others scrambled over them, sometimes trying to avoid the bodies if they could... Moaning in anguish, volunteer after volunteer fell to his death. Their fanaticism led them forward, and death was the banner they carried. And so, there were more martyrs for Allah. Then others stepped over them, pushing, stumbling, falling, and scrambling to get back up, over the bodies of their brothers in arms. Just the day before, they had shared bread and cigarettes. And that day, they ran over one another until there was a bridge of living bodies, torn and cut, stacked on one another after agonized pain had finished them. The attack ran through the wired canal to reach the third defense line. There,they reached a row of bunkers, from which Iraqi soldiers fired shots, shooting into the dark without any care for sparing ammunition. The chaos of the automatic fire silenced the attackers, yet there were the cries, groans, and screams of the dying. During that night of screams and despair, air planes howled and dying men struggled through their last breaths; even I did not dare to get into that meat grinder. I stood along with several other people from our volunteer squad "without brakes," and did not proceed inside. For the first time, our direction took us backwards – we fled, and we retreated. Two days later, the Iraqi position was fully conquered. We had actually managed to gain control of the impossible fortifications that had stood in our way. We established our paths and put clear Safe Passing signs in the minefields. The water in the canal was completely drained, and you could see the protective structures made lethal with the large number of blades and tangles of barbed wire. The canal was full of whole and partial corpses, frozen in the most ridiculous positions, with the most awful grimaces on their faces. As I was looking at the lifeless bodies of the young men, some of whom I knew, that same question arose in me again, "Is this what Allah wanted from us? Is this what you have for us, Allah? Running over mines, dying, cut by metal star blades and barbed wire? Was this what you, God, wanted!? Live human sacrifices? All of this death, all of these corpses?" It was all so meaningless... with what seemed like a plague of endless death. People continued to die all around me. Lots of people.Constantly. I had lost count of how many by then, neither did I want to count. Nonetheless, there were those I couldn't forget. Like this one brother in arms who patrolled with us along the Kiruna River. A smart man, educated, and of good upbringing; he was even fluent in several languages. We talked about our homeland. He was from Isfahan, a Persian millennial city, the capital of some old empires. He told me about his family and children, and asked me if I had a family of my own. "Nope, but a beautiful girlfriend. One day we will have a family and children," I answered, showing him a photo of Afsaneh. "She is beautiful," he agreed. He told me he used to be a tour guide before the war. He had friends in Europe and was planning to emigrate there with his family. He told me the kind of business he wanted to start there, what he wanted his children to become. The best education was in Europe, he would explain, looking at me, and I would nod in agreement. Just as he was dreaming, he gasped, paused, and collapsed. I leaned over him; a sniper had got him right in the head, splashing his blood onto me and my clothes. I held his head in my hands, looking into his eyes, the flicker of life that once burned bright disappeared within an instant.

Another time, again during patrol, an Iraqi with an RPG slung across his shoulder suddenly jumped out at us, prepared to shoot. How did the enemy manage to get so close, that unexpectedly? There wasn't any time to think, you had to run and pray to God that you don't get hit. We ran in zigzags, like crazy men chased by wild animals, as he fired the RPG at us. A boy was just in front of me, just slightly off to my side, when I saw the rocket flying toward him, cutting through his right arm with its fin. His arm twisted like a propeller, and he collapsed on the ground. I threw myself down next to him, embraced him with one arm and began to drag him away. I kept up, trying not to lose his arm since it had twisted, and twisted in his socket. I didn't even know what was keeping the arm attached anymore. When we reached the first possible shelter, I grabbed his hand and adjusted it as much as I could. I kept tearing pieces of his clothes, tying them tightly around his shoulder to stop the bleeding as much as was possible. He was in so much pain that he fainted, not feeling anything anymore as I kept dragging him, stopping intermittently to cover his wounds. Panting, I thought to myself while I was trying to bandage him, "It is better not to feel any pain while leaving this world." But he didn't leave the world then. He turned out to be quite a tough one. It was incredible; they managed to save him before he had lost too much blood. We did have very good physicians in Iran. They even managed to recover his arm, which had hung about lifeless in the socket for so long – even to the extent that he could use it again with limited movement. I had never needed the service of the military doctors. During that whole time on the battlefield, people continued to fall like flies all around me, and still, somehow...as if something was protecting me... I survived one attack after another. Nothing, however, could save me from losing the illusions I had,once, so diligently constructed.

The end of my illusions

I went home during a leave, the sweetest 15 days. I went out around the neighborhood in the evening. As I was standing on the street one day, talking to some old friends, a black Mercedes pulled up in front of us. It was big, polished, and bulletproof. I couldn't think of a single friend who would have such a special limo. Not to mention that in the years that followed, these black cars primarily got me into trouble. Inside, to my surprise, was a bloke I once knew from the neighborhood. He greeted me and asked me to get in. I examined him suspiciously, and I recalled that his father used to work in the least classified level of some secret service of the revolutionary militia. "Was this what they drive here?" I thought to myself. I saw the way the others greeted him with mixed feelings of fear and envy. It caught my attention, and I jumped in. He gave instructions to the driver, and with a content grin, he responded to the look on my face. Clearly, he could read the logical question betrayed by my expression,"Where did you get all this from?" He began to explain how his stellar status had come about, and how he got to drive around in this Mercedes. His father had advanced his career in the militia quite rapidly, and thus, he had been able to get a job in the special services, working directly for the Ayatollahs... So this was how he got into this sweet deal. Every Ayatollah had his own circle of trusted people; actually, it was more like an entourage of free loaders who served him. In return, he looked after them and their families and made sure they lived by an incomparably higher standard than the rest. "Was this why we had the Revolution?" I thought. Before, we used to say that the Shah was stealing, and that's why he was taken down. Yet, the Shah was just one, while the Ayatollahs were five. Of course, the boy looked pleased. Was there any reason not be? As he spoke and explained, we arrived at a party with others like him. He introduced me to them, as if he was showing me off, but in actuality, he was praising himself. "This is Ali, the bulletproof lad. Ali fights against the infidels. Yes, this is him. We grew up together. We are really good pals." Nodding to the rest carelessly, I checked them out very quickly. Conceited, haughty, puffed-up brats;all of them thinking they were a big deal. They had never been in battle, they didn't know the smell of gunpowder, of blood, or death, or shit. I could tell there was lots of money involved. They had taken several wives, the most beautiful girls. Whatever girl they laid their eyes on, she was theirs. "Martyrs' widows." As many as one wanted. The Ayatollahs had even founded a national social organization that looked after the widows whose husbands were killed at war. How noble of them to help the widows of the shahids. How did they help them? For some, there were handouts. For others, the most beautiful ones, they were taken as wives. Their husbands had died in the war for Allah. These men took their women in the name of Allah to look after them... I thought of my dead friends, declared shahids... and I looked at these spoiled little brats, with their harem of dead men's wives. Why did my friends die? To serve their beloveds on a silver platter to these guys? And again, inevitably, thesame question rose up once again like a chorus, "Allah, is this what you want? Is this what you expect from me? To die for your name, so that Afsaneh can become the next wife of one of these brats who cannot even look me in the eye?!" God could not be a selfish, sadistic, brutal, and ruthless tyrant who fed on the blood of those who believe in Him. I didn't believe in this kind of a God. I simply couldn't. These self-absorbed excuses for men, who prided themselves on being so accomplished, had never held a dying friend in their arms. Their expensive clothes had never been stainedby the blood of their brethren. These sissies, who considered themselves as being so big and bad, began to praise me: "Good for you, Ali, you are an example. Allah needs people like you... " They began asking me about this and that, fussing around and strutting like cockerels in a hen house. I was squinting cringing inwardly, I couldn't stay in their presence... And then I saw her. She was there, among the rest, Daud's girlfriend! He had shown me her photo! I bowed my head, and I left without saying a word. I could feel their confused glares upon me, but I didn't care whatsoever. Allah needed people like me? What about them? Didn't he want people like them too? To go and to die in combat? Why weren't any of them blowing up into pieces? Didn't they want to fight for the one true faith? Up there, 40 virgins were waiting for them. All of a sudden, I realized that hodjas' children never went to war; they stayed in the mosques and hung around their fathers, pretending that they were helping them. They didn't seem very eager to be martyrs and go to heaven.

All these smart asses sure had me for a fool. Obviously, I, myself, voluntarily accepted playing the part of the moron. For more than a year now, I had been at war, primarily on the battlefield. Folks in the neighborhood had started legends about me. They would say that

I was bulletproof, that I always got out of deadly situations alive, even out of the worst ones. They would narrate tales of how people around me would die left, right, and center, but death always passed me by.They were all fantasizing that I was immortal... This was quite good for my ego, but later on, I would discover that people had always needed legends. They needed to inspiring legends that they could pass on. Legends that they could reinvent and include themselves in, if possible. That night, as I stood on the street watching a war veteran with his legs cut off, shuffling along on crutches, reaching out for alms... watched how those black polished cars passed him by as if he were a tree... That was the end of my illusions. That very night, the holy war was over for me, forever. Allah might need me, my heart surely needed God, but I no longer needed Allah. Allah was no longer my God. Henceforth, if I were to take part in any jihad, it would be my own personal one, for my own personal gain.

Run, Ali, Run!

Drugs in our neighborhood of Afsarie didn't come from only one particular place. You could find all sorts of drugs from all sorts of places – some were good, others had a bad rap. This source of drug abundance was located in the so-called Golden Crescent, a vast cross-border area between Iran, Pakistan, and Afghanistan, where nearly 90% of the world's opium is produced. For instance, the opium extraction from one acre in these poppy cultivation–favourable lands is four times higher than that of its competitor, Morocco. This opium fertility explains a lot of things. One of them is the old tradition of opium use in Iran. In fact, opium has been most common in these regions since ancient times. In the old days, our Persian kings smoked opium. One becomes confident, energetic, and clear-minded when smoking opium. It's actually very good, especially if you are over 40 years of age, and even little children know this. If younger, you don't really need it as much; but still, there's nothing wrong with its consumption. Heroin, on the other hand, is a completely different story. It's nasty, and it makes you feel like a filthy rag; it's quite a heavy drug, and it is highly addictive. Some people from the block did heroin. They didn't really look like people any longer. They were ready to do anything, even sell their own mother, just to get their hands on another dose of their substance. It wasn't seen as cool or macho, and nobody had respect for them. Hashish is quite different – completely harmless, and one can smoke it as much as they want. It just makes people feel better and better. It's natural, just grass, nothing more. Personally, I started the hashish business out of pure coincidence while hanging out on the streets. There were no cafes, discos, or bars to hang out in, so we would just roam about the street, looking around. One man passed by, and then another, looking for hashish and opium. "Can you find me a good deal?" Of course, I could. I knew where all the dealers were. And so, the job was done. I'd never been lazy. I'd had a lot of jobs, although, none of them were for long because I always managed to get myself into fights and trouble. Nonetheless, it was not laziness, and I had never been lazy. My mother used to sigh and say, "Ali, it's as if you have ants in your pants. You can't sit still." Indeed, I was always moving, looking for something more, something more interesting. And drugs definitely sparked my interest. My parents could hardly make ends meet, let alone give me pocket money. So I quickly found my way around my new trade. The clients were happy, and they contacted me again and recommended me to their friends as well. In time, the orders multiplied.

The power of drugs

I began gaining customers' trust, and it made me feel quite important. Cash started flowing into my hands and my pockets filled quickly. I took orders from the army as well. Some of my clients were chiefs and officers. I knew exactly what I wanted to do once I returned from the war. My boyish enthusiasm was not enough anymore; I was tired of feeding on the crumbs of others. My days as an errand boy were over. The contacts I had built, the money that passed so easily into my hands, the amount of drugs I dealt with, the energy and courage I felt, paired with the loss of all religious delusions I had been under –they all added up, and I quickly gained positions and territories. Soon after, I took over the drug market in the main street of the neighborhood, the Bismerti. I surrounded myself with some serious guys; in fact, they actually started to follow my lead, seeing my capability. We gradually built up a solid system, a well-oiled machine. That was how I took over. We became the heads by offering the best deals. Thatwas how it went in Iran. Whoever had the best deals became the leaders. I mean, what kind of boss would one be if he couldn't even find the good deals. Top quality and quantity, good pricing, and voila – you were the boss. Knowing this, I quickly began dealing with direct suppliers. There was this guy named Mohammed, an experienced Afghan who imported drugs in Tehran directly from the Golden Crescent. He provided me with the best-quality deals. No more going over anyone's head, no more underhanded spoiled goods, no more tricks with rising costs. The best product was coming directly into my hands. That's how the lads and I got to selling premium-quality deals. Mohammed supplied some other dealers in our part of Tehran with the same product. Exactly the same deals. But they were way too greedy. Their opium packets were smaller, yet they charged more and the quality of their business was a lot worse. Soon, they started losing clients, as more and more people preferred to deal with me. Sure enough, very soon I began to get visits by some of these other mad hatters who were hardly doing any business anymore, thanks to me. "Ali, what're you doing, man? Business is not going well because of you. We have no clients, no money." I had no intention of withdrawing. I had figured out how to make the drug supply successful, and that was how I was going to do it. The competition itself would decide who was going to get the clients. "Are you making any profit this way?" "Obviously I am making profit if I am selling at this cost," I would reply. Unsatisfied, they would leave bitter, passing threatening looks in my direction. But I didn't care. It had been a long time since I had cared about what these dimwits, who thought they were so tough, wanted or thought. They didn't know how to be tough. None of them had been through what I had endured on the battlefield. Everyone who had been in military combat had either failed to come home or had come back with missing limbs. Everyone but me... I anticipated that they would strike, and, in if it was to get to that, I was ready to strike back in a way that would forever remain etched in their memories. But, they were well aware of my character, and they knew how wild my boys were. I guess it was owing to this that they never actually made any moves against me. Neither the young aggressive traffickers, nor the older players on the field dared to touch me. Besides the war rumors about my immortality that I found to be a bit hilarious, there was another thing that restrained the older dealers. It was my brother Daud's reputation of being a political opponent of the Ayatollahs' rule – this, in itself, had earned him enormous respect in the underworld. That's how it was during those days – the thugs, hoods, and con artists in Iran showed respect for the political enemies of the government. The respect for my brother overflowed onto me and safeguarded me with extra protection. This is when I began to feel very powerful, and it all stemmed from the power of drugs. Influence, money, reputation... My mother began to catch on. She could tell something was going on, like every mother can when her children are up to illicit. She always had an unerring eye over her children. What I was up to wasn't hard to figure out anyway... A boy my age coming home with pockets stuffed with money. My pants had these large side pockets, and they were always full of money, literally overflowing. "Ali, what are you doing?" She would ask in distress, always standing in that tiny little hallway with her hands on her hips. "Nothing, mother," was my usual reply upon entering. Always nothing, only nothing, as if she couldn't see or didn't know. "Ali, be careful. What you're doing is not good." "I am not doing anything, mother." "Ali, don't you dare buy anything for the house with this money! It will go in the bin." Indeed, she never accepted anything I tried to buy. I bought food for the family. I wanted to help. I tried several times. Nope... she always refused. She did not even let the food inside the house. Mother did not want any such help. So I stopped. I could not change her mind or persuade her to accept it, and, of course, she could not stop me from doing my business either. My father gave up as well. I was old enough to stand up to them. Some of the guys my age had even got into tiffs with their fathers,raised their hands at them even. The Revolution had given power to my generation, and our old men had no choice but to keep their mouths shut. Times had changed, it was our world now. From sunrise to sunset, my father worked at a fruit stand that belonged to someone else. He hardly made any money. I was making more than him. Way more. Thanks to the money and the reputation my chums and I had built for ourselves, the older hustlers, former gang members from the block, would even invite us to their parties. Usually parties were set up on the roofs of one of the houses of these old-time thugs. The roofs in our neighborhood were flat and surrounded by walls, and hence, one could freely enjoy privacy. We would go to the roofs, watching out for the militia. Alcohol, hashish, and opium – we had it all, stacked in stacks on the roof. As we drank and smoked, we would check on the situation, a head or two peeping below from the top. Being invited by the older big shots was considered a matter of real distinction. We had gained true recognition, and this helped us stand out amongst the other gangsters on the block. We, being the youngsters, provided the alcohol and the drugs. Our business was booming; the older guys weren't making as much as we were, but they enjoyed the ride. Having had the rich experiences of getting arrested and being sent to prison, they told us their alluring stories –first, to show off, and second, to warn us what it would be like if we ever got arrested. "They beat you till you bleed and pass out," they would tell us. "They want you to betray the others, and most importantly – to give away the source where the drugs are coming from. You should keep your mouth shut, otherwise you are out of the game. Once you're out, there is no getting back on the wagon, you have lost the trust."

Shish kebab detention

There was a lot to learn from these older daredevils. I remember some of the tips they gave me. For example,the wisdom that you either smoke the dope, or sell it;never do both. You try doing both, and you will surely fail. They were right, and I would learn this later at my own expense. As for Iran, I never went to jail for drug possession there. They never caught me. The way I did things was simple, yet effective. My mates sold the drugs and collected the money. I saw my pals and the dealers alone. No witnesses. There was no way of proving my involvement, andso, no one ever could. I did get arrested once, but it wasn't for drugs. It was for getting caught red-handed while stealing a car. It happened only because I had broken the iron law those old wise guys had given me. I had started smoking the dope. When stealing, your mind needs to be sound, and your reflexes, quick. But I was high, and they caught me there, right on the spot. I had no way of getting out of it. Stupid, huh? Arrested and hand-cuffed, I was stripped naked; they were looking for drugs on me. They did a very thorough check. There were many cases where deal-ers would deliberately provoke the police to arrest them. Once in, the dealers supplied drugs to the detainees. They would place the dope in a small plastic bag and swallow it. Once they were in, they would induce vomitingto get it out. The other way was wrappingthe dope in plastic and sticking it up their anus... Drug addiction is a medical sickness, and couriers have always been extremely inventive when it comes to hiding the dope. For this reason, every detainee had to be checked thoroughly. The common room held about 150–200 people. There were a few small rooms along its sides, but without doors or beds. It was a kingdom of lice and disgusting smells. The adrenaline rush from the crime had long passed,leaving you with only that nasty smell and that dirty floor you got to know very closely. You also got to know some of the people far too closely and personally... as you heard their screams and shouts from the basement. They deliber-ately beat people close to the common area so that the other detain-ees could hear the screaming. Listening to that, you knew the kind of torture and beating to prepare yourself for. Not that one could ever really prepare oneself for that heinous a torture. The Iranian tradition of beating prisoners date far back to the ancient times. One of the classic contemporary specialties is called "Shish Kebab" wherein you have to sit on the floor and bend your knees so that they touch your face. Stretching the arms forward, the wardens handcuff your wrists and slid a stick underneath your knees to lift them up. Following that, you end up upside down, with the soles of your feet facing up. The wardens then ask the detainee their usual tricky question, "What is your shoe size?" No matter what number you give them, the guards respond, "Well, from now on, it will be double." They like to try and crush you mentally, andthen, the physical abuse begins. Mercilessly, with a leather strap, they beat the sole of the inmate's feet until they fill with blood, becoming so blue and swollen that, indeed, they practically double in size. The inmate is then released, although,by this time, it's impossible to walk. The wardens still continue to beat the person, forcing them to walk on their feet. Then, they take you into a tiny hallway with a slippery floor made of cold concrete whereyou have to walk with your swollen feet until they go down to their normal size.But this doesn't happen,they do not become any less tender. Meanwhile, your body freezes. Thereafter, the guards take you back inside, do the shish kebab, and yet again, they beat you with a leather strap. One can hardly bear such pain. Some guys would come back and admit that they couldn't do it one more time, and that they would end up confessing... Others returned completely smashed from the beating, admitting they gave themselves and all the rest away. Of course, everybody respected the tough ones the most. I was one of them, and I had to pay the price of my loyalty by enduring a lot of beating over the years. Still, I never gave away my friends, or accomplices, as the investigators, prosecutors, and judges liked to call them. I found out years later that those friends did not always return the favor.

At that time, however, everything was still going fine. I was eventually allowed to go, and the drug business was booming. We did business with respect and accuracy. We knew how to invest into relationships with the right people. We made some valuable friends, the most important among whom were theones from the Drug Abuse Agency. They were good and savvy guys. They realized that we were serious businessmen, and they treated us accordingly. Whenever they confiscated drugs somewhere, they immediately contacted us, nobody else, and sold the merchandise to us at a price much lower than the one on the market. It was a solid deal for both the involved parties. They got cash, and we got stash that we were able to sell almost instantly. No one could beat our prices, and we were still making good profit. The best part of this relationship was the fact that those who were responsible for catching us had spread their umbrella to cover us. We were safe. Things were going well, and there was nothing to complain about. This went on for about a year...

Cash and profit

About this time, Akbar came into the scene. Being about 10 years older than me, he was a leader among his peers, just as I was among mine. Despite the age difference, he and I were both on the same wave length. Goofy at times, we moved quickly and vigorously, always getting things to work in our favor. We made money from everything. So much profit came our way. Being around Akbar, I fell for something besides drugs. It involved my passion for motorcycles and high speed. We would pull up in front of a bank on a motorcycle and wait for the people to come out with full bags. Some of them would have withdrawn money to purchase property, whereas some to start a business. There were no credit cards at that time, it was all cash. When the people walked out of the bank, we would snatch their bags out of their hands and speed off. The security guards at the bank did not care about what was going on outside the bank. The tellers had done their job; they had handed the money over to the customers andit was the customers' responsibility afterward.

Perceptive people like me and Akbar were always able to reach an agreement with the militia, especially because we had built the right network of contacts. Those relationships brought a certain guaranteed peace. So with this venture, we made money out of nothing. Just cash, all profit. I rode the bike, he snatched the bags, and off we went as quickly as possible. By the time the people even had time to process what had just happened to them, why they were standing there empty-handed, we had had left the scene already. I got to ride really good motorcycles, constantly getting new ones, thanks to my friend, Tagi. Tagi stole motorcycles, as I guarded the stealth. He worked at a mechanic shop where he would dissemble them, repaint them, and sell them to new buyers. I rode a new motorcycle every other day.

Sure enough, my mother noticed and her suspicions increased. She would ask, "Where did this motorcycle come from?" "A friend gave it to me just for tonight," I would quickly answer. "I'll do a couple of laps, and tomorrow, I'll give it back." I would go out, jump on the motorbike, start it very slowly, and then, once I was a good way off from the house, I pushed that thing until it roared like a beast.

Motorcycles make you free, hard to catch, strong, and fast. The horizon is yours, and you can go so fast that you are nearly untouchable. They equal advantage and power. Not surprisingly, the Mujahidins, for example, would use extremely powerful motorcycles as weapons in their attacks. Riding on powerful motorcycles, they would come out of the blue and throw a hand grenade into a limousine belonging to one of the imams. By the time the bodyguards in the escort cars had any chance to act, the riders hadsped far ahead. This is how a lot of bombings were carried out and many people were killed. Hence, the authorities tightened the restrictions on powerful motorcycles. Getting a license was quite tough. One required to havea special license for vehicles with engines that surpassed certain parameters. Besides, getting a registration done was very difficult because of the strict regulations. Even once registered, one was often pulled over for inspection. The militia knew the owners and, if necessary, they could easily track them. The Honda 125 was convenient for us. All guardians of the Pasdaran drove the exact same motorcycles, which were designated to them upon employment. Growing a beard was my next step, and then, I looked just like a real "Pasdaran." This motorcycle, however, wasn't the most powerful, so it didn't work well in certain situations. Then, we began looking for a more powerful one. At this time, I met a friend who had a Suzuki 250, but he was afraid to ride it! He didn't have the balls to drive such a hefty bike! It was just luck that he was completely okay with us borrowing it in return for cash. We could then carry on our business. We made very good money this way, and so, compensation was never a problem. Akbar and I were completely in tune with one another's thoughts, and we were heading down fast. So fast that I didn't think I would live to see my 40th birthday. That's what I would tell my classmates and childhood pals whenever we would get together. They spoke of wanting a family and children. Some wanted 5 children or 10, others wanted 12... These were boyish fantasies to me. I used to tell them, "I don't know about you guys, but if I make it to 40 with this lifestyle of mine, it would be a God-given miracle in itself." They couldn't wrap their minds around what I was saying. They had a normal life, some had even graduated from school. At that time, I still had normal friends, normal people who worked in honest jobs. One of them even became a tailor, and I felt so proud of him. Having a tailor for a friend was very good, it made it seem like I could be a normal person too, at least to some extent. His name was Manuchehr. He moved to Australia. Meanwhile, I was getting very close to the people I worked with. That's usually the way it works out, right? Like this dodger, Tagi, for example. He got me into the business of stealing motorcycles, and he also taught me how to smoke hashish. When he'd offered me hashish for the first time, I'd jumped up and caught him by the throat. He had started turning blue, just a little. "What are you up to? Are you trying to turn me into a drug addict?" Wheezing, he said, "No, not at all; hashish is not a drug any-way. Am I a drug addict because I smoke hashish?" Frankly, he didn't look like an addict. "Ok, let me try," I agreed. And I loved it. Besides, it was entirely innocent and harmless. The harm would eventually come, but later. At that time, it was time for partying and adrenaline rushes, time to make money and get ready to marry. Earning cash helped me gain confidence that I would be able to marry. I kept see-ing Afsaneh, though less frequently than before. I had become bolder and more assertive, and she was more responsive. Believe it or not, this is how we got to our first kiss. Luckily, her parents didn't find out, or they would have certainly killed her. No question about that. The risk involved was great, especially for her, yet this was the most certain proof of her feelings for me. Besides being beautiful, she was smart as well.She never asked me unnecessary questions about my speedily improved financial status. Afsaneh was not raised in a royal palace. No, she was a girl from the block. That's where we met, and she knew how things worked.

The murder of Mehdi, the butcher

It was a night like all the rest. The night after a good day. We had made some good money, and so, it was time for us to unwind and treat ourselves. We had bought some home-made brandy... illegal, of course. It had always been illegal. The brandy was very strong, so we needed some soda to mix it with. There was a soda shop on the block – its owner used to import Coke, Fanta, and Sprite from Turkey. Akbar rolled up in front of the shop in a sleek Peugeot 504. Right then, we saw another gang. Rascals like us. Good fellas. Some-times, we did business together. We shook hands and started talk-ing when they asked us if we had first-class opium. "Of course. First class is all we have." "In a couple of days, we'll need two kilos. Can you give us a good deal on it?" "Sure thing, we offer the best deals on the block. Best quality, best price." We gave one another a pat on the back, everyone was happy. One of the boys was Mehdi. His family owned a butcher shop, which is why we called him Mehdi, the Butcher. The nickname came from his father, who was the best butcher on the block. Their business was booming, selling lots of meat and making big bucks. Until Mehdi was birthed, his father's only grief had been not having a son – in some Islamic countries, it practically makes a man a failure if he is without a male heir. What kind of a man couldn't have a son? It was shameful to have several wives, each birthing only daughters. Daughters couldn't get you anywhere. So with his whole mentality, Mehdi's father had done everything possible to achieve his dream of bringing into the world his long-awaited male heir after eight daughters. This alone showed that he wasn't the one to give up easily. Mehdi had been this long-awaited male child, heir of the clan and the family business. This had built his domineering confidence and belief that he was allowed everything ever since we were all children. He knew that, no matter what he got himself into, his father would get him out – it had already happened more than once. Mehdi's father would always bring money and fix the situation whenever his son messed up. Whatever this daddy's boy did, whether he beat someone or seduced a girl, his father's money suppressed any grudge or trouble from the authorities. Mehdi himself was not lazy. Since he had been a kid, he had always helped his father. He had perfected his butchering techniques and had learned to use a knife with great skill. This ability, combined with his unbridled temper and his father's financial protection, led people to avoid any conflict with him. People generally preferred to keep their mouths shut about the trouble he caused them. He and I had always showed consideration for one another. I didn't want extra trouble, and he avoided bantering with me because he knew me too well. So, on that night, there was absolutely nothing that foreshadowed the events that were to take place in the following minutes. We scanned the drinks available and bought some sodas. I took the bottles and went out. Akbar stayed inside, still talking to Nader. Mehdi and Nader were friends just like Akbar and myself, always together, always brewing trouble. Skipping from one topic to another, out of good will, Nader offered Akbar a girl who happened to like Mehdi and was waiting for him in the car. Mehdi, on the other hand, did not want to go with her alone and had invited Nader. Now, Nader invited Akbar, who was supposed to invite me, if I was willing to join them. Akbar hated such stuff, so he just refused the offer and went out. Unfortunately, as he passed Mehdi's car, he peeked in and saw the girl waiting inside. It was Shahla! Shahla was the wife of one of our very close friends who had recently gone abroad to work. How could this stupid woman do such a thing? Akbar came to me and started narrating what he had seen, infuriated. I couldn't understand any of it, he was so angry. He explained his rage to me later, but it was too late. Before I could even say a word to him, he stormed angrily toward the car, opened the door, and started yelling at Shahla to get out and go home. Then he charged back into the shop. Seconds later, he darted out, chased by Mehdi, who bore a knife in his hand. "Why did you mess my things up with Shahla?" Mehdi was also cursing at Nader. Nader had no idea about Shahla's marriage, but we knew Shahla's husband, and Nadar had made an inappropriate offer to the wrong people. Such a dumb, messy story... Later, I often thought about it, and asked myself if I really had to get involved. Was it really my business? Everything happened so quickly, there was no time at that point to think about anything. Holding a knife in his hand, Mehdi, the Butcher, was chasing my mate Akbar, wishing to kill him. I pulled my knife out and stood right in front of Mehdi. What else could I have done under those circumstances? I wasn't going to let him kill my friend. While Akbar tried to get his knife out of our car, Mehdi and I got into a messy tangle with our knives. Nader bolted towards me, hit me in the face, and pushed me down to the ground. I was much shorter than him, you see. Right then, Akbar jumped in to protect me, and this time, he held a knife in his hand too. One kick and Nader was on the ground. Akbar was a very strong man. He thrust his knife towards Mehdi, who withdrew quickly. As Mehdi protected himself, he stabbed Akbar in the neck. Akbar screamed out and grabbed his throat with his hands, leaning forward. I was already back on my feet and stood right in front of Mehdi again. He didn't look like himself. He had the look of the devil in his eyes, ready to cut throats. I imagine I looked the same way to him. He swung his knife, he was very quick. I managed to protect my throat from his knife, but I wasn't fast enough to protect my face. The blade split my lip all the way to the chin. I felt the knife literally scraping my bone. Akbar jumped up in front of me and flung his knife toward Mehdi at the very same moment that I swung my knife as well. One of the two blades sank deep into Mehdi's neck. He gasped, clutched his throat, made a step forward, and tumbled down at my feet. I leaned over him, terrified, praying for him to still be alive. But it was too late. His eyes were rolling backward, his body was shaking with deadly spasms. Numerous questions raced through my mind at the speed of light: Why has this happened? I never wanted this to happen! We had nothing to fight over! Did I want to hurt him? Yes! Did I want to defend myself? Yes! Did I want to kill a boy from the neighborhood? No! Not even him, the unpopular Mehdi, the Butcher! I didn't want to kill him! Leaning over his body, I could see life leaving him, forming a growing puddle of blood all around him. During the war, I had always thought about this – there is so much life in the human body, yet it only took seconds for it to slip away. Then, there was no spirit left. Just a body. I was holding him, shaking his body, "Mehdi, Mehdi!!!" It was useless. It wasn't the first time someone had died in my arms. I looked up at the others,seeking some final hope, as if I was waiting for someone to tell me that that wasn't happening. Nader was horrified, he started withdrawing slowly. Akbar was holding his throat again, pressing it with his hands. Blood was oozing through his fingers... And then, I knew I had to run.

Run, Ali, Run!

We got into the car. Whenever we were in trouble, I was always the one driving. I liked Akbar's car. A powerful vehicle. I knew it intimately. I always pushed it to its limits. Roaring and fuming, the car would try to pull away from me, but I would always master it and make it submit to my will. There was no time for anything else then but to press on that gas pedal as hard as I could. We had to disappear from the neighborhood. There was no time; it had to be right then. Not realizing that this might be forever, I just continued to press on that accelerator. We left town, and were driving on the open road. We were both shaking, our bodies completely pumped up on adrenaline. My face was bleeding, Akbar's neck bleeding, and there was the death we had just caused and witnessed... We were rattled. I pulled over and turned on the lights inside. "Let me take a look at that wound, Akbar." Although he was much older than me, I was the one with the war experience. He pulled his hands away from the wound and stared at me. "It's not that deep," I told him calmly. "But you definitely have to get a few stitches. Otherwise it will be very difficult for the blood to stop." Relieved, Akbar nodded. Looking at my chin, he said, "We have to get you stitched as well." At this point, I looked in the mirror to see a deep open wound,starting from my lip all the way down to my chin. My clothes were soaked with the blood dripping on my chest. "Listen," I told him, "We'll find a needle and thread and we'll do it ourselves. I'll stitch yours, and you'll do mine. It's not that complicated. I've done it in battle. If you don't know how, I'll show you." Akbar agreed at first, but then he began to plead, "Listen, it's not going to work. We need a doctor to have it done properly." "What doctor are you talking about?" I got angry with him. "They'll call the law dogs right away. The first thing the cops do is to warn the hospitals to keep an eye out for people with the same wounds and give them a call if anyone shows up. While they're stitching us up, the boys in blue will come and arrest us." Then, Akbar told me he had a friend who could take us to a doctor, in complete discretion and safety. "We can trust him, listen to me." I agreed. He was 10 years older than I was, and he had more friends in various places. Off we went to find his friend. At first, his friend was shocked to see us show up covered in blood like that, but he agreed to help us. "You're lucky. The doctor's on duty tonight. I just have to check to confirm." We drove to the hospital and went behind the building. "You wait for me here, next to the fire exit," he said and went in to look for the doctor. "If he calls the cops, I'll find him!" I told Akbar, clenching my teeth to bear the intense pain from the wound. "He won't," Akbar groaned, holding his neck with both his hands. His friend turned out to be okay and didn't give us away. The doctor stitched both of us up, even though he wasn't very enthusiastic about it. We left through the back door and disappeared into the night. We hardly got any sleep in the car that night. Early in the morning, I went home, got myself some clean clothes, and took off the ones drenched in blood. I told my mother, "Akbar and I got into a car accident last night. Put these clothes in the wash." In a way, it was true. To some extent, the murder from the previous night had indeed been an accident. However, during that time, the jacks had caught a friend of mine and had forced him to reveal my whereabouts to them. Apparently, they had already found out about Mehdi. Nader had told them everything. They were already looking for me. They knew me well – I didn't sit still and was constantly on the go. It was easier for them to find someone who would betray me as opposed to roaming around the myriad neighborhoods of vast Tehran, losing time. While my mom and I were still talking, early in the morning, a stranger came to our home and told us all about it. He said, "So and so has sent me to apologize on his behalf, and to tell you that in an hour or two, he's bringing the jacks here. He's pretending he doesn't know anything for now, but he's only trying to win you enough time to escape. He'll have to tell them. They know that he knows, and he doesn't have a choice, but he's sent me to tell you that you must run right away because the cops are on their way!" He told me all of this in front of my mother and disappeared as quickly as he had appeared, afraid that they might catch him at my place. My mother realized something terrible had happened since the police were looking for me. She called one of my sisters and instructed her to hide the bloody clothes I'd come home in, and she began wiping up the blood traces I had left. I had to run.

After the murder, Akbar and I decided to hide in JadehChaloos, a favorite recreational area with many people who lived in Tehran, including us. It was located between Tehran and the Caspian Sea. We knew this exceptionally beautiful and picturesque place quite well. Home to many camp grounds, it attracted thousands of people every Thursday and Friday, the weekend observed in Iran. We had wonderful memories associated with these remarkable gorges, steep slopes, and marvelous panoramic views, spreading from the hills to the sea. We had always gone there as tourists, just to chill and relax. We had never thought we would gothere as wanted criminals, driven away by fear and uncertainty. We spent nearly a month there, sleeping in Akbar's car during the night. We also used his car to get arounduntil we left Iran. At the time, there was no computerized system to verify whether a certain plate number had been filed in the crime registrar, or if the car owner was wanted for a crime. They only checked for documents. Ourpersonal documents and car papers were clean, so there was no reason to be detained. Even back then, Tehran was a 15-million metropolis, a huge city, mainly occupied by houses and small four-to-five–story apartment buildings. It was a vast area, making it very difficult to track down someone wanted by the jacks. Besides, we never spent the night in Tehran. We entered the city at dusk, in the twilight, and left around one or two o'clock after midnight. It was most dangerous when we would return to our neighborhood, the familiar streets, our own homes, and the ones of our relatives. My so-called friends from Basij were lurking everywhere. There were informers and spies who would call them if they saw us. Yet, we still didn't know how to escape from Iran. We had never thought about it before, we had never left the country before.

Akbar assumed control of that move. Being older than me, he knew people in various circles, some quite quirky and exotic. One of these circles was a group of Iranian gypsies who looked just like Pakistanis and even spoke like them. In fact, they spoke several languages, including Arabic, Persian, Turkish, and Urdu (the official language in Pakistan). Akbar had come across the brother of a girl from the block who was married to one of these gypsies. That's how it worked in Iran – somebody had to vouch for you, otherwise you were nobody. So we got to them. They had strong connections everywhere, and they knew the smugglers across the border because they used them regularly. When their sons had to enroll in the army, the smugglers made arrangements to get them out through the Turkish border. All they needed was a passport, and then it was simple. They issued us passports – fake ones, obviously. We still had to wait though, until they actually made the passports, and this delayed us by nearly a month. We worked directly with their boss – Abbasi, a skinny 40-year-old, polite, and intelligent man, along with being an extremely brutal scoundrel, of course. The boss of the scoundrels was not the oldest but the most cunning, just as it was in our crews. The best thief is always the boss of the thieves. Abbasi was our man, because he controlled everything; he had connections with the smugglers and the counterfeiters that we needed as well as with the other gypsy families. Apparently, we were not the only ones who had a problem he could take care of. He had problems of his own too, and he turned to us for help. They were being racketeered by another gypsy clan that was taking a large share of their profit.

Being stronger and more violent, that clan mainly dealt with robbery. Abbasi could protect neither his people nor himself. They desperately needed brave boys to stand against those bad and dishonest people who were trying to control the money they had earned with great risk and tension. Of course, we responded positively to his request. It was a good deal for both the parties. We agreed to be their guards, and in return, they had to give us a percentage of their profits. I had already prepared my boom stick, a Llama 7.65, made in Spain. Akbar was also armed. We were still waiting for our passports, and at last, they were ready. It was time for parting. Parting with my home, my family, my Bismetri Street, my neighborhood, my Tehran, my homeland, Iran... and my love, Afsaneh. It was getting more dangerous to go back to our neighborhood, as more and more people were being sent to look for us and our homes were under constant surveillance. We knew that if we were to get caught, we would be doomed to the gallows or an inevitable shot to the head. There had to be a way to make my departurebearable, and I just had to find it. I'd always managed to procure solutions and had always found a way out. It was the same this time. I took a big strong hit of heroin. For the first time, I used inebriation as a way out. I had always felt sorry for people who turned to drugs for a way out. Smoking heroin was addictive and stupid, or that's what I thought. But it wasn't dumb. It wasn't dumb at all. It was a top-notch solution. Thanks to the heroin, I was able to say my goodbyes to everyone. My mother, as usual, became suspicious the moment she saw me. "Ali, what's going on? Are you ok? What did you smoke this time? It was not hashish, was it?" I couldn't lie to her. A mother cannot be deceived when it comes to her children, unless she, herself, decides that a lie about her child suited her more than the truth.But that was not the case with my mother. My father just looked at me, shook his head, and looked down at the ground. I wonder how he felt then– to see me following the footsteps of his youth? What had it cost him to stop in time to create a family, a home, and children? What would it cost me to stop? My aces from Bismetri responded like men, of course. And that is what I expected from these tough guys? "You'll be fine, you have always been. It'll take some time, but then you'll be back. We are here waiting for you. You'll always be our brother." We hugged like brothers, and they left. The customers could not wait forever. The most difficult was to part with Afsaneh. What could I have possibly told her? How could I have explained to her that instead of being together with her in Tehran, I had to leave the country and that we would have to be apart? I comforted herthat it was only going to be a short and temporary separation. "Once I get to Turkey, as soon as possible, I'll send you everything you need – money and documents – so you can come to me. No matter where I am. Then, we'll get married." "We will get married," she repeated as her eyes filled with tears, "We will get married." "And we'll have children," I said. "We will, Ali, of course, we will." "But now I have to run, Afsaneh," I said, holding her hand as I was trying to convince her. "Run, Ali, run," she nodded, biting her lips, and I dared to kiss her,our second kiss. And then,Afsaneh smiled with tears in her eyes and took a step back because it was time...

The following night, our new friends, the frauds, introduced us to the smugglers who took Akbar and me out of Iran through the mountain enroute to Turkey. By foot, we passed the border between Iran and Turkey at Hoy. Some guys in a Jeep were waiting for us there, and they took us to the villages near Van. We went down to the lake, took a deep breath, and looked around. Then we looked at each other, smiles finally diffused into our serious faces; we jumped up and down and embraced each other, happy that we had reached our goal and had saved our lives. Shouts of joy and relief! No one would look for us in our new whereabouts, no one would arrest us, no one would hang us, no one would shoot us in the head... But then, our celebration was short-lived, as we looked at one another again. What now? Now that we had escaped, what was our purpose from that moment onward? We had no clue. Where to? We didn't know that either. We didn't need to think over it for too long though. When you don't know where to go, you head to the capital, Istanbul. What would we do there? What we did best. When you don't know what to do, you do what you do best. Having been close to my parents, I had somewhat remained mindful of their commands. "Be reasonable. Don't do anything stupid." They annoyed me, but they still wielded influence over me. Now, all barriers were off. My life's long escape had begun. In the next years, as I ran from the law and from myself, others would be running from me as well.

Zeyfur, Sampal, and Hartahort

The initial enthusiasm of being free started to fade quickly. Living in Istanbul with a measly 30 or 40 bucks in our pockets hardly brought any joy. We had to figure how to make ends meet. Lucky for us, that new city was the size of Tehran, and we knew how to thrive in a big city. Stealing a bike there wasn't any more difficult than what it was in Iran. Istanbul had so many neighborhoods and so many banks and "business" opportunities. People withdrew money daily. Everybody dealt in cash, especially since credit cards were not common then. We needed cash. When short on cash, you either realize that you don't need much to begin with or you find a way to get some. We found a way. Eventually, we were even able to buy two Mercedes Benz, one for each of us.

Months passed, and we were doing better with every passing day. That meant that it was time for a change. The better we did, the more careful we had to be, so as to avoid screwing up and getting caught. The sense of imminent danger never allowed me to relax. I was adamant about not bringingAfsaneh into alife filled with uncertainty and danger at every step of the way. In order to support a wife and a family, above all, I needed to provide peace and security, not just money and a passport. I already had the money needed for our own passports; Akbar and I had found these Iranian guys who were top experts in the field of counterfeiting. They put your picture on a stolen passport to make it look just like a real one. The passports looked completely legal, not just to us but also to the customs officers. These counterfeiters were professionals, and we had no problems with their work, except for one thing.

Somehow, the counterfeiters missed something that didn't seem like a big deal to them.They put Akbar's photo on a woman's passport! This made Akbar very upset. Actually, he was quite angry. When they brought us our new passports, a grumpy look swept over his face that made me curious. I took a quick look before he hid it away; I saw it and started laughing. The name on his passport was *Arvane*. In Farsi, *Arvane* literally means "wild violet." I looked at Akbar, and then I looked away,still laughing. Then I laughed even harder. I tried to control myself, but I couldn't. I was laughing like a horse. Hee-hawing and neighing at the top of my lungs! He knew why I was laughing, so he didn't bother saying anything to me. Frowning, he opened the passport again, looked at it angrily, and put it away. I looked at him, giggling, "Excuse me, what was your name again?" I was teasing him, "Man, I knew you were wild, but a violet? Come on!" I kept guffawing, dying of laughter. Akbar looked at me, trying to get me to shut up,"You've got the wisdom of the whole world coming out of your ears, huh?" (The name on my passport was *Farsad*, meaning "wise.") "I don't know anybody more stupid than you. This is how far your wisdom has brought me," Akbar quipped. "Wild violets can't offend me, just the cultivated ones." I kept laughing; it was uncontrollable. I was trying not to go overboard though;we weren't the kind of guys you should tease. Being wild was what had brought us to that place. Of course, there were some advantages to our cavalier lifestyle – dope and girls. I wasn't dreaming of marrying any of them, and it's unlikely the girls were really crazy about us. We drove fancy cars, showing off, but it wasn't stability that we offered.

We could feel that the time to leave Turkey was approaching. We had turned into a breed that could not stay in one place for a long time. Like our friends, the Iranian gypsies, even if we didn't entirely want to, we needed to move on. Moreover, these gypsies who had taken us to Turkey had been asking us to accompany them as bodyguards in Bulgaria. It didn't take us long to decide that we were going to take them up on their offer. Two things were clear to us: we had to get out of there, and we always made easy cash when hanging out with them. We came to the Bulgarian border in the summer of 1990. I remember the FIFA Soccer World Cup was being held in Italy at that time. I didn't watch soccer much, but everyone talked about it. You couldn't ignore it; even as we were going through the border and entering Bulgaria, it was all we heard about. Getting through the Bulgarian border from Turkey with fake passports was proof that our counterfeits looked legit. The Bulgarian border has always been, and still is, quite difficult to get through. In prison, I met guys who had travelled all over Europe without a problem, yet they got caught right at the Bulgarian border with their fake passports. Stories circulated of people wanted by the Interpol, who had crossed borders everywhere, travelling from country to country withoutever getting caught, having been caught right away upon reaching the Bulgarian border, trapped in a Bulgarian prison waiting for the Interpol to pick them up. That wasn't the case with us. We crossed the border with no problem and met up with our friends, the gypsies.

How to milk a cow

Honestly, Abbasi's guys had invented such a good scheme; I wasn't a bit surprised that they were making big bucks. They were smart enough not to do business with the Bulgarians, saving themselves from the danger of getting into trouble with the local authorities. They lived on the outskirts of Sofia[3], deceiving foreigners, predominantly Turkish workers travelling to and from Western Europe. These gypsies conducted highway robbery in a very well-mannered way.Their preliminary preparation was spot on. They spoke several languages fluently, including Turkish, English, Persian, and Urdu. Even in the Turkish language, they knew various dialects. They had carswith false license plates from whichever nation they wanted, be it Germany, Austria, Holland,or Swit-

---

[3] Sofia is the capital of Bulgaria

zerland. Turks travelled to-and-fro mainly in these countries, and the use of these license plates helped to gain trust by appearing legit. Moreover, the whole scheme seemed quite believable. A woman would sit on the front seat, a child and a man in the back, either Akbar or myself. Thus, prepared, we would embark into the hunting grounds, the Sofia-Belgrade Road, the Ring Road, the Trakia Highway, or the road from Plovdiv to Svilengrad. Scanning parking lots and stands along the highway, whenever we spotted foreign workers, we pulled over right next to the victims, took out some food, and put it on the hood of the car. We would start chatting with them, telling stories of how we had worked abroad for years and now were returning home. We'd even dine with them to show respect and further pull in their attention through conversations. After that, we pulled out wads of money, thousands in various currencies – Austrian Shillings, German Marks, Swiss Francs, or Dutch Guilders –and would ask the victims piteously, "You see, I have a child and my woman in the car. I'd like to buy them something. I only have large bills. Could you please exchange it for some small change?"

We knew very well that the Turks wouldn't have small bills either. They would have exchanged their small bills into large ones before leaving. They worked for maybe two or three years and were headed home to invest their savings in their home country, either buying land or property or starting a business. We only wanted to make the victim feel sorry. The victims would then pull out wads of large bills to prove that they would like to help but couldn't. At that moment, the first goal would be attained– getting the victim's money out of his pocket. The deceiver would then look carefully at the wad and say, "Hey, man, give me that *zeyfur*, I'll pay you triple." "What is a zeyfur?" the victim would ask. The truth was, this was simply a trick; the word had no meaning. Sometimes, for a change, we would also use *sampal* or *hartahort* instead of zeyfur. Zeyfur, sampal, and hartahort – all of thesewere just verbal *Sim Sala Bim*, some *abracadabra* of the gypsies, to fascinate unsuspecting victims. Of course, to the victims, it was explained that a "zeyfur" was a very rare banknote, and that as collectors, crazy about the zeyfur, or sampal, or hartahort, we would give anything to have these invaluable bills, lying, "You don't even know what kind of treasure you've got in your hands," and then, would add, "Can I just see it?" At this moment, curiosity and greed would prevail, and the victims would hand over their wad of money to the deceiver. Second goal – check! Having gotten a hold of their money, the skillful hands of the deceiver were in control now. While checking out the bills one by one, the deceiver magically would steal a few of them. These frauds had incredibly dexterous and fast fingers. When the magician's sleight of hand was through, the wad of cash was returned to the victim, but not before the deceiver held the wad with both hands one last time. It was a psychological maneuver, a working scheme, tested thousands of times. While looking at the hands holding the money, suddenly, the victims would look up, surprised, into the palmer's eyes, as if asking, "Why are you not letting go of my money?" The deceiver then hands the wad of cash to the person with one hand, while the other hand would withdraw, pulling out some bills twice as fast with the ringer finger. Always, the same thing would happen – the victim kept his eyes on the hand giving back the wad, not on the other hand with the stolen notes. The final take brought in about one-third of the wad for the thief – for a 100-bill wad, it meant about 30. Everything happened so quickly, the victim the victim could never catch a whiff. If, accidentally, something went wrong and the victim got suspicious, the deceiver returned the money back playfully. If the situation got worse, then either Akbar or I intervened. That was why we were there and the service we got paid for. Usually, we had no problems; everything went smoothly, and these skillful gypsies with their dexterous fingers made huge amounts of money. On top of that, they never killed the cow, they just milked it, taking only a part and not all. By the time the victims realized what had happened, they couldn't do anything about it. These deceivers stole with such finesse that often, the victims wouldn't even be able to connect the incident with money that was missing, and instead, they grew suspicious that perhaps their relatives had stolen from them.

Through the genius of the *zeyfur*, *sampal*, and *hartahort*, deception, and the dexterity of their hands, these magicians own houses and properties in Iran worth millions of dollars. It took them only a few summer months to make such a large fortune. Today, these deceptions don't work in Bulgaria, thanks to highways that are much safer and the installation of surveillance cameras in many places; also, information is now made available to travelers on the internet about gypsy trickery. Times have changed, but back then, it used to be a very profitable business.

Abbasi would bring in roughly 200,000 German Marks a month, worth $100,000 USD in today's market. The others made similar amounts. Business was booming. They paid for bodyguards, and there was enough money for everybody in the group; we were all friends and partied to the hilt. Over time, however, these gypsy business partners began trying to cheat us. They started hiding money from Akbar and me,something that naturally made us nervous. It became obvious one time when, right after the job was done, upon entering the car,the deceiver gave the stolen money to his wife, who immediately put the bills in a plastic bag and straight into her undies. No matter how fast the deceiver was, we could tell that there were not hundreds but thousands in cash. Later, we were told, "Here is your share, 100 German Marks; this time we only raked in 500." Yet, we had clearly seen the thousands he had handed over to his wife.We began to get a little uptight. "Hmm, let me see, perhaps my wife made a mistake," said Abbasi, pretending to be naive, giving us yet another bill. That didn't make us any happier. How could they steal from their own bodyguards?

In general, things began to go downhill, and in the end, with all respect to the ladies, financial logic prevailed, thus introducing a new practice – a daily inspection of the bags. The fact that the stashed bags of cash could not leave their assigned hiding place at request created extra tension. Therefore, parting with the gypsies became inevitable, albeit reluctantly on our part.

One-sided termination of the agreement

The gypsies persistently tried to shake us off, hiding and changing houses constantly. We didn't let this deter us, as we tracked them down and harassed them. Akbar and I always found their dens in the most brilliant ways. For example, we built connections with the pimps at the clubs who would supply prostitutes to the gypsies. We would wait in the car for the girls to come out of the clubs, and as soon as they did, we would go and bump into our former so-called friends. What hustlers! How dare they lie to us and steal our wages! When we pursued them, we would switch cars every so often to avoid recognition and to foil our attempts at retrieving our due pay. It was our source of income! Why should we allow them to steal from us poor workers? We chased them down, demanding our fair share. We had considered the unwritten agreement we had had with Abbasi and his company as being valid for an indefinite period of time. It was their problem if they did not need to use our services any longer.

Things got more serious when one of their guys tried to fool Akbar. Akbar brutally beat him for it, breaking ribs and one of his arms and leaving his face badly swollen. Akbar gave him a good beating, nearly to death. Apparently, that was when the hustlers' family committee got together and decided to lodge a formal complaint with the police against us. They went on to do everything possible to get us arrested and convicted. We found out in time, but it forced Akbar to immediately flee Bulgaria. He had to go, first, because he was the one who had committed the crime; and second, because he had acquired a mandatory registration card given to everyone who was temporarily residing in Bulgaria at that time. I had not received one as yet since I was having some trouble with the law. I couldn't leave the country legally, and quite frankly, I had no reason to leave it illegally. I decided to hide until the danger had subsided.

I hardly had any money left when I went over to Reza's to hide. Reza was a friend from Iran. He let me stay at his place for a few days, but his money situation was worse than mine. "Give me a hundred dollars," Reza said, adding, "Within a few days, some smugglers will have a job for us, so we will make some money. They will give us a hefty advance payment, and there you go. Then I will pay you back the rest." "Ok, here's a hundred dollars," I told him, leaving myselfwith hardly anything. As a guarantee, he gave me his passport. Being friends was one thing, but playing by the rules was another. Anyway, he kept his promise. He was gone for two days and came back with an appointment date with the smugglers. The next day, we went for a meeting at the cafe in the Slavia Hotel. We sat down, and I ordered two coffees and a sandwich – just one because Reza had already spent the hundred dollars to pay off an old loan, and I had only a few coins left. I felt sorry for him because I knew I would be fine, but he was a chump who would soon would be left with no money again. We divided the sandwich. I put some sugar in my coffee, stirring it with a spoon, once, twice... Suddenly, at that moment, I felt two guns against each of my temples and heard, "You move, we'll blow your head off!"

It was apparent these guys weren't joking. They were serious. I did not move. They had me nailed to my chair. Handcuffing and frisking followed. I was clean, no weapon on me that day. Head down, I was pushed into a waiting police car. I thought about Reza and how unfair it was that he was also being arrested because of me. Damn! In the car, I began to plead with them, telling them that he was not guilty, he only happened to be there by accident. Not that anyone paid attention to me, but I kept insisting and went on and on, even after we entered the police station, "Let him go, he is innocent." They took me to a room where Reza was already sitting in a chair, surrounded by a few policemen. I asked for a cigarette. Reza pulled a full packet out of his pocket and handed it to me. What did I see? "Rothmans King Size."Hmm, how come? He had no money for coffee that morning,but then, he was pulling out fancy cigarettes. In Sofia, one could only find Rothmans King Size in the Japanese Hotel and nowhere else. I thought of Abbasi, who only smoked that brand.

"You smoke some real good cigarettes," I looked at Reza, who lit my cigarette and pulled back guiltily. As I took a puff, the investigator asked me to admit to the allegations of armed assault, robbery, and infliction of grievous bodily harm. We used the help of an interpreter to make sure we understood each other. How could I have admitted to that crime when I knew that the punishment was 15 to 20 years of imprisonment, and I hadn't even committedthe same? I answered, "I don't know what you are talking about. I'm innocent." They did not even bother asking me again. They turned to Reza, "Tell us the story again." This guy I had shared my food with, my friend, Reza, who I had felt pity for, the one I had pleaded for because he was innocent, opened his mouth and began. I couldn't believe my ears.

The story told by Reza the traitor

He told them everything, going into great details about how Akbar had told him about the gypsies' tricks, how he had stabbed one of them, how he had hurt the other one, and how we had made arrangements to blow them up the next time. I thought I was going to pass out. I interrupted him, speaking in street talk, so that the interpreter wouldn't understand, "What is it that you are betraying me for? Do you know what will happen once I get out?" I asked him, furious. He just looked at the floor, and kept on and on.

Later, I found out what had happened. Reza spent the hundred dollars I had lent him. Somehow, he had gotten to hear about Abbasi and the gypsies who were seeking to hand me over to the police. Reza had gone to them and had made a deal to betray me and Akbar! They gave him a thousand dollars under the condition that he would arrange for them a meeting with me at a café where the police would catch me. What a perjurer! With Akbar gone, it was just me. This so-called friendhad given us away for a mere one grand! "How could you be so gullible, Ali, and so stupid?" I kept asking myself.

After Reza finished, they pulled me into a cell, alone. A few hours later, they pulled me out of the cell and into another room. I went in. Four people were standing there, lined up. "There you go, an identity procedure," I said to myself. They pushed me into the line. Two policemen entered the room with a witness, an Iranian gypsy. Abbasihad paid him to testify against me. I'd never seen this man, and he'd never seen me. How was he even going to recognize me? Abbasimust have told him about the deep scar across my chin. Of course, the moment he entered, he took one quick look at all of us and immediately identified me. He came close and pointed at me, "This is the man who beat my friend, broke his arm, his head, his ribs, and took his money." This was the charge for the armed robbery committed by Akbar, but since he was gone, it had all fallen on my shoulders. This false witness was looking into my eyes, continuing with his lies. I couldn't hold myself back, I told him in Persian, "Liar! Once I get out of here, I'll find you and do to you all the things you lie about me having done." He stepped back, shouting to the policemen, "He's swearing at me!" That made me even more furious because it wasn't true. There was no swearing in my vocabulary. I told him, "I'm gonna knock your block off if I find you." This false witness told the police he was Pakistani, and they believed him. Just because he had a Pakistani passport didn't mean he was a Pakistani! He was a pure-blooded Iranian gypsy! The worst part was that he was a hustler and a liar! What else could I have even expected being in my situation? I was handcuffed and stuck there.

My recently severed friends had two witnesses against me, and I knew they could pay for and bring as many witnesses as they wanted to. I was being charged with everything Akbar had done in addition to all the things I had done myself. This was all running through my mind as I was being locked up. "Ali! Ali! Locked up like a fool!" I could not believe it. In the interim, they put me in the lock up by the West Park Bridge. There were four or five beds, but more than 10 Vietnamese. Early in the next morning, I was taken back to the police station and put behind bars. I stood by the door, checking everything out. "I have to come up with something, I have to," I kept telling myself. I noticed the guarding sergeant kept getting up and going to the office several times, literally popping in just for a minute, or for even less than that. What was he doing in there? Watching a game or a movie? I didn't know, and I didn't care. Even if it were only for a moment, I liked that he left me alone, regardless of the fact that I was already behind bars. I looked carefully, nobody else was guarding me.

No cameras were present in prisons at that time. I started examining the lock very thoroughly. Then, I observed that the key had most likely been turned just one time, and that the lock bolt was barely keeping the door shut. I thought to myself, "What if I pushed a little here and there? I might be able to open it." To my happiness and their misfortune, there was a loose door lock and a distracted sergeant standing between me and freedom! Apparently, they didn't expect someone to attempt an escape right in front of the guard.

Prison break

"Think, Ali, think!" Nothing left in my pockets! Everything was taken. Oh! I always had a paper clip in my back pocket. I checked it, and there it was! Good! They had missed it when frisking me. I took it in my hand, and with my face glued to the bars, looking out, I unfolded it behind my back. I stepped back a bit, and began to discreetly work on the lock bolt. I pushed gently; the bolt was loose. There was a gap! That was it! The sergeant got up and went to the office again. Let me try now, I thought. I pushed the bolt harder, and at the same time, I pulled the door towards me. It opened! I didn't expect that. I was so shocked; I locked it again. Who would have imagined that this stupid door would open so easily! "OK, Ali, calm down! The sergeant didn't see anything. Breathe. Here, he is coming back, not suspecting anything, patience. Wait for him to get up again to go back to the office. That's it; here he goes inside the office." Then I pushed the lock tongue with the paper clip, and the door opened; but this time, I pulled it back without closing it. I'm not crazy to make the same mistake twice. I was just standing there, pretending I was doing nothing. Pretending that I was locked in, but I was not. And then, I carefully countedthe seconds it took my careless guard to get up and go into the office. I did not have a watch on me, and so, I counted slowly. The first time it was 19 seconds; the second, 21; the third, 19 again. Ok, that was good. It was enough time. I just had to wait a little while. "Breathe, just breathe." The next time he shut the door behind him, I opened my door calmly, left the lock up... without any rush... and then quietly closed it behind me. Then, I walked through the hallway without drawing any attention to myself, and then out into the yard, "Breathe, just breathe." I turned around the corner, and off I went! I vanished from that place like a bat out of hell! "Run! Run! Run!" I kept telling myself. I zigzagged through a few streets as far away from the lock up as I could. I turned sharply at a corner, slowed down, kept walking, and then I disappeared. I found a safe place to hide in, sent news to some faithful friends, and they gave me some money.

In a few days, I started looking for Abbasi and his gypsies at their usual hangouts: a hotel downtown, several other hotels in the districts of Simeonovo and Dragalevtsi, a house behind the Romanian Embassy, on the Ring Road, on the road from Sofia to Slivnitsa, on the highway from Sofia to Plovdiv all the way to Svilengrad. Interestingly, I couldn't find them anywhere. "Of course they are gone," some friends of mine informed me, laughing. "It's not surprising. An hour after your escape, they went to the police station with more witnesses against you. The policemen were frantically running back and forth, and Abbasi found out you had escaped a little earlier. The very same day,Abbasi fled with all of his crew!" Hmm, I didn't know these people were so fast. However, just be to sure, I looked around some more; truly, there was indeed no trace of them. The traitor, Reza, had a passport made immediately and fled to Austria. I never saw him again. Years later, because my understanding changed, I realized it was good fate I didn't find any of them. At that time, what could I do? What I did best, of course – sell drugs.

In Bulgaria, I got drugs from some Iranian tourists.We had an arrangement to meet at a hotel where they were staying at. I went to pick up some hashish and to see these guys. Having received my product, I started chatting outside in the parking lot. I had made some quick money that made me feel little more relaxed. Wrong! The problem with quick money was thatitlulled my attention. I accidentally caught a glimpse of a man whose face I recognized. He was looking around randomly; I felt something was off. I was certain that I had seen him before; I couldn't remember his name but could recognize his face. Typically, I am not good with names. I've had so many fake passports that I know a name does not matter. Faces are much more difficult to alter than names. I never forget a face. As we were talking, I told the boys calmly, "Now, do exactly what I say. Stay close together in a row, I will slowly turn around, and walk away. Just stand still." They got together. I turned slowly, and then, calmly headed to the nearest bus stop. I just needed a little lead. If someone was coming for me, I couldn't be caught. I walked slowly, wearing an unbuttoned summer shirt, when suddenly, a bearded man I was passing jumped upon me. Apparently, he was a cop. At that moment, I pulled myself away sharply, leaving my shirt in his hands and started running shirtless. I lost my balance and stumbled to the side, which slowed me down. Right then, the face I had seen in the parking lot struck me. He tackled me, and grabbing me by the waist, he shouted, "Where do you think you're going?" "If you didn't catch me, you would have no idea," I thought angrily, as I was handcuffed.

Once again, I was back at the police station.This time, straight to the second floor and to a different room. I scanned the room, just in case. Not a chance, the door was heavy, complete with a sturdy lock. The sergeant saw me scanning and giggled. "Forget about it," he said. "This time there's no way out. The officer who was on duty when you had run away the last time is guarding you tomorrow. He'll give you a good old beating.

Why did you run away during my shift?!

Do you know what shame he's had to bear because of you? The police chiefs have teased him relentlessly, thanks to you. As for the sergeant who was guarding you, he was fired!" Okay, I got it. It was going to be a horrible day the following today; not that that very day had been easy, but at least it was drawing to an end. I looked around and saw my shirt, tossed on the sergeant's desk. "Can I have my shirt back?" "Yes, no problem," he replied, and handed it to me. I checked the pocket; the hashish was still there. That felt real good, a beam of light in those two dark days. There was something there to make me feel good at least. I would have some hashish and rest. The next day, the offended officer showed up, hastily walking. I could see his chest rising and falling, he was panting with anger. I'm sure somebody had notified him that I had been caught the previous night. No doubt he had hardly slept in anticipation of the beating.

He got to it right away,without even bothering to wait for the other shift to leave. This guy had huge hands. Man, it was impressive! It was as if he was kicking me with his feet! He hit me once and glued me straight to the wall. Next, he punched me so hard that I went flying into the opposite wall. I can never forget that beating. He kept shouting at me, "Why, why did you run away during my shift, you idiot?" As if I had meant my previous escape as a personal insult. I never understood why some people take things so personally. I had to do it during somebody's shift, right? The beating was heavy and so was his swearing. I was right!I had only reached the morning and my day was already turning out to be awful. Later, it would turn out that this officer was a real cool guy. We even became friends; he liked me too. Whenever we talked, later, he would always say to me, "You're cool, you idiot, why did you run away during my shift?" He kind of stopped swearing at me because we had become pals. He could not figure out how I had managed to procure a passport from Kuwait when they had caught me. How did I get it? It was funny; it got me thinking.To be honest, I had never even noticed it. I got transferred to the Sofia Central Prison. Before the investigator left for his summer holiday, he sent me there to ensure that I would still be around when he returned. He got his wish, but they couldn't prove anything. There were no witnesses, no fingerprints, and no evidence, nothing that could be used to convict me of a crime. I was imprisoned for six months and some days and was finally freed.

Meanwhile, Akbar returned. He came to pick me up, and off we went together again. Our friendship was great, but the heroin brought it to an end. Akbar smoked so much heroin that sometimes, he had no idea what he was doing. He didn't remember, and he didn't care. His case wasn't closed yet. I didn't know when they might decide to reopen it and lock me in again instead of him. Besides, between the two of us, I had always been better at dealing with money. I always kept my arrangements and people knew they could count on me. No one could count on him anymore. He was dragging me down with him, and that was bad for my business. I told him, "Akbar, we must go separate ways. I'll give you 6-7,000 Deutsche Marks. Head toward Western Europe and deal with your life. They are looking for you here. They'll lock me up instead of you again. I've had enough." He didn't agree with my advice and went back to Iran. I never understood the kind of foolish confidence that led him to do that. Soon afterward, my Iranian partners told me Akbar had gotten arrested and was put on trial for the murder of Mehdi, the Butcher. A few months later, I found out that he had been sentenced to death and then hung and shot in the head almost immediately, according to the Iranian protocol.

During that time, strange things that I couldn't explain started happening to me. For instance, there was this one time when as I was walking and smoking heroin, and out of the blue, I saw a sign that read "MARIBOR"[4] with a digit of some kilometers beside it. What was happening? I was lost. Where was I? I turned around and saw something like 30 scared Africans looking at me.

"What am I doing here?" I asked them. No answer. "What are you doing here?" I asked.

They answered, "We don't know. You are the one taking us to Western Europe. That's where we want to go."

"What? Have I gone mad? I've never seen youbefore!" I became angry. I didn't know what was going on.

Right then, a group of furious, armed men jumped out of the bushes, holding guns at me, yelling, "You crazy man! Where are you going? Where are you taking these Africans? Don't you know there is a war going on in Yugoslavia right now? Everyone's fighting. We're killing one another! You want to die too?"

"Hey, hey, I don't know what's happening; I don't know these people. I've never seen them before!"

"Don't you understand, you fools! Go back to Bulgaria!"

I turned around in the direction opposite to the sign. Behind me, the Africans continued after me. Where did you say I was taking you? Yeah, right. I kept walking, smoking, and wondering about this nonsense; whether it was real or a dream. How in the world did I get to *Maribor*? How bizarre! How completely bizarre! Where was my head all this time? It was probably my searching heart. Who knew? I always had a searching heart. I've always wanted to see, hear, and to try and touch new things. I was always searching. As my mother always said, "Ali, it's as if you have ants in your pants. You can't sit still."

I said to myself, "What a minute! What's going on here? Can a man help all these people get to Western Europe when he, himself, has not

---

[4] Maribor is the second largest city in Slovenia, West Balkan Peninsula

been there? Let me check it out and see for myself what it is like there."
I left for the Netherlands. What was I looking for? What was I missing?
I didn't know, but one thing was clear, I had no peace within. I spent
six months in the Netherlands in a village close to Tilborg, next to the
Belgium border. My intention was to acquire citizenship. Of course,
I did underhanded things again – selling drugs and fooling around. I
didn't understand why people went to the Netherlands. I didn't get the
attraction. There was nothing special about it, so I returned to Bulgaria.
Something about Bulgaria drew me back. As much as I tried to stay
away, I always came back. That time, it was because of a girl – Rossi.

What is your gender?

We had met just before I had left for Tilborg. It was a crazy kind of love.
"I will go there," I told her, "and I'll send you an invitation." Bulgarians couldn't roam freely around Europe back then, they needed vi-
sas. Rossi, simply put, was beautiful. She had black curly hair through
which her green eyes shone like gems. She was mad about me.

It was amazing that such a pretty girl was so crazy about me.
As I responded to her love, it became even crazier. I told her, "Rossi,
Tilborg is so boring; there is no point for you to come over. I'm moving back." What I didn't tell her was she would need to have a visa,
and I couldn't help her out with that. Of course, I had the option of
helping her illegally. However, I cared for her way too much to let
her get involved in all my underworld dealings. My golden rule was
to never work with ordinary people, and she was ordinary. Working
with ordinary people in the past had always messed me up somehow and had created problems. I only worked with law-breakers.
There were no mistakes that way. Anyway, it was bad enough she
had fallen in love with a brute like me. Generally speaking, tough
girls are crazy about bad guys. They are absolutely determined
to screw their lives up, hanging out with guys like me, and there's
nothing that can stop them.

"Come back, Ali, my love. I can hardly wait," she would say. I could hardly wait to see her too, but on the way back, I decided to pass through Switzerland. It was not a shortcut or anything but just that some guys had invited me there. Birds of a feather flock together. They were friends, and so, I had decided to stop by and see them. I thought that it was a good opportunity to do business and make money. I entered the country without any problems, using an Italian passport. According to my new identity, my mother was Romanian, and my father, an Italian. Everything was fine until then. I had no problems all throughout Europe. The passport was a high-quality fake. I had it made in Romania on my way to the Netherlands. Prior to that time, I had used a Turkish passport. I left Romania with that Italian passport and had travelled all over Europe. And then, I was in Zurich, Switzerland. We got ourselves into some trouble there, and the police came to check our passports. "Here, go ahead, check," I said, handing him my Romanian fake. The officer checked my passport, and, to my horror, he burst into laughter. He looked at me, looked at the passport, and kept laughing. What was going on? Why was he laughing? Man, it made me furious, standing there, not knowing what was going on.

"What's so funny?" I asked him.

"You want to know what's funny?! I'll have to check if you've got a penis," said the cop, still grinning.

"What? What did you say?" Chills ran down my back.

"I said, I'll have to check if you've got a penis," said the cop, softly stressing that last word. "You've got a female name on your passport."

"What do you mean?" I couldn't understand.

"Well, according to your passport, you are Michaela Nitu," said the cop. I looked at the passport. He was right! It reminded me about the time when I had made fun of poor Akbar, the wild violet, but at least he had known that was given a girl's passport. In my case, I had not even realized that Michaelawas a female name. At that moment, I realized what a stupid thing I'd done. The cop started showing my passport to the other cops, leafing through the pages, showing off all the stamps from all the other countries, proud to the marrow of his bones that he had been the one to catch me. A stupid situation! If only I could have gotten a hold of those dumb asses who had made my passport then! Those gypsies! *Zeyfur, sampal,* and *hartahort*... I chuckled to myself as they handcuffed me and forced me into their police car. I was to be stuck behind bars until I would agree to tell them who I was and where I was from. I was locked up until my identity could be completely clarified. All I had was a fake passport. I didn't have other documents. What could the Swiss authorities do but send me back to Iran?

A voyage to the gallows

On a cold spring day, they put me on a plane, and I was sent off to the gallows and the bullet in the head. I was going to join Akbar in hell. Where would my lifestyle have taken me except to hell? I looked out through the window as the plane descended for a landing in Istanbul. I thought to myself, "When one doesn't know where to go, they go to Istanbul." I loved that city, and back then, even more. I loved it to death. I didn't really want to continue my flight. Istanbul was irresistible. Nonetheless, I continued on from Istanbul to Tehran, all aboard and into the air.

"You're stuck, Ali, you big smart ass, you'll be hung at 30 because everyone pays for their sins. Remember what you used to tell your friends, "I'll die before I turn 40," I thought to myself, "If the court speeds up the trial, you might die before you turn 30." I was thinking about all this when we landed in Tehran. The city felt strange and foreign somehow, but that was no strange city. Thatwas where I was to be hung shortly. Perhaps, I should have felt some sorrow or should have reminisced my homeland a little. But no, I felt nothing. That place was no longer my Tehran, and I was no longer its homeboy. I was locked up in ZandiGasr, a prison known to be a very bad place for perpetrators of very serious crimes. There was no escape from here. There was no way I belonged to that place. They forced me into a room, and there he was, my uncle! He was my own flesh and blood! He was waiting for me on his feet. He threw himself at me, almost engulfing me in a giant hug! He hugged me hard, right there in front of the guards, while I was still in handcuffs! I hadn't expected that.

My uncle was one of the people who always wanted to prod me on the right path. He had spanked me as a child, reasoned with me, talked to me, but nothing ever worked. No one had any luck teaching me, but, oh, how this man loved me like his own child! He knew how much my mother loved me too, and that amplified his concern for me. He had done everything he could back in the day to try to get me on the straight and narrow, but with no success. Somehow, he had managed to do something else successfully.He was one of the few smart men from the Shah's rule who had managed to not only survive during the Ayatollahs reign but also gain influence. Now, holding me tight in his arms, he burst into tears and whispered in my ears fitfully, "Ali, my son, I swear by my life, by my very own hands that hold you now, I'll get you out of here." He nearly brought me to tears. The guards had to pull us apart and take me inside.

My uncle's presence was a ray of hope. He must have known about my arrival and had arranged a strong connection to allow his visit in ZandiGasr.That itself meant a lot to me. What promise he made to get me out of there? I felt hope like a drowning man clutching at a straw, although, in hindsight, this is an improper comparison because, although I really was drowning, my uncle's word was never straw. A clever character like my uncle would never give false hope in a situation such as the one I was in. No, not to his nephew. He must have already set a plan in place. I strongly believed that. To kill time, I started looking for things to do. I began working out –push-ups, crunches, and similar body-building exercises. There was plenty of space. To my surprise, the prison was huge and in good condition. It had nothing in common with the stinky cell at the police station where I was locked up the first time and had experienced that shish kebab routine.

Welcome to the Prison Fortress

ZandiGasr turned out to be much bigger, cleaner, and brighter,even more than the Sofia Central Prison in Bulgaria where I would be locked up in the coming years. Shoes were not allowed in the cell and were meant to be left out in the corridor. We wore shoes when we were taken out for a walk in the designated area. Each block had its own area, and there was zero communication allowed between inmates of different blocks. Escape was out of question. This was *ZandiGasr* after all; its name means, "Prison Fortress" in Persian. How could a man even fantasize about getting out of there? If he did muster the imagination, how would he be able to do it? "Money," my uncle told me during his next visit.

Money has been well-received anywhere, at any time. He was quite convinced that, in our case, money would open the doors of the fortress wide enough for me to sneak out. How was he going to do it? He never told me that, and I never asked. That was his business. I had to help him with some cash. After all, it was my life that would come to an end if we didn't make it on time. Speed and money was what we needed. "I've transferred money to my mother throughout the years to help my family. About $60,000 USD in total," I told my uncle. I had used a very primitive, but nonetheless, effective payment system to transfer money internationally. Whenever someone who was originally from Iran needed money in Bulgaria, I would give them the cash. Simultaneously, their relatives in Iran would give the same amount of cash to my relatives. On the phone, they would hear us say, "I gave it. I got it." Then, from Iran, we would hear the same, "I gave it. I got it." With this "give/get" banking system, about $60,000 had reached my mother. I knew her; she would have hardly taken a dime from it. She could tell where it came from, and it would have been a great compromise on her part to even accept it. I knew she would not have spent it.

Not surprisingly, in the end, money went where it had come from, from crime to corruption. Ali, the big hustler,who did business throughout Europe and made big bucks that eventually ended up in the hands of judges and prosecutors. I was grateful that my parents were even willing to let that money be used to help me then. My uncle took care of the whole situation. As far as I understood, there was not much resistance from the key people in charge. I just waited while everyone around me shouted like crazy. The FIFA World Cup in the USA had begun and the Bulgarian team was beating all the other teams. Not that I cared about soccer. I was never keen on it. All the prisoners were going mad about this championship. Everyone was teasing me, "Hey, you, Bulgarian fella! Your team is winning again! Look! Look what they are doing! They even beat Germany. Look at Stoichkov, Letchkov, Balakov, and Kostadinov" Prisoners and guards alike had the names of the Bulgarian soccer players on their lips. "Soccer doesn't interest me," I would reply plainly. "That doesn't matter. Watch some anyway! It might be your last World Cup," one of guards joked. You come across all sorts of jokers in prison.

Rossi, I love you to death!

Anyway, instead of losing brain space over such din, I chose reading Rossi's letters, which managed to reach me even there in prison and made me feel more eager for life and love.

"I'll die if you don't come back to me. I don't want to live without you," she wrote, and that brought tears to my eyes. If I did not go back, it would only be because I had been executed. I did not want death, neither for Rossi nor me. My heart knew that this woman loved me with her whole being, and this endless love gave her power over me. It made me hers. I wanted to be with her. I proposed to her from the bottom of my despair. From ZandiGasr, I wrote, "Rossi, I want to marry you! Please promise me you will marry me when I return. I love you to death!" This was the first woman who had ever cared for me that way, and I could feel that care deep within me. Being completely consumed and genuinely dedicated was a maddening feeling, especially for someone like me who had lived in a world of lies, fraud, and robbery all his life. This was all going on when I was facing the gallows! Why couldn't fate have been a little more generous? "I want to marry you, my dearest Ali, I want to be with you forever," she wrote back. How could I watch a World Cup? My heart thumped, I was ecstatic, but not because of the World Cup. Anxiously, I dreamt of Rossi. I longed for Rossi. Nothing else burned in my thoughts like Rossi did! Fired up in the madness of love and fairly glowing with flames of passion within that drowned out the football euphoria without, I was jolted by the voice of the guards who called me in to, asking me to pack my belongings. I was being released! My uncle was waiting for me outside to take me home to my mother and father. Two days later, I flew to Sofia through Istanbul.

There was a little less than $6,000 left from the $60,000. Bulgaria screamed out to me like never before because Rossi was waiting for me. We could not live without each other. And so, we ran to the city hall to get married as soon as possible. We lived happily and wildly, but also modestly due to the unforeseen legal costs of my life-saving matter in Iran. That didn't bother me. I knew I would always be able to think of something. I always had and always would. *Zeyfur*, *sampal*, and *hartahort* – I remembered those artistic hustlers and a slight smile appeared on my face as my wife's body touched mine. If I'd ever been close to happiness, I think it was right then.

A Tool in the Devil's Hands

True happiness is not real. Or, when it is, it's short-lived and gone in a blink of the eye. This is how it went between me and Rossi. After months of passionate, crazy love, cracks began to appear between us. Something cold blew through these cracks, wearing our togetherness down and making the distance between us even bigger. We didn't give up on each other; we didn't turn our backs on our marriage either. Yet, somehow, with our arms reaching out to grasp the other, the crevices between grew larger and deeper. We saw it happening, but we couldn't stop it – each one sinking in our very own swamp. Hers comprised alcoholism,mine, drug addiction. Smoking dope made me feel good; it gave me peace and confidence. It cleared my mind, and it helped me think straight. Within a few hours, I would feel even worse than I did before, andso, I'd take another dose. Then, I could be myself again. Without it, I simply couldn't be myself. When sober, the reality around me would become unbearable. Another smoke and I was myself again, drowning in my heroin addiction – this hadbecome me. Without anything solid to grab hold of or to step on, can one drowning person help another? The only thing I could do was watch – watch as both Rossi and I sank deeper and deeper. Especially, as I continued to break that one golden rule of those old dogs in Tehran, "You either sell drugs, or you use them. But you can't do both. Try and you'll ruin yourself..." My relationship with Rossi was the first to fall victim... my first failure. Although the drug business had been going well, there was one problem – there were some inconvenient witnesses, and I couldn't bear the thought of going to jail again.

Then came the day when I planned on getting rid of one of them. I had sworn to myself that I would never let a witnesses live; I would never leave a loose end. All my problems came from witnesses. My friends would ask me to protect them against gangsters. I would risk my life to save their asses, and they would witness against me! I paid a visit to the calabooselike this because of my own stupidity. "You can't get any more stupid than this, Ali. You are a fool, a big fool. You think you are a smart ass, but you are always the one getting screwed. You get locked up, and they're out there free."

Faster than a bullet!

This is what happened between Denis and me. "Please, Ali, come with me. I have to meet this guy, but I'm scared something's going to get screwed up." Screwed up? It couldn't have been any more screwed up that what happened! If I hadn't gone to protect him, I'd have still been still free. But I failed to factor in all that then. I was caught in a trap like the last fool on earth. Why? Cause Ali was always the tough one. Always loyal.Always there for his friends. What did Ali do this time? He went with a friend to protect him and make sure that his friend would not get robbed. Nothing crossed his mind; nothing told him that something was off. It all seemed like a simple job, like all the other simple jobs that were a part of his everyday world. The dealers got the drugs from his house located in a village close to Sofia. This guy was supposed to show up and exchange cocaine for more heroin because there was a cocaine shortage in the Bulgarian market. On the other hand, Denis had plenty of heroin. A simple swap. No money involved, nothing to be worried about. It was supposed to be simple, no big deal – just a swap. You'd think if there really should have been a problem? No, why would there be? Yes, I should have seen the red flag. If Denis was so freaked that he was asking me to be there "just in case," I should have been more careful. I should've just said no. But I went, because I was tough, and I didn't care. I was on guard, with my eyes and ears peeled. When, in actuality, I was at the wrong place, at the wrong time, with the wrong people. And that wasn't my first time. All the troubles I'd ever gotten myself into boiled down to my own lack of discernment. Within minutes of entering the place where the meeting had been arranged, that same fate was to strike me once again. So we were sitting there, waiting for this guy, killing time with small talk. Denis looked down at his watch, fidgeting nervously. Downstairs, at the entrance door, his guard waited for the guy. The swap was to be done unarmed, that was the deal. The guard was to check him and bring him up. I looked at my own watch, as I thought to myself, "Come on, where's this guy? I have things to do." I stood at the wall by the door from which he was going to enter. He would see my friend, but not me. Once he was in, I was to stand behind his back, just in case. Including the guard, it was supposed to be three to one, good as gold. The bell rang, which meant he must be coming, and everything seemed fine. But it wasn't! That guy entered the room with a gun in his hand, pointing straight out. A Љkorpion machine pistol. I knew the weapon in his hand very well. A big hairy hand with a massive, heavy gold ring embedded with a huge black stone held the gun. The moment he stepped in, I jumped on him. He was a big man, huge, just like the weapon in his hand and the ring on his finger. However, not expecting my move, he swayed. We took hold of each other, rolling over on the floor. The pistol flew out to the side. He managed to push me away, but I threw myself towards the pistol and pulled it back with my hand. As I stood back against him, I heard Denis say, "Watch out!" Denis had grabbed the guy but couldn't hold him. Being stronger than Denis, he pushed him to the side and threw him onto the floor. He aimed at me with another gun, the muzzle pointing straight at my forehead. He must have had two guns! "This bullet's going straight through my head," I thought in that split second. Hurriedly, I moved to the side, heard a shot, and felt the bullet flying through my hair, sliding against the skin of my head. "Faster than a bullet! Bulletproof, I am!" I fell on my back. Looking up, I thought, "Let's see what a smart ass you are!" I shot him straight in his heart –

one, two, three shots... After the fifth shot, his eyes slipped away, his knees bent, and he collapsed on the floor. He was not much of a smart ass after all. I looked at Denis, shaking like a leaf. "We have to run, Ali, we have to run!" He began saying it over and over frantically, pulling me to the door. As we ran down the stairs, that same bitter thought echoed, "Run, Ali, run!" I jumped over the guard's body lying at the entrance door. Later, I found out that the guy had used an electric shock on the guard. He had planned to kill him after he was finished with Denis and after he had taken the heroin. Later, I found out a lot of things. Denis had begged me to help him in case something went wrong, and I had gone because Denis was my friend... but I had no reason to go. They didn't owe me money; there was nothing in it for me. But Denis, whose life I had saved by paying the price of commit- ting a murder... Denis, my so-called friend, had made a deal with the prosecutors against me. This was the bitterest part of all. One fine day, I was the fool who wouldbe charged with the murder. Since I had been the one shooting, it was easy for him to make a deal and set me up. He was going to be free, and I was going to be locked up. I confessed to the shooting – there no way out anyway. Anyway this, anyways that. Anyways, it wasn't fair for me to have to pay for the whole thing. He was the one who had gotten me into this mess, and he got out clean, throwing me under the bus. If I hadn't been there that day, he would have been dead, and I would have been free. And now? I was locked up in the dungeonbecause of him. Because Ali is tough.Because Ali is a faithful friend. "You are a fool, Ali, a fool! You're not a smart ass, you're a fool."

I swallowed the bait and got caught

I couldn't believe it when they caught me. They pulled me right out of my bed at fivein the morning, as I was still sleeping, dreaming in La La Land. I couldn't believe that because I was sure that neither of the other two involved would speak up. Yuksel, the guard, was a tough guy from the Razgrad area. He'd been caught for drugs a few times and was familiar with the good old beating of the cops. He had several arrests lined up in his file, as well as some scars on his back, yet he had never scoffed up any information. As for Denis, it seemed completely out of the question! It never crossed my mind that Yuksel would open his mouth, or that Denis would make a deal with the prosecutors against me. How did all of that happen? Mansur, the guy I killed, had told his girlfriend that there was a swap arranged and had mentioned Yuksel's name, which she had remembered. When the news got out and she was interrogated by the police, she mentioned Yuksel. The cops had checked Mansur's mobile, had gone through the last dialed numbers, had found Yuksel's number, and had caught him. He had told on us and had disclosed them everything right away, down to the way we looked and the distinguishable features we had. Subsequently, the cops had caught Denis. I had heard about it and my head had gone spinning. Phew! I had never imagined that he would spit my name out. Why would he do that? He was the one who had gotten me into that mess, and I had saved his life. It wouldn't make any sense for him to betray me... How could I be such a fool?! My *friend* had made a deal with the prosecutors right away. "I didn't shoot him. It was Ali, he shot him." And so, the cops from the Special Forces, pulled me right out of my bed at five in the morning while I was still sleeping. "Good morning, Ali, congratulations on your arrest!" They pulled me down on the floor, handcuffed me, beat me, took me to the car, and off into custody. Once at the station, they tied me to the cell radiator and continued to kick and beat me until I fell back on the floor. I got to know the floor very well. It was dirty. It was also the very bottom. They kicked me again. I was used to living there, on the floor, with the kicks... Close to my face, I could see the shoes of the people inside. There were all sorts of shoes – new, fancy, worn-out, polished, old-fashioned, dirty... The shoes that entered the cell at that moment belonged to a boss. They made the other shoes jump in salute. I sighed with relief – usually when the boss comes in, the beating stops. "Do you know where you are?" I heard the voice wearing the shoes. "No," I replied. "It's the room where we killed Amir and Merdat... You know them, don't you?" I shuddered. These were scary shoes... and then they left the room. Of course, I knew Amir and Merdat very well... we were friends. That had been back when I had left for the Netherlands, and I had tried to get them to come with me. "You go, we'll be there in a month," that was what they had told me. They were Iranian drug traffickers who had some dealings with the Police. They acted like people with special protection, doing their business without being disturbed. Their area was downtown Sofia, the underpass of the National Palace of Culture. Their smooth proceedings continued until one day, something happened in their apartment. According to official information, three cops from the Anti-Crime Agency had gone there for a passport check. Previously, the police had spent six months tracking their address, though it was well-known to every drug addict in Sofia. When the cops rang the doorbell, Amir and Merdat had been sorting drugs inside. As a result, the table in the living room was covered with brownish powder. The two casually opened the door and began talking with the cops. The cops had then insisted upon performing a search, and that was when the Iranians had opened fire. One of the cops was killed, the second one died later in the hospital, while the third one was severely wounded but had somehow managed to call for assistance. Later, the third one had recovered. Amir and Merdat had managed to escape and went to hide out at a client's house. They had tried to contact one of their girlfriends at her workplace, but the cops who had spent the last six months tracking their address already knew about this girlfriend. So they had been waiting there at her workplace, tapping the conversation, thought they failed to detect the whereabouts of the killers. Two weeks later, again according to official information, Amir and Merdat were shot near the National Palace of Culture, as they had resisted arrest when the cops tried to detain them. Then, I found out that hadn't been the case after all. Not like I could trust the cops, of course, but I could put myself in their shoes. Shooting a cop was a sure suicide. No cop would ever let the killer of their mates live, nowhere in the world, and that was clear as a bell. Even now, three years later, they couldn't help but remember this bloody double murder... and they still couldn't forgive. "You're in the room where we shot Amir and Merdat..." So I must have been within a hair's breadth from being shot when I was arrested. Yuksel and Denis must have told the cops that I was the leading character in the operation – a dangerous Iranian, most likely armed. Later, when I looked back at those events, I thank the Almighty that the cops came to arrest me at five o'clock in the morning while I was still asleep. I was so dumbfounded when it happened that I had no clue what was going on. If I had been more aware, surely, I would have resisted, and surely, I would have been killed. When they beat me... man, it felt like every one of my ribs were breaking under their blows. When you get beaten up that way, you must breathe slowly, inhaling softly, to keep the ribs aching to a minimum. I was in pain... my kidneys and my arms were hurting... I couldn't walk. They threw me into the cell like one would throw a sack of potatoes... I knew I was still alive though, cause I could feel the pain. Had I been dead, I wouldn't have felt the pain. There was this young man in the cell who helped me move from the floor to the bed. He asked me, "Why are you here?" "Illegal gats," I answered. I wasn't in the mood to explain why or what... He looked at me suspiciously. "They wouldn't beat you like that for possessing illegal weapons." The guys from the other cells started knocking on the wall, asking "Is the Iranian there with you?" "Yes!" "Do you know who he is? Read the newspapers and you'll find out". So my cellmate read about me in the newspapers, and then he just stared at me. "Illegal gats, huh?" Obviously, he'd found out everything. I realized they were going to send somebody to kill me. It was not going to be a cop, but Mansur's father was surely going to send someone. There, I found out who the guy I had shot was, why he was so brutal, why he hadn't followed through with any of the arrangements he'd made, and why he walked in there, ready to kill left and right. I also learned why Denis had been so scared about meeting him, and why he had insisted that I accompanied him, 'just in case.' I learned that Mansur's father had the reputation of a trusted person (insider) in the Bulgarian and the Turkish Special Forces. Moreover, he had a strong influence in the underworld. He was one of the key people who exercised control over the export of amphetamines and Captagon from Bulgaria to Turkey, using a well-known company. Established during the time of communism, these channels were still effective. Mansur's father had made a promise that I would never leave the cell alive. He was rich and powerful enough to make sure that my persecution would play out exactly the way he wanted it to. It was no wonder that I spent so much time in solitary confinement. I was constantly on guard, even in my sleep... as much as I could, of course, because there was no one who could fully protect me, and many who could get me killed. I had to be the most careful when going to use the toilet – thatwas where it was the easiest to meet people. Ivo Karamanski[5] was one of them. He used to tease me regularly, "Hey, the Immortal One, where have you buried the drugs?" "When we get out, we'll go there together and dig them out," I would also reply with a teaser. It felt good to still be alive. Time goes by much faster when you're not alone. I was transferred from custody to the Sofia Central Prison, cellblock #1 – the site of all who are accused or convicted of serious crimes. There, time came to a standstill. I was completely alone. I was allowed five minutes each in the morning and the evening to use the restroom. There was a bucket in the cell for the rest of the day. We in-mates were also taken on a one-hour walk in the area assigned to our cellblock. I was mortified to find out that some of the guys had been there for years. I'd been there for a week, and I already thought I was going mad. There was no one to talk to. I could hear voices coming through the bars from the upper and lower floors. The guys in the shared cells would talk loudly with their faces pressed to the bars. I learned a lot about the prison and the world outside, thanks to those guys. They were way more informed than a guy like me, stuck alone in isolation. That was how I found out

[5] Ivo Karamanskiwas a reputed Bulgarian mobster and acolorful underworld character in the Bulgarian Mafia. He and his bodyguard were gunned down in 1998

that the guys in the shared cells had started working out in preparation for a coming competition among the prison cellblocks. Push-ups, arm-wrestling, long jump… That caught my attention.

Pushups against dark thoughts

I said to myself, "Ali, seize the moment. When you get transferred into the shared cells, you'll see who'll measure up." I started working out – doing push-ups until there was no strength left in me to keep going. Only then, I could escape from the dark thoughts that haunted my mind and could get some rest. I hadn't been taking care of myself before I was convicted, and since I had become a drug user, my physical abilities were slacking. The exercise began to cleanse my body from the toxins of the drugs. At first, I did several sets per day – each one comprised 10–12 push-ups. I did them slowly, I took my time, there was no need to rush. Slowly… up – inhale, down – exhale.And again. Up – inhale, down – exhale. I could tell I was alive. Inhale, exhale. Up and down. Though there was more down than up. On the floor, on the bottom. How did I get there? And again, inhale-exhale. From 10 push-ups in a set, I went up to 50 and from 10 sets to 15. Then 16 sets… then 17… Day-after-day.Inhale-exhale. And up, and down. It's better not to think too much, especially in solitary confinement – it will absolutely drive you nuts. "Stop thinking, Ali, stop. There's no point. Whatever you're thinking doesn't make sense anyway." I got to 1,000 push-ups a day, and up. Inhale-exhale. 1,200. Up-down. 1,300. When I reached 1,500 a day, I stopped going up. 30 sets of 50 push-ups. These workouts saved me from the abyss of madness. There was no other way I would have survived its clutches. They kept me alone, locked down in solitary confinement for over a year. Usually, it was about six months to a year in solitary confinement, depending on the crime and one's mental state. Inmates are closely monitored through their stay; their condition, and the way that they handle themselves every day is noted. They investigate to be sure that they don't transfer an inmate to a shared cell where he might know someone, so as to prevent any opportunities to conceal evidence or to threaten witnesses, and more. I spent a whole year in complete isolation. I didn't cause any trouble. On the contrary, I behaved well, too well even. I wondered if that had something to do with Mansur's father. The ongoing I had heard about in relation to his company made me sure that I would be killed on any given day. So I worked out every day, trying to ignore these thoughts. The harder I worked out, the better I felt. When your mind is occupied and tired, there is no time to think about being killed. It became freezing inside the cell. During the winter, it was -10^0C to -15^0Coutside. There was no window, and the bars were covered with plastic. To get some fresh air, I would pull the plastic down. Once it got to -15^0C, and I had to pull the plastic back up because it was really cold. The inmates would put on all the clothes they had. And then, again, push-ups on the floor to total exhaustion, 30 sets of 50, a total of 1,500, beginning right after my morning trip to the toilet and finishing before the afternoon trip. When they took me out in the afternoon for my walk, I was already finished, ready for a shower. It was -15^0C outside, but I was still pouring cold water over myself with a hose. The rest were wrapped up in their layers of clothing, shivering and looking at me in disbelief, "Ali, what are you doing, man? You'll freeze!" But I didn't freeze, in fact, I was far from freezing. I got accustomed to the cold, and ever since then, I have always enjoyed winter. I had to put myself through strong physical pressures, such as that, in order to stay sane. Being in jail back then was very difficult – especially being in solitary lockdown. Nowadays, conditions are much better, but back then... there were three men who had hanged themselves while I was in. One of them hung himself right behind the door, creating a door stopper from the inside. They couldn't get in to take the body out. Those who wanted to take their lives always found a way. They would use small razors to cut up sheets and blankets, twisting them into ropes... That is what happened when you got to thinking too much. I worked out, and hardly did any thinking. All I had to do was to keep up with these push-ups... down on the floor. I knew the floor well, and I knew that I shouldn't stop. Inhale-exhale. The prison guard checked on me every few hours. I didn't pay any attention to the rustling noise that came from the peephole every time they checked on me. I didn't care, let them look. Inhale-exhale. Up-down, 1,500 push-ups per day. Six months later, following yet another look through the peephole, the lock clicked and the door was opened – this wasn't on the schedule. I stood up and looked toward the door. Whatever was coming, I wanted to meet it face-to-face. It was the guard, a strong, sturdy man, who had walked in. He kept his eyes on me and blurted out, "Man, I have great respect for you." I was stunned. "Why's that?" I blurted out as well. "I've been watching you for the past six months. You never stop working out. When you don't work out, you have a book in your hands. On their path to degradation, the others turn into animals, they rape each other. You work out and read. I just wanted to tell you – well done!" And he left. These encouraging words came out of the blue. When in jail, people tend to forget lots of things – encouraging way of speaking is one. And so, when one of the guards approached me, an inmate in solitary confinement, with respect, I was left stunned and speechless. "Well done!" I hadn't heard a good word in a long time. That was what I thought about when I laid down to rest, and then, I decided to read a bit more. And again...Inhale-exhale. "I am alive!" Up-down. "How did you get here?" According to the law, the charge pressed against me would either have me imprisoned for 15 to 20 years, or get me the death penalty. There was a moratorium on the death penalty at that time, but the words had not been removed from the written law until then. The death penalty was abolished three years later, and I was still locked up! They couldn't keep an inmate for over two years without sentencing them, yet they held me for nearly four years!

Did you kill Mansur?

Indeed, from the very first day, although I was the new one, the other prisoners had great respect for me. Usually, new inmates have to comply with the older ones. This rule has always been obeyed. And I found the rule being obeyed when I was transferred into the foreigners' squad where the regime was lighter. I had to wait for more than three years for the transfer. There, a guy came to me with the following invitation: "Please join us for a cup of tea, to meet some people." It was the Turkish inmates who wanted to see me. The clever ones among them, might I add. "Ok, I'm coming," I replied. Rules are rules. Respect is respect. That was true for cellblock #13 too, which was made up of foreigners expecting to be issued with a verdict. (Cellblock #10 was made up of foreigners with issued verdicts.) When they saw me, they were completely dumbfounded and suspicious, as if they were looking at an alien. I'am just shy of 5' 7".The intensive daily workouts, along with the food shortage had made me lose all my body fat. I had turned into a stick figure made of muscles and tendons, skin and bones. They kept their eyes on me, scanning me up and down, and then, they looked at one another. Their ringleader was in his mid- 50s, donning a waxed moustache, a clever bloke. Squinting his eyes at me, he asked me in plain Turkish, "Did you kill Mansur?" Apparently, somehow they had found out that I spoke Turkish. I examined them each carefully, then looked at him and replied, "It just happened that I shot and he fell. God put an end to his life by my hand. How He'll put an end to mine, that I don't know. Only He knows that." He kept staring at me in disbelief and said, "You see, Mansur was a brutal man, and we had some problems with him. He used to kill his partners just like that, just to take their stuff and their money. I, myself, know about eight murders that had been committed by him that way. They were good people, and he killed them like dogs." I didn't comment. Whatever happened between me and Mansur was done and over with. Not a lot of talking is required when speaking about something so serious anyway. They asked me a few more questions. I gave them short answers. It still felt weird and strange that they knew me, that I was the one that people had told them about. "One last question," the Turkish bloke went on. "Mansur owed me some money. 70 grand. We were told he carried that money with him the night you shot him." He paused, waiting for a response. Our eyes locked, I replied, "Ask the one you gave your money to." He nodded. The conversation was over, and I was back in my cell. I went through the conversation in my mind... They had to know that I was telling the truth. I had no problems with these people after all. I began to relax a little. Being in a shared cell, we would chat with one another. Time passed much faster this way.

I even began to make plans for the time when I was to finally get out, plans for drugs, money, and parties. One day, as I was dreaming about those things, Meyaz came to me.

Dad passed away

Meyaz was a Macedonian who spoke Turkish; that was how we communicated. At that time, having a mobile was still uncommon and quite expensive, but I had given his mobile number to my mother in Iran, just in case. It's not like one wants to be contacted under such conditions. But they did contact me. I remember it as clear as daylight. Meyaz came in the cell, made a sign to the others to leave and keep guard unless one of the guards came suddenly – that was when I found out about the mobile in the cell. Then he looked at me, "A woman rang and told me she was your sister. She wants to talk to you. Get ready, she'll ring again." He turned his head the other way. The phone rang. It was my sister! "Ali, I'll be frank with you, I'll tell it as it is," she said and started crying. Nothing, but the worst crossed my mind. "Dad has passed away." She could hardly speak, choking through her tears. I felt a sharp deep pain pierce through my lower back that made me sit down. He had passed away a month ago. They had just found the courage to tell me only then. I hung up and threw the mobile. I was heartbroken; my whole being was aching. I cried. The others asked me what had happened. After a couple of minutes, they figured it out and left me alone. I cried for a month. I couldn't calm down. Locked in mourning, I hardly put anything in my mouth. The following days, I barely ate or worked out. I mourned. That was all I could do. My insides were filled with barbed wire, thorns and nails, pain and horror. I said to myself, "If that guy hadn't got me into that mess of his, I would have been able to go to Iran while my father was still alive and be beside his deathbed. I'd have said my last goodbye, honored him respectfully with my presence in his final hours on this earth." People in Iran have great respect for their fathers, a Father is viewedas an institution, and we bow down before our fathers. Because of all the stupid things I had done all of those years, I had gone astray from him. My lifestyle had separated us temporarily, but now his death had parted us forever. I was never going to see him again. Because of that fool, my friend, I was behind bars! Because of him, I couldn't send off my father. All because of him!! He was free; I was in jail. Then I made a promise. "Once out, I'll find him and kill him. I am not leaving any witnesses behind." If I had the slightest doubt about someone, a bullet in the head would follow. I got a barbed wire tattooed on the bicep of my left arm. It was my only tattoo. For every murder after, I got a drop of blood tattooed onto my barbed wire to remind me of the death of the traitors, as well as to remind other people that Ali doesn't forgive treachery. At that time, I began working out even more. I had turned into a machine – boxing, push-ups, crunches. At 34, I felt like a wolf, bitter toward the whole world because my dad had died. It was the chair's fault, the Turks' fault, the bed's fault, my fault, the prison warden's fault, the inmates' fault. I blamed everyone. I was hungry for revenge, blood, and death. If somebody looked at me the wrong way, I beat him. If he was physically stronger, I would fight till we bled or until they pulled us apart.

I didn't care how huge they were, I just wanted to fight, and nothing could stop me. The last one I had almost beaten to death was the head of the cellblock. Prisoners would choose one person to represent them before the Prison Committee. We had chosen a guy from Turkey. I chased him while he was trying to run away and caught him right by his cell door. I had beaten the crap out of him. As I looked up, inside the cell, I saw the supervisor of our cellblock#13. Such a fine woman... What was such a fine woman doing in the prison? Anyway, she worked as a social worker and supervisor of cellblock #13. As they pulled us apart, we started quarrelling, and I was sent to my cell. There was a punching bag there... and I kept punching it so hard that it started to tear apart, and the sand began seeping out. There was blood on my knuckles and blood on the bag. No one dared to come close to me, to say a word, or to try to stop me.

The day following the incident, suddenly, I sensed someone standing behind me. By the looks of my inmates, I could tell it wasn't one of us. When I turned, I saw her, the supervisor. I was naked from the waist up, all covered with sweat. "Put some clothes on and come with me," she said. I threw a T-shirt on and remained standing. "Pick a book and follow me," she added. "Where am I going?" I asked. "It's for your own good, Ali, come with me." Usually when people told me they were doing something for my good, it was a sure sign not to trust them. For years, no one had done me any good. Nevertheless, there was something in her voice I hadn't experienced in a long time. There was kindness and compassion for me. She didn't feel sorry for me; it was compassion she offered. Somehow, she was grieving for me. "Where?" I asked her again. "Into the cooler. It's for your own good. If you keep going like this, you're going to ruin yourself. I know you're suffering from the loss of your father, I know you're upset. You might kill someone. If you keep going on like this, you'll spend your whole life in jail." She was right. That was where I was heading. Only, I knew how much anger I had been accumulating. I knew she was right. It was better for me to spend some time in the cooler. I looked down and followed her. After that, this woman came to see me every day. She didn't have to. She brought me coffee and cigarettes, which was prohibited. She talked to me like a person. It wasn't prohibited, but that never happened either. "Nobody's to blame, Ali. Nobody has power over death. You shouldn't blame yourself. It's nobody's fault. Every person will leave this earth. This was your father's time. He raised you and looked after you, doing his best. But he's gone now... You should be proud of him and not blame yourself about anything." Her words were like a balm, gently applied upon my wounded soul. Day-after-day, the words of this kind woman were healing the wounds inside of me. Her gracious presence squeezed the poison, oozing it out from my soul. It was like a spiritual detox, though it was only temporary. Two weeks later, when I was sent back to the cell, I was much calmer.

Forgive me, I'm meeting someone else

I continued to work out, until one day, Rossi came to visit me. She was different, she wasn't my Rossi –rather cold, almost like a complete stranger... I could tell she was having a hard time telling me why she had come to see me. She wanted a break up. She was seeing someone else and could no longer wait for me. Fearful of my reaction, she blurted out those words as if she was saying them at gunpoint. She expected me to lash out. "This shall pass. I don't want us to break up." I, myself, was surprised at the words that came from my mouth. I didn't want to let her go. I loved her so much. I had already said too many painful good-byes in too short a time. She was taken aback by my reaction, and I could tell that she had expected something completely different. She had hoped that I would reject her because of my pride, jealousy, and hurting reputation, and it would be all be over quickly, even if it was an ugly ruckus. But it did not happen that way. I got up and walked away. "Think about it," I told her before I left the visiting room. But she had thought about it already. We never got together again. A year later, without my consent, she got a divorce through the official channels. This break up cut yet another connection I had to something good and bright, my connection to the woman I deeply loved and was deeply attached to. And I knew how much she cared for me. Or... how much she used to. Now I was alone. There was no warmth that could soften the hardness that had taken hold of my heart.

I was released on bail on December 31. Happy New Year, asshole! Well, there was at least one piece of good news. I already had a job. It was arranged while I was still in the dungeon. I had met a crime boss, and we had gotten along quite well. He was released before me but was killed before I had gotten free. Nonetheless, his promise was kept. They rang me about the job despite the fact that he was dead. He was a man of his words. He had to collect some debts. Whenever there were problems in debt collection, he would send these huge guys with big necks to claim from the debtors. Most people were intimidated by these huge mobsters, wearing black sunglasses and black clothes and driving black SUVs. That was the style back then, and it worked beyond a doubt. Anyway, the mobsters weren't always able to get the job done. There were tough people out there who had no fear and were ready to open fire – that was when our brigade was sent. We were not huge like the other guys; our average height was some 5' 7", but we always got the job done. Even the most stubborn debtors paid back as soon as they would hear about us. Nobody wanted to get a visit from us. At that time, I was extremely evil and good at terrifying people. Darkness gripped my heart, and I was a very special tool in the devil's hands.

Vengeance for the witness

A whole year passed by like that. It was autumn then, and I thought, "This is the best time to finish him." He had gotten me into this, and tomorrow, because of his testimony, I was going to be sentenced. But

I wasn't going to let that happen. The barbed wire on my arm was eager for its first drop of blood. I had thought about it for a long time and had come up with an action plan. I already had a gun, of course, the serial number was deleted, and there were two full magazines and sufficient extra bullets. All set for action. That night, the guys and I from the gang had a great time – lots of alcohol and drugs. I drank whiskey, snorted cocaine, and smoked heroin like a crazy man. Everything came in huge amounts. Ali was gone. Alcohol and drugs combined make you lose yourself. You become someone different, even a complete stranger to yourself. You lose control over yourself. It's as if a separate consciousness takes hold of the mind that belongs to you when you're sober. As if you are outside your body, looking at it externally. Yet, surprisingly, you find that you're still the one who commands your body to move. It's as if somebody else is inside. It's as if you've gone absolutely insane! There, I decided that it was time for action. I got in the car, a fast flashy Opel Senator. I called a girl who worked as a prostitute in a widely-known club in downtown Sofia. My girl, so to say. She always knew she could count on me. There were money, drugs, and parties. If I needed her, she was always there for me. This is how it went this time too. She dropped everything the moment I rang her. She was a very beautiful girl, in appearance and countenance. This time, I didn't need her for sex. I wanted her to come with me, so that she could stand at the door while I went about my business. I was going to ring the doorbell while she stood in front of the peep hole. He was going to see her and open. He would never open the door for me. She asked me if I had ecstasy with me when she got in the car. I gave her a pill. I took one too. I had already taken two. While she was browsing through the radio channels in the car and was trying to find some music, I leaned my head on the steering wheel and said to myself, "If You are there, and I am wrong in doing this, please stop me and don't let me get there." I think, deep down in my heart, I didn't want to commit another murder. I had never wanted the previous ones either. My ego and my pride, however, reminded me that I was being treated like a fool, having to sit in prison because of someone else... Besides, it felt as if the inertia of killing was pushing me along the road – one, two, three murders... One more or one less... Who cared anyway? Either way, I knew I was going to hell. There was no way for redemption for me; no going back for a murderer like me.

So I was driving to a village near Sofia, to my so-called friend's house. From the outside, it looked like any other village house, but once inside, it was clear that it was not. There were reinforced doors that added additional security, but I knew how to get in. I always could and always did. No matter what, I would find a way. I thought about this as I was on the road to the village with the girl in the passenger seat. Whether it was indeed me who was thinking, or whether I was so drunk and high that someone else was doing the thinking for me, I was going to figure that part out later. Subsequently,I looked in the mirror and asked myself,"how in the world I did get so far?!" Right then, as I was taking a turn at 110 mph and could hardly keep the car on the road, suddenly, I saw a four-wheeled wagon in front of me. At that moment, time flew in slow motion, and the air thickened as if it had turned into jelly. I saw everything clearly. I saw a man and a woman in the wagon, a girl and a boy next to them. "I'll make it," I muttered under my breath and turned the steering wheel sharply to the left to avoid collision with the wagon. I went into the oncoming lane, and right then, in the thick air that blew around me in slow-motion, I saw a car coming toward me. I saw the face of the driver in the car. The man and the woman next to him looked at me with their eyes wide open with that look on their facesthat one has when one realizes they are just about to die; but their mind was refusing to accept the inevitable. I knew that look, I had seen it before. I could either hit the car in front of me or hit the wagon. I had to choose. To sacrifice the two people in front of me or the four people in the wagon. Whichever choice I took, everyone would die. As for myself, I knew I was dead this time, because like always, I didn't have my seatbelt on. I never enjoyed driving with the seatbelt on. So there was nothing that would hold me back from death. Then I turned the steering wheel even more to the left, all the way. The car lurched to the side, hit the guardrail and ripped it; it tore the fence on the bridge we were on, and then I heard a scream. It was the girl sitting next to me. We were flying mid-air. "Well, one thing is sure... I won't be making it to his house. That guy will definitely live today. Not sure if I will. But I am sure my prayer was heard, and there is someone up there. And this someone didn't let me commit another murder." That was my last thought before we hit the ground.

Are there other people in the car?

I was walking among the freshly cleaned narrow streets in the Zanjan market. The huge silver trays on the stalls were laden with fruits and veggies. The freshness of the summer morning fragrance was all around – aromatic apricots and peaches, smiling like the sun, cracked sun-ripe melons and frosted watermelon slices, fresh peppers and tomatoes, zucchini and eggplants arranged in circles, piles of onion and garlic, green beans and sweet corn – the abundance of the East overflowed through the stalls of this wonderful market in Zanjan. I was walking along the artisan shops, the pride of Zanjan, well-known far beyond the borders of Iran. I was in awe of the shining colorful Persian carpets and the skillfully crafted slippers covered with beads. One could find all sizes here. The market had been buzzing since dawn; vendors were praising their merchandise, selling two for the price of one. Buyers were looking and frowning. "It's expensive, down there they sell it for less," they said, passing by andthen returned and continued bargaining loudly to try and get a good deal – that is why they were there! Some of them would not buy anything; they were out for a walk to feel alive and to get someone's attention. I thought I was like them. So I walked slowly, browsing through the small artisan shops. Coppersmiths and their gleaming copper vessels – from the smallest coffee cup and the tiniest coffee pot to the huge cauldron where one could boil a sheep... just about anything could be found there. You could also spot the famous Zanjan knives and daggers, the ones with the gleaming blades and the magnificent inlaid handles. Proud creators of this whole splendor, some of the artisan knife-makers were working as we spoke, and sometimes, they glanced at the passers-by. As I kept walking and looking around, I found myself in front of a shabby workshop, a little different from the other ones. The knife maker was pressing the blade of a dagger onto the rotating flint, while yellow-reddish sparkles were flying to the sides, creating somewhat of a juvenile festivity in the busyness of the work day. He smiled to himself. The boy in me was enjoying the stolen festive moment. And then, the maker pulled the knife away from the flint, carefully touching the sharpened blade with his thumb... Thereafter,the man turned and looked at me, coming close toward me with his blood-covered dagger in his hand, shouting, "Are there other people in the car?" "What people? What car?" I was confused, thinking... One could hardly pass another in these narrow streets... there was not enough space for the people, let alone a car... "Are there other people in the car!?" the knife maker shouted even louder, as he raised his hand with the dagger, and with a few lightning side-strokes, cut my body into pieces! I didn't believe my eyes; this could not be real! But the pain was real! This excruciating pain led me back through the labyrinths of my mind, and I opened my eyes slightly. Somebody was cutting metal near my head, and yellow-reddish sparks were flying all around. I felt an increasinglyexcruciating wave of pain flood my body. Someone was yelling at me, "Are there other people in the car?" I wanted to say that I had never seen this scary master-maker of Zanjan knives before, and I did not know him. I had not done anything to hurt him, and that I did not understand why this was happening... And what car they were asking about... But I couldn't speak. Then, upon hearing somebody moaning to my right, I opened my eyes a little more. I could see hair covered with blood, someone's long hair among the smashed metal pieces. The girl, the car crash... I couldn't see the girl, just the hair covered with blood... "Are there other people in the car?" A stronger moan came from my right. "Yes, yes, there is a woman in the front seat!" several voices shouted. What were they talking about? What front seat? Just a pile of mangled metal, screeching and grinding.Then two hands were able to reach me, then they grabbed me and started pulling me out. I wanted to help them; I tried to stretch my arms and legs forward to lean against something hard, so that I could push myself out. My hands were listening to me, but my legs weren't. I looked down and I saw my legs gruesomely twisted to the side, not obeying my will. My right leg was dangling strangely below my knee. I saw the broken femur among the bloody pieces of flesh... the ankle of my left leg was twisted just like a hockey stick. At this moment, I was able to push myself out. I felt strong, because I pushed myself sharply and high above the car. So high that I could see the ambulance in which they later moved my body. I saw the ambulance racing down the road; I saw the cars around slowing down and making way. I saw the siren blinking and wailing, hysterically. Then, suddenly, it became dark... then even darker and darker... a thick, viscous darkness, and then, there was nowhere to hide... I was turning into darkness... darkness and fear... darkness turned into fear, and fear turned into darkness. I became darkness and fear. Likewise,an endless horror began to consume me.

Light at the end of the tin tunnel

But then, I saw light that quickly turned into a tunnel, a tunnel with dazzling pure light. I started sinking into it more and more until the light filled everything around me, including my entire being. It did not irritate my eyes; there was no need to squint, and I was not afraid... I felt peace and calmness overtaking me. The nicest place I could have ever been in. I did not want to leave; I wanted to stay there forever, in the light. That light felt so kind and friendly – it wanted to meet me, "What's your name?" "Ali. What about you?" Then ... a slap! "What's your name? Stay awake!" "Ali," Then I thought, "Stop slapping me!" Yet another slap! "Stay awake! What's your name?" I opened my eyes slightly, and saw my body rocking, bouncing left and right in the ambulance. The doctor did not want to leave me alone; he kept slapping me. I did not have the strength to answer him. Who cared about my name? I liked the light in the tunnel, and that's why I was going back there. I wished I could stay there forever, but the slaps kept coming. "Stay awake!" What's your father's name?" "Ibrahim... Just leave me alone!" I wanted to be where the light was. As if he had heard me at last, the doctor left me alone in the light. But that was not the same light; the one now had nothing to do with the pure graceful peace I had just been a part of. That new light was painful,it hurt my eyes and made my body ache. The neon lights on the ceiling above me were moving fast in a line. The stretcher carrying my body, was moving through the hospital corridors with people running alongside. They were pulling the rings off my fingers – stuck to my flesh, to my swollen knuckles, and they didn't want to come off... they kept pulling harder, and it hurt even more. I felt my clothes being ruthlessly cut and stripped away... all of them. The belt around my pants was giving them a hard time. Everything was wet and sticky with blood; they cut the pants with a knife, the belt too. Grateful, I was drifting away again, losing consciousness, but not completely. I heard surprised and slightly upset voices, "He's waking up, he's awake... the anesthesia hasn't worked." "You're waking me up, I want to sleep," I was thinking. "How do you expect the anesthesia to work with the amount of drugs and alcohol in my system...?" They put a mask on my face, and all of a sudden, I inhaled dreams, peace, light... I was so grateful for the hands that put the mask on my face. I could see Afsaneh, and I was talking to her. My love, beautiful like a fairy tale, with blond hair and green eyes, she was smiling and talking to me, and her voice was like a bubbling brook... "My love, you're still so very handsome, just like the first time I met you. Your face is carved into my memory, and I often try to see it on the faces of my children. I can't see it, my love, because none of my four children have your features, because you're not their father. Ali, that's why they don't look like you. Believe me, I waited for a passport and a plane ticket for so long 'cause you had promised... remember, that night when you left? I wanted to be with you wherever you went. In your Bulgaria... or anywhere... just to be with you. I waited and cried. Then, I met someone my parents approved. He is a good man, Ali, and he loves me very much. Over time, I have learned to love him too... in my own way. Not the way I've loved you, Ali, so deeply... But he looks after me and my children; he is always with us... And gradually, my hope that you would send me a passport and a ticket turned into fear that you might not do it after so many years... More than 20 years, my dear... You are so handsome, just like that moment when we first met... Don't be angry with me, Ali, ok? I couldn't wait any longer..." As I reached out to touch her face, to tell her how many times I had looked for her, how many times I was told that she had moved away with her parents... Then I found out she had gotten married. That was why I stopped looking for her, but she was still so beautiful after all those years... just like before. I wanted to tell her that I was happy for her, happy that she had met a good man, and she had children... certainly, they were as beautiful as her... I wanted to tell her not to blame herself because I didn't stay alone either, and I met a woman who had loved me enough to have married me. But my lips were moving without making a sound; no voice came from my mouth. "Poor him, he's delirious, must be dreaming..." Afsaneh said thoughtfully, as if she was not talking to me and kept saying, "He's dreaming, talking in his sleep..." and her image started fading away, melting into the light... until it was completely gone. "He's talking in his sleep," I heard a stranger's voice and gently opened my eyes. This light that shone on me was so painful, an aching kind of light, as if handfuls of razor blades were being poured over my eyes. I wanted to cover my face with my hands to protect myself, but I could not. My hands were fully stretched along my body, firmly tied with ropes. Pipes were coming out of me, all wrapped up around me. The collision with the steering wheel had broken four of my ribs, minimal damage of sorts. It was because I had not put my seatbelt on. Like always. My left leg was broken, so it was hanging in the air with some weights balancing it in a specific position.

Where is my right leg?

I could not see my right leg, but I had this weird unpleasant feeling, as if my toes on my right foot were all stuck together in something dirty, something like mud... you know, when walking barefoot in mud, before you wash your feet, when the mud is still there, all dry? That was what it felt like. I felt dizzy, and everything seemed blurred. I saw a nurse in the room, and I called her utilizing all the strength I had left. "Nurse, nurse..." She came immediately. "What do you need?" Right then, another nurse entered the room. I told her, "Please get a wet cloth and put it between my toes." "Which foot?" she asked. "My right one," I replied. The other nurse pulled her back, whispering something in her ear. Even though I was dizzy, I could tell something must have happened. I couldn't get up, because my arms were tied down on each side of me. But I lifted myself sharply with tremendous effort, and over the sheet, I could see that my right leg was shorter. Much... much shorter. I couldn't believe it. They had cut my leg off. I refused to believe it! Then I became unconscious again because of the pain. I came back to myself, and slowly realized that I no longer had a foot, no longer had toes... when they had amputated my foot, the nerves got bundled up together, creating the illusion that my toes were dirty. I looked sideways and saw the girl lying next to me, tied to the bed. She was all covered with pipes as well, sleeping. I looked at her, mortified about the moment when she would wake up and see that her left arm, from the shoulder down, was gone; it had been cut off...

I started thinking about committing suicide, considering different options for how I could end my life. But they kept me tied to the bed... A psychologist started visiting me, to talk to me... Then they began giving me morphine. They had figured out that I had used it to get stoned, and that milder painkillers would not help. The effect of the anesthesia was long gone, and severe pain was gnawing at my insides after the surgery. My right leg was stabilized in a fixed position and I had to stay still and up, so it did not dry up. That was what the doctors said. "Be patient, be patient, it's for your own good, just wait," they kept ranting. I did not mind at all any more. I could easily wait. Under the influence of the morphine, I could endure anything.

It was only then that I had just begun to realize what had happened during the car accident. The collision had been so hard that the engine had come loose and had smashed through into the car. The edge of the engine had cut through my leg as if it were a knife and my flesh was meat... the entire bone was cut... The car had rolled several times onto its roof, turning into a mangled mess of metal. That was why they had kept asking if there were other people inside. The car was so banged up that they could not see anything through the metal wreckage. When they managed to reach the girl, they were able to get her out without her arm, it was already cut off.

The thought of suicide was a constant nuisance. It had been the worst day of my life to wake up and see my leg gone. I couldn't get over it. Literally speaking, a large part of me was gone. I would never have the same speed and agility that I had been so proud of and famous for.

"Why did you let me live!?" I began to cry out to whoever was up there. "Is this life? You should have just taken it too!"

You Won't Catch Me Alive!

There was no way I could keep doing what I used to. When they cut off my leg, they also cut off my agility and quickness, something that I needed now more than ever before. The streets were now controlled by the Shopi[6] – they were the new head honchos of the drug trade in Bulgaria. It had been years since foreigners dominated the market, and now the Bulgarians had taken over. If you wanted to work, you had to go through the Shopi. If you wanted to get around the Shopi, you had to be ready to risk your life and place your bets on your luck and your abilities. I was always ready to take risks, I always in luck too… but I wasn't quick anymore, and I knew that I would never be again. This had become clear to me when once, I was confronted by a gang from one of the neighborhoods. This gang had started selling drugs for their own profit – something that was no longer allowed. Times had changed then. Everything had to go through the Shopi. It sucked, of course. I was grumpy, frustrated, and in despair. If I had still had my leg, I wouldn't have given up so easily. I would have given these goons a hard time, but I was alone, and they were many in number. Even worse, as if being left completely alone wasn't bad enough, I wasn't even whole anymore. Leg-less, I felt awful. I had literally lost a piece of myself – a big, important piece at that. A piece that had previously allowed me to run and jump, to escape or attack, I had been quick… It had been my pride. It was clear that I couldn't work like that anymore. I had to come up with something. When it got tough, Ali always came up with something… If I couldn't do it in Bulgaria, then I'd go abroad. I decided. London was calling out to me. It was a big city, like Istanbul and Tehran. I knew how to find my way in that kind of place, and it would be much harder to catch me there too. A smart aleck like myself

[6] Shopi is a regional term, used by a group of people in the Balkans, self-identifying as Bulgarians, Macedonians and Serbs.

could find a thousand things to do in a metropolis like London. My new passport arrived. My new name was Ivan Ivanov, a very common Bulgarian male name. I didn't want any mistakes this time. The passport was very well-made, a Bulgarian passport, and it looked original. I left for the Netherlands to see my old friends first. They had already become Dutch citizens and had successfully adapted to normal lives, working in regular jobs and living like ordinary people. I was going to break a very important rule of mine – never work with normal people. There is always something they misunderstood, and then, things always went south. Whenever I did business, I did it only with criminals. Usually, there were no problems with them. But these old friends of mine still remembered me, and they welcomed me warmly, wanting to help me as much as they could. After I stayed with them for a few days, I headed for Calais, France, where the main flow of immigrants to England passed through. To legally enter the country, you were required to have a visa, but it was very difficult to get one. So I came up with something easier. I knew there had to be a way out. Now, of course, there was. At first glance, it seemed like an easy feat… for a healthy person with two legs, that is. But for me, something that would have looked so easy before, was downright impossible then. I decided to check out what the other smart alecks were doing in order to get across the border illegally. I had to do my research so that I could devise a plan for myself.

En route to the dreamed-of England

What I understood was that I had to sneak up behind a truck passing through the English Channel, get underneath it, and hold myself on somehow for the rest of the way. It wouldn't have been a problem for me – I was fit and strong at this time…had I only had my two legs. But that wasn't the case anymore, so this wasn't going to work the way that I wanted it to. That brought me down. The life of a disabled person is difficult, especially for a criminal with my level of experience. So I had no other choice but to come up with more difficult things, and by that, I mean legit things, and that was very sad, of course. I had no idea how I was going to do perform that feat, but I knew I would come up with something. I had always done that, and I was going to do that again. So as I was standing there, envying the two-legged lucky ones who happily hung onto the trucks on their way to dreamland England, my phone rang. An excited Bulgarian friend of mine explained to me that in the last couple of days, the UK had changed the visa requirements for Bulgarians. "What's changed?" I asked, intrigued. So what I found was that if I flew to Bulgaria through Great Britain, I would no longer need a transit visa to stay at the airport in the UK. So I could enter any UK airport completely legally? It worked perfectly for me. It was high time I received some good news. Then I had to figure out what the protocol would be in order for me to stay in England as an immigrant. My friends from the Netherlands told me that I had to be very, very careful with the preparation. If the Immigration Services found out what country a person had arrived from, as long as human rights were respected in that country, they would deport him back. I would be boarding the plane in the Netherlands, so they would surely send me back there. Humans' rights are surely well respected in the Netherlands, even a little too much, if you asked me; but, nonetheless, that was not where I wanted to be. What did I need to do to prevent myself from getting sent back there? It was a little hard to believe, but I learned that the Immigration officers searched one's belongings thoroughly, and, based on their "findings," they would decide what country one had come from. So I had to be sure to only have things that were made in the UK. Everything, even my chewing gum, should be from there. Change, sweets, chocolates, cigarettes, newspapers, magazines, souvenirs, and anything else – there shouldn't be any giveaways from other countries in my belongings, otherwise I would be deported. When it came to possessing US dollars, Euros, and British Pounds, there was no way that would give me away because these currencies were used in many countries. There was something else that was very important – I had to avoid airport surveillance cameras at all costs. From the moment I got off the plane, to the time I got to the Immigration Office at the airport, I had to remain invisible to the cameras' eyes. Otherwise, they would track me down and find my arrival flight and which country I had come from and send me back there right away. This "transit" of mine in the UK was actually just an open door for me to figure out how to stay, and it was my job to get to the Immigration Office in order to secure this. So I landed in London with a very clear action plan, holding a duffle bag with some clothes and some money – that was all I had. Upon entering Heathrow Airport, I put a hat on my head and glued myself behind two men who were much taller and bigger than I was. In this case, my short stature actually served as an advantage. I walked right behind them to the first restroom. I stepped aside with my head bowed down, went into a stall, and tore my passport into pieces, flushing them down the toilet.

Mr. Ivanov – Nobody

I was now officially nobody. Mr. Nobody. "Very well, Mr. Ivanov, very well," I was thinking contentedly as I changed into the clothes in the bag. Then I turned the bag inside out – it was reversible – casually passed through a few more restrooms, throwing my old clothes away, one by one. The bag was the last item I threw. Now I just needed to exchange my US dollars into British Pounds, to buy me some cigarettes, chewing gum, and a newspaper, and wait for the plane to Sofia to depart. I stood there, chewing my gum, carelessly looking at my watch from time-to-time. I was not in a hurry, in no rush to catch the plane. I was near the gate, waiting to see that plane leave with my own eyes. "Last call for passenger, Ivan Ivanov!" I was playing deaf. When the plane took off, I waved it goodbye, joyful as a child. Now I could safely fulfil my duties pursuant to the laws of the country by going to the nearest Police Office, telling them I was an immigrant with no passport who was obliged to surrender to the Police. They didn't seem very excited about it, but after they realized I was from Iran, they found an interpreter who spoke Farsi. "How did you get into the UK?" an arrogant cop with rosy cheeks and an overbite started interrogating me. "I'm on my way to Canada," I replied sincerely, "But the smuggler who promised to arrange everything set me up, took all my money, leaving me without any ID." "Where have you come from?" the rosy cheeks asked me vainly. "I've no idea," innocently I said. I could tell they weren't falling for it, but I wasn't offended. I knew how professionally deformed cops are – even the most innocent citizen in the world would somehow be flawed in their eyes. I, on the other hand, was not the most innocent, so I understood when they decided to check everything on the airport cameras. It is a huge airport, so it took a while to get through all the records. One hour, two hours – nothing. I was sitting, waiting patiently. After all, the cops were just doing their jobs, and I had to show some understanding, right? More time passed by, they watched the security footage, but they still couldn't find me anywhere. Turning almost red now, the rosy cheeks came to me and said, "Look, we'll leave you alone, just tell us how you entered the airport. It's September 29, 2001 today. You know what happened on September 11 in the USA, you must have seen it on TV. So, if you were able to enter the airport without us seeing you, it means that there is a security breach, and that we should fix it. Tell us how you did it." Nodding and looking sympathetically, I replied, "I was promised by a smuggler to take me to Canada but..." At that point, the cop just waved a hand at me, and turned around. He didn't want to listen to me anymore. Well, what could I do? There were rules and principles. If lying, you must do it till the end, believing your own lies even. Until finally, the cops gave up asking – for no other reason besides the fact that they couldn't prove anything. I continued to repeat the same thing to the other cop who came for backup and took over the interrogation. "I don't know how I came here, it was dark in the cargo compartment, the smuggler brought me here and told me to sit and wait for him while he got himself a coffee. I waited and waited... I went to look for him when I realized he was gone! That was why I came to your office." "But how did you enter England?" they kept insisting. "In a special secret compartment on a truck trailer all the way from Iran... that's how I came," I replied. Meanwhile, they checked my belongings and saw they were English. No label said they were bought at the airport, the receipts were gone; I had thrown them away when I bought everything. They could not catch me and did not know where to send me. Iran wasn't, and still isn't, on the list of countries where human rights are respected. They looked at each other, made phone calls here and there, got angry... shrugged their shoulders and paced about nervously. I sat patiently, looking as innocent as I could have looked. They asked me again, "Just tell us how you entered the airport." "I'm tired, my leg is killing me. Don't you see I'm disabled?" I replied.

Kicked out from the Heathrow Airport

Finally, they got really pissed off, opened the door and kicked me out, "Go to the Home Office." It wasn't very nice of them to treat a disabled person that way. "Where's the Home Office?" "The same place where it has always been. You'll find it. If you managed to come here all the way from Iran, and we can't figure out when and how you entered the airport, you'll definitely find your way there." Even though they didn't know me, they were right. I would think of something, and somehow I would be fine. I called my mates in the Netherlands, so they could help me with the address. There was no internet or mobile services yet. They told me the exact street and number; I wrote it down, took the subway and headed straight to the Home Office. The address was correct; they hadn't moved in the last few years.Once there, I filed an application form with my real name, the procedure for my emigrant status began, and they gave me a temporary residence card. After that, everything began to fall back into place – drugs and all the other shit. I checked out Camden Town, Seven Sisters Road, North London. I came across some guys from Jamaica and Greece, good guys, smart alecks with a solid presence in the market and well advanced in their businesses. They owned illegal poker casinos and hosted black market betting of all kinds, right from soccer and cricket to horse and dog racing. I knew they did the drug deals there as well. The Jamaicans controlled the streets in these areas too. The street dealers got the dope from them and reported back to their suppliers. So, as a wholesaler, I was interested in these guys as potential clients of mine. I had to find them and meet with them. And that is exactly what I did. I found them, and we met. Of course, I was recommended by suitable people. Once recommended, the doors always swung wide open. We met at one of the "black" casinos, and got straight to the point about the trafficking organization and all the details that went along with it. Unfortunately, the conversation was a little uptight at first; there was a misunderstanding that turned into a squabble. One of them happened to be a bit more nervous, pulled out a gun and shot my right leg twice. He stood there, waiting for me to curl over and fall down because both shots were accurate at close range... but instead of falling, I looked at my leg and shouted at him, "What do you think you're doing!?" Two blows of the fists, and he was on the ground. Horrified by the fact that nothing had happened to my leg, he collapsed without resistance. The other guys stood between us, yelling at us, telling us to stop... To stop what? As if I was the one shooting! I was relieved he had shot at my prosthesis and not at my good leg, or my ability to walk would have been completely screwed beyond repair. Well, after they calmed down, we sat down again and continued our discussion. Afterward, they told me they were quite intimidated by me when they saw that nothing happened to me after they shot me. They did have the right to be frightened... I would have been scared too had I been in their position. How could they have possibly known that they had shot at a piece of prosthesis? I also had a gun on me then, but I didn't pull it out because if I did, I would have shot them all. When I shoot, I don't aim for the legs, I aim at the heart. But what man with any common sense would kill his precious prospective clients? I was sure they would realize their mistake, and that's exactly what happened. Soon after, we got to an agreement about business matters, and we burst into laughter over the awkward shooting situation that had just passed. They turned out to be really cool guys, with a great sense of humor too. We even became friends.

My head is wooden too

"Any other part of your body that's made of wood, just so that we don't aim there when we shoot?" they asked me, laughing. "My head is wooden, don't shoot there," I replied, laughing as well. We were enjoying ourselves, cracking jokes, and having a good time. And the business picked up, and in rolled the money. Everything fell into place. With money, the girls, the drugs, the alcohol, and the parties all lined up for me again. At this point in my life, I had started to make peace with the emptiness inside of me. I had stopped looking for something particular that would fill the void within. ifeveryone around me lived their lives that way and didn't give a damn,then I must have been doing something wrong in responding to the calls of my searching heart. Why should I worry? I just had to live my life. And I did so for a long time, long enough to believe that it would always be like that. But the thing is, "always" never lasts forever. Everything ends because there's always someone that screws it up. It happened again – a guy with 50kg of heroin, travelling through Bulgaria, was arrested in England. Now, we're not talking about 50 grams, but 50 kilos! The Services must have been working seriously and somehow reached a breakthrough. If this guy started talking, they would have hit the other sources of imported drugs. That was why we had to act. Obviously, we had to stop our import temporarily, and this was at a time when things had just started going well. Bummer... That's when this Iranian guy contacted me. He was safe; we had done business together before. He asked me if he could stay with me. After the Bulgarian heroin arrest, things were unsure, and he was afraid that they might arrest him too. "Sure thing," I said. He arrived together with a Cyprian, Fanos Christou, and brought 10kg of heroin. That's how I met Fanos. Him and I clicked from the very beginning – birds of the same feather. He looked credible, experienced, and competent when it came to business. As we talked in greater length, I could tell that he was a serious international player, with a broad vision and extensive business experience... And by that, I mean all sorts of business. I had the feeling that he's operated with big bucks. You either have the feel for big bucks or you don't. He definitely had a feel for it, and I liked that. That was what got me to listen to him carefully – he didn't look away, but straight into my eyes when he talked, he was very convincing. "I need a serious partner," Fanos said, "My recent partners in Bulgaria pulled a fast one on me, and I have lost all my connections there. A little bird told me that you are a serious man who can be trusted. If you and I can make a deal where you take over the channel through Bulgaria and you provide good stuff and good deals from Turkey, you'll make some big money, man, I'm telling you. I have lots of serious clients in England, that's where I'll come in" I looked at my Iranian friend, who had been listening quietly up until that moment. He nodded – so I could trust Fanos. "Ok," I gave him my answer a few days later, while I had some time to really check him out. "You should know, I have a pending case in Bulgaria, and this might cause a problem. If they arrest me at the border, upon entering the country, and take me to jail, you'd better not leave me there. After all, you're the reason I'm going back." "I won't," he said. "If they lock you in, I'll be there for you."

"Ok, then. I'm going back. Get ready for action." I packed all my gear from my place on Seven Sisters Road and off I went to Heathrow. Fanos knew some people in the Home Office, and they got my documents ready in no time. This time, everything was legal. I arrived at the Sofia Airport, and sure enough, once I got to passport control, I was asked to wait. Then, a few guys in uniforms pulled me aside.

Back to jail

I was annoyed that they had handcuffed me right away. I hadn't been at the hearings for the trial of Mansur's murder, so I'd been declared missing. There I was again, back in jail. I'd had enough of this, seriously! Being in jail was not the best way to spend my life. All the extra hassles with lawyers and all the legal formalities were absolutely beginning to irritate me. Luckily, that was when Gabriella came into the scene. Before I left for England, we had been together for some time. She served tables at the restaurant I owned in Sofia, on Lion's Bridge. A very beautiful girl. I was single at that time since Rossi had already been granted official divorce despite my reluctance. She had gone down her own path – she would have been crazy to spend her whole life visiting me in prison. Those months right before I left, Gabriella and I had started seeing each other. While I was in England, we talked on the phone, but then she told me she'd met someone else, and they were living together. Later, I found out that she had gotten pregnant, and had a son with this guy. Then she rang me to tell me he'd left her, and that she was looking after her son on her own. I didn't know how she was doing, so after being arrested at the airport and being sent to jail, I decided to give her a call. Thankfully, she came right away and started working with lawyers, trying to sort everything out for me. I stayed in jail for quite some time. Being in remission repeatedly, the case of Mansur's murder was full of procedural violations. While waiting, I contacted Fanos from prison and made the connection between him and these guys – they could do the job until I got out. But they turned out to be unreliable – they added some crap to the drugs and downright screwed everything. They ripped him off. Again, no channel and no stuff for Fanos. During that time, I was placed under house arrest. That would've been fine if I had a home, but I didn't, and respectively, I had no address to give to the court. Thank God for Gabriella, who let me use her address. So I moved in with her, and we started living together. She worked, and I looked after her boy while she was at work. Of course, I also did some chores around the house. As life went by, one day she told me she was pregnant. How could she be pregnant? I could not believe it, for no reason other than the fact that I'd never imagined myself having a child. Even when I was very young and still in Iran, walking on crooked paths, I told myself that I wouldn't live to see 40. How could I have a child of my own, how could I look after a child if I could not look after myself? "I'm keeping the child," Gabriella said sternly. "I want to have this child and I will. It's too late for an abortion anyway. I didn't tell you earlier on purpose." "Keep the child, I don't want you to have an abortion, I never said that…" I replied, a little confused. How could I burden a child with a father like me? "Gabriella, a child with a father like me is like a child with no father. You know the way I live." "I've already made up mind, and that's it," she cut in. Okay, if she really wanted that. And I kept quiet. I decided not say anything else, lest she thought I was trying to convince her to abort the child. I would not mention that one of my greatest fears was that my child would be shot while someone tried to kill me. And there was something else that worried me too – what kind of child could a man like me have? A child with birth defects…? It was good that I had no money for dope during my house arrest. So I started hoping that all would be good with the pregnancy and the delivery. Meanwhile, some appeals about the case were processed, and Fanos was looking for me, giving me a hard time. He needed some stock because his clients in England were getting impatient. The market demanded supply and regularity. I got it, and I tried to contact the most serious people in the business, people I'd been trying to avoid working with. We'd exchanged some favors but had never done business together, until then. The most serious people were also the most dangerous ones, just like these guys. If we screwed it up with them, a "sorry" wouldn't work. So I told Fanos, "We'd better not screw this up, these guys aren't to be taken lightly." "No, we won't screw it up," Fanos was positive. "On the contrary, everyone's gonna profit from the deal." So, then, I sent news to the guys while I was waiting for the final verdict on my acquittal.

My son is born!

Time flew by... Gabriella was getting quite far along in her pregnancy and was now in her ninth month. Because she had some complaints during the pregnancy, the doctors wanted her to stay in the hospital, just in case. So I went to visit her, brought her whatever she needed, made arrangements with the doctors to look after her, and made sure she would have the best team operate on her during the delivery. During the rest of my time, I was doing my business, of course.

One morning, as I was on the go, the phone rang at 9 am. It was Gabriella. "It's a boy, and all went well." I jumped like crazy!!! "How many doctors, how many people were there at the delivery?" "Four," she said. Right away, I bought four bottles of whiskey, packs of cigarettes, and chocolates – the way it should be for an occasion like that one. And then, I saw him for the first time... the baby, my baby! So small, tender, so pure... such a small and sweet being. I had no idea how to behave or what to say... I was afraid to touch him, afraid that I might hurt him with my rough hands... My joy was overwhelming. I'd never experienced such joy in my entire life, and I simply didn't know what to do at all... I knew I must have looked weird and funny, but I did not care... which was also unusual for me. Maybe all fathers behaved that oddly in the first minutes and hours of their child's birth, but for sure, I must have been one of the funniest new dads.

I'd bought a pile of things for the baby – a stroller and a crib, lots of clothes and toys... And then I called Fanos and told him, "I have a son, I'm taking some time off. When I'm ready, I'll call you." "Congrats!" he said, "When though?" "When I'm ready," I replied and hung up. I had a son! Nothing else could be more important to me then. And I fussed around Gabriella and the baby... One evening, she asked, "Do you want to help me bathe him?" "Help you bathe him?" I repeated, a little confused. "I'd love that, but I don't know how to do it... I've never done it before..." Smiling, she showed me and handed me the child... I wanted to take him, but my hands were trembling... Looking entreatingly, I did not know exactly how to hold him. "Here," she said as she kept smiling. I didn't know what was so funny to her, and if I could, I would have vanished, feeling embarrassed... Holding a child with my hands... How could I hold him when I knew what I'd done with these hands? I was a low-life criminal, and my hands had shed blood. How could my hands hold this little pure being, such a beautiful and gentle angel? "I can't," I looked at his mother, pleading with her. "Take him, you're his father," she insisted. As she said that, I gathered some courage, and took him just like she showed me how to. I put my open hand under his bottom, and his little head on my forearm. My hands were shaking. "Hold him on the side in case I drop him," I told her. She smiled again. As for me... I was angry that I was so helpless, yet grateful that she was standing there, close to me and the child ... just in case. I began to pour water softly over him... and the baby was so calm, blinking, and looking up at me. He was even smiling at me. I didn't know why, but he was smiling. Then it struck me – I realized how badly I had always wanted to have a child. I had always wanted – with all of my heart – to be with this angel. That night, as I watched the way the mother dried the baby and put his clothes on, I heard my heart say, "They'll never catch me again and send me to jail. I won't let them. I'll always be here with my son. No matter what happens, even if they shoot at me. They better kill me and finish me, rather than make me live away from my child." With those thoughts in my head, I looked at him until he fell asleep in his crib next to our bed. Such a sweet, loving baby. And then we fell asleep as well.

I was deep in slumber when a fighter jet flew over me, and the siren began to blare for a bomb attack. I immediately jumped on my feet, searching for my gun and the keys for the ambulance. I was on the battlefield, and yet again, those Iraqi infidels were attacking us during the night! Move fast! Where were my shoes? But... there was no gun, no keys, no air planes... I was in Gabriella's apartment, and the baby was crying right by my head. "Where's this voice coming from, my son?" I wondered as I ran to rinse his pacifier, hoping the sirens would stop once I put it in his mouth. Luckily, the baby fell asleep again quickly, along with his mother who had gotten very exhausted over the last few days. I was still awake, sitting in bed, hovering over the baby. "Do I really have anything in common with this wonderful child? I'm his father, so I guess I must. Deep down inside of me, there must be some good left since my child is so pure and innocent. My son, my son..." And I just watched him sleep ... the entire night. I didn't sleep that night.

I was so happy, constantly cooing over him those few days, playing with him, washing him, and talking to him... I helped Gabriela with whatever I could – I took the two children out – our baby was in the stroller, and her other son from the previous relationship, I held him by the hand. The three of us went out for walks in the nearest park; the neighbors looked at us with admiration – what a caring father! It made me feel so good; I was pleased with myself. It's true. I wasn't doing it in hypocrisy or for the neighbors' approval – that was the least of my worries. I did it out of love. Anyway, no one knew me there. But those who knew me started losing their patience. Fanos kept ringing "to remind me," as he put it. Then, he became more impatient. My money was almost gone, and I could hear my empty pockets calling me. I hated not having money. I had forgotten what it was like not to have money since I was a child, and I didn't want to remind myself. Then I made the contact between Fanos and the most serious guys I knew – the ones I had told him about earlier. Very reliable guys – Kurdish guys who kept their word. If they committed to a deal, you could count on them. Whether it was to deliver drugs or to smuggle people through the border, or to put some thick headed people's brain back into its gear – I could count on them for just about anything. But I had to be sure that my part was executed to perfection as well – arrangements, money, deadlines – everything to the T! Compared to these guys... Fanos seemed a bit more "artistic" and scattered than what he needed to be in this business, and this made me a bit tense. He was from Cyprus; that was how Cyprians were. Either way, he was a British citizen and had grown up in London. Who was I to pick on him? It wasn't like I was any better. It was important for him to take care of his part in the deal; the rest was none of my business. So we made arrangements between the Kurds and Fanos. The price difference of the drugs between Turkey and England was huge. There was no time to wait. It was time to move. We discussed the way the profit would be divided amongst us. I vouched for Fanos, that he would do his part, and then, the guys would deliver the drugs directly to him in London. Top stock at top price.Fanos started the distribution around the neighborhoods using the Jamaicans. He informed me that the trade was good, and that all was well as it should be. Perfect! I rubbed my hands happily, expecting 50 grand in British pounds, quite a good amount. I started making plans about what I would do with it. What Fanos would do with his money was his business. The truth was, he made some really good money for himself out of this deal, bless him. Our part with the Kurds was 150 grand in British Pounds. I rubbed my hands – it was lots of money. If we would live a simple life, that money would last us a long time. I would be with my son and Gabriella; then I would decide what I'd do next. I'd definitely come up with something. Then, the deadline when Fanos was to give us the money got closer. There was two days to go. I tried to ring him, but he wasn't answering or calling me back. I did not particularly likedbeing in that situation because it was making me a little nervous. I rang him time and again. After five or six missed calls, that guy finally picked up and explainedwhat had happened? He had gone to a casino and gambled all the money away there; he hadn't expected that to happen… "What will we do now?" My heart sank as I saw everything getting screwed. Fanos had no money to pay us off, and that was very bad – the Kurds would not leave things unsettled, and neither would I. The question was, who would get a hold of whom first, and how we would get our money.

Kidnapping the British citizen

"What matters is not what we'll do, but what you'll do," I told Fanos. "The ball is in your court, so you'd better sort things out." And I hung up, but I knew I had to come up with something too. As I was smoking on the balcony, I saw these black SUVs pull over in front of the building, some people got out, looking up. It was the Kurds. I quicklywent downstairs. "Fanos played the money gambling in a casino… is that true?" they asked me. "That was what he said to me," I replied. "Whether it's true or not, I haven't seen any money my way." They nodded understandingly and said, "Ali, bro, we know it's not your fault and he's to blame. But you also know the rules of the game. We know you, you vouched for him. Whatever you're go-ing to do, now is the time to do it. We're expecting our money from you. No offence, but you've got a week." That was what they said, and I knew I had seven days to live. I knew these people, I could not hide from them anywhere. They would find me if they set their head to it. What was I to do? I was still under house arrest, and I had no money – we had no money for bread, let alone a 100 grand in British Pounds. "Think, Ali, think." I had to think fast, but the more I thought, the more stupid were the plans I came up with. That's what happened when I though too much, too hard and too fast.

I rang Fanos, explaining calmly, "Mate, the guys want their money. They found me, they'll find you too. You've met them, you know them, and they mean business." "But I don't have the money, I gambled it away," he said. "Look, then come straight to Bulgaria. I have made arrangements to get stock from another place. Once you sell it, you'll make enough to give them the money back. This time there'll be no profit for you. We've got to fix this mess." That was what I told him, lying through my teeth. Nothing was arranged. It was not like it was the Camden LockMarket. What stock? If you screwed up once, no one else was going to give you any more stock. We all knew each other. They could tell what sort of person you were. So there was no stock, no nothing. But he did not know all this, and he got hooked to the bait. It was easy to believe me anyway, since I'd never lied to him before. This was my first and only time lying to him, and it was because I was forced to... That was his fault. Fanos arrived at the Sofia airport. Since I suspected the English Services might have followed him, I decided to secure myself and not meet him at the airport. If they followed him, they would catch me as well, and I did not want to risk another arrest. Fanos arrived, I gave him a hug like a valued guest, and he was – he owed me lots of money. Then I picked up his luggage kindly, we got a taxi and headed to the Mladost District. We stopped at the open market and paid for the ride. We had gotten out over there on purpose and had crossed to the other side – it's a road with two separated lanes of one-way traffic. If someone was following us by car, there was no way to keep on our tail – they would either have to pull over and walk after us, at which point we would see them, or they would simply lose us. I looked around, and we disappeared between the apartment buildings. At that point I was positive that no one was following us. On our way there, I took his phone and threw the battery away. So, we went behind the market, between the buildings where two of my mates were waiting in a car – Harry and Nasko. We put the luggage in the car, and Fanos in the trunk, and off we went to the mountain. The house where we would stay was located in the villa zone of the VladoTrichkov village. It was December, we had just had snow the previous day, and so, it was a little harder to drive. The seven-day period was about to be up the following day, and the Kurds would soon arrive to get their money. I went to an arranged meeting, the SUVs arrived, and I took them directly to the house. I showed them Fanos, tied-up inside, and told them, "Here's your man. Don't think I'm lying to you. I'm not the one that has your money. Give me some more time until you get your share." They had been sure that I had taken their money and was lying to them. Nobody trusted anyone in our underworld business. Trust and brotherhood were empty words. No trust or brotherhood existed. When they saw him, they calmed down and gave me more time. Then, I gave him a phone to call someone in England to provide the money. I had thrown his phone away while we were still in Mladost – otherwise, we could have been tracked, and I was not stupid enough to let that happen. So Fanos called his son-in-law, a Spanish guy, and asked him to send him 100 grand of British Pounds. He asked Fanos, "Why do you need so much money urgently?" Fanos replied, "I want to buy this house by Sofia, it's a good bargain, send me the money quickly." Indeed, the money arrived. The Kurds took it, and went their way. Phew, at least this was all settled, I could finally relax then. There was very little money left over for me, just a bit of pocket money. I said to myself, "Let me go home, and leave this money with Gabriela and the children."

Don't go! I have a bad feeling!

Rushing, I went inside, left the money, and I was about to go out as she grabbed me, "Ali, don't go, please, stay here. I have a very bad feeling about this. Please stay here!" I was in shock! I took her hand, pulling back gently, looking surprised, "What are you talking about? Don't say that. What you say might actually happen. Everything will be fine, just give me a little bit more time. After this, I'm done with this lifestyle," I told her. The truth was that she had no idea what I was doing, but she could tell that my job was dirty. She was not stupid. No woman is. When a woman falls in love, she loses her mind temporarily, but even then, she'll surprise you. Actually, that's exactly when she might surprise you in the most unpleasant way. Anyway, I left and went up to the villa, thinking, "Fanos got them their money, he would get me my money as well. Then I would let him go, well and sound. It never occurred to me that some of Fanos' relatives might contact the cops because Fanos was in this mess himself. After all, he had organized a drug channel. They wouldn't call the cops. So I was at peace about that, but I wasn't at peace about the fact that I still hadn't gotten my money yet. I made him ring his son-in-law again, "Didn't I tell you to send me 50 grand?" His son-in-law started muttering, asking questions. Then, in front of me, Fanos told him, "I gambled, and I lost it. The people want their money. They won't let me go unless I pay them back." The guy, still muttering, promised to send the money. He didn't have the money then, so he needed some time. Three days, and the money would be there. "Okay, we can wait three more days." And then, I saw a big black Jeep Cherokee passing by the house slowly. I didn't like that at all. "What's this Jeep doing? Have you seen it before?" I asked Harry. "No worries, these are some soccer players from the village, they come to one of the villas to get high and have orgies. I know them," he replied to me with great certainty. After all, he was a local, and it was him who had made the house arrangement, and I trusted him with the logistics. "Okay, so we're okay then," I said, trying to forget about the Jeep. Since we had to stay in the house longer than was planned, we needed to buy some more food. The food in the house was almost gone, so we had to go to the village to get some more. We started debating over who would go into the village. One of us would remain in the house to guard Fanos while the other two went to the village. Of course, as usual, I didn't want to stay in one place, just like my mother used to say, "Ali, you cannot sit still… as if you have ants in your pants." Harry didn't feel like moving, so he decided to stay. At the same time, Nasko insisted on coming because he wanted to talk to me. Off we went. He was driving – I couldn't drive a stick shift with one leg. We were moving slowly because it was snowing again, and we could hardly see the road. So Nasko began to tell me about this really great deal once we got the money back, and how, in no time, we could make big bucks. I was listening and thinking, "This is rubbish." And I looked around, looking into the side mirror and adjusting it to my view. As I was listening to Nasko, we got close to the village, and I could see the black Jeep approaching us from behind. They started giving us some pressure by flashing their high beams. They tried to overtake us. I told Nasko, "These villagers are playing cool; don't let them overtake us." Until then, I was still choosing to believe what Harry had said – that these were soccer players from the village. We kept going and got to the central part of the village. There was more room there, so the Jeep overtook us, abruptly cut our path, pulled over, and stopped sideways in front of us. Out of the window, I saw the barrel of a Scorpio machine pistol – now that seemed funny to me. "Are these dumb heads trying to rob us? You serious? Now it's about to get hot under their asses," I thought as I pulled the gun out of the glove compartment in front of me. It was my favorite – PSM pistol, cartridges with shifted center of gravity bullets. The bullet can enterthearm and leave through the head,making it ideal for close-range fights. I also had two spare mags… They would see now when I turned their fat bodies into Swiss cheese! How was I to know that after the second call, Fanos's son-in-law had called Scotland Yard complaining that his father-in-law was kidnapped in Bulgaria? The British authorities gave our mobile numbers, i.e., my phone number, to the Bulgarian authorities. They found out it was me and had planned a joint operation with Scotland Yard and the Bulgarian authorities. Via the mobile operator, they detected where we were, they found the house, and by then, they had plenty of information on who we were. This was why the Jeep was after us... The Jeep that Harry had kept dismissing, "No worries. It's fine." But it wasn't fine anymore then, when a hooded guy with a POLICE sign on his clothes came out of the car, and then two, and then three... commandos from the specialized Counter-Terrorism Squad. "There you go, Happy New Year," I told myself, "we are caught". I knew, very well that these anti-terrorists were not trained to catch criminals when there was a kidnap. They were trained to shoot down all the hijackers and take care of business on the spot. "There's no time to lose," I thought to myself in those few seconds. I was a lost man; I was no longer afraid of death. After all I'd done, my soul was doomed to hell anyway, and there was no salvation to be secured. It was clear that they would probably kill me, they obviously knew everything. I would not make it in the snow and the rocks around, and it would be almost impossible to run away. Maybe, if both my legs had been fine, but there was no way then. It was true, I had two magazines, but they had a whole brigade in full combat gear. They would riddle us with gunfire while we were still in the car, turning us into minced meat in seconds. However, I was not going to surrender without a fight, I thought to myself as I took the gun into my hand. I looked at the commando closest to us. Why hadn't he put his helmet on? I wondered, as I turned off the safety switch of the gun. At this moment, the image of my son appeared before my eyes. I wanted to see him grow up, and if something happened to me then, I questioned how would remember me? Dying in a shootout with the police, after killing one or two cops? I put the gun down, and we got out of the car with our hands up. They pushed us down on the ground and handcuffed us, kicking us as hard as they could... brutally... then they left us to lie there in the snow for half an hour to cool off. We started shivering. Then we got pushed into a car, two commandos guarding us. One of them said, "You're lucky." "Yes, very lucky," I replied, hardly able to speak, because I had three broken ribs, and the pain was making it difficult for me to breathe, "Yes, you caught us just like chickens in a pen, right before New Year's Eve." The two commandos looked at each other and the second one said, "I don't think they know about what happened in the house." So we found out that when they went into the house, Harry was immediately shot, according to the official version, because he tried to resist. Only God knows what truly happened there. But the truth was that, if I had stayed there to guard Fanos, I would have already been dead. But there I was, having dodged yet another death... apparently I really was Ali, the Immortal.

Why did you kidnap the British citizen?

And so, they sent my immortal dumbass to jail. All sorts of officers came to see me, like children, looking at me as if I were an animal in a zoo. And they scolded me. I mean all of them – all dressed up in their suits, edgy and furious. I was always suspicious, even more so of the guys in uniforms. So I looked at them, wondering what was making them so upset. One of them, the most furious of all, looked at me, asking, "Do you know who I am?" I looked back at him, thinking, "I don't know who I am, let alone who you are." And I replied, "No." "You'll soon find out," he threatened me. I kept silent. "Why did you kidnap a British citizen, you idiot? Why didn't you kidnap someone from Albania or Turkey... or somewhere else? Why from the UK?" At that point, I got a little angry. There was just no pleasing people! They were angry with me because I had kidnapped someone from the UK!? Why from the UK, you want to know? Well, only because it was a British citizen who had lied to me and had stolen my 50 grand, even when he gave me his word! If the idiot were a Turk, I would have kidnapped a Turk. It's not like I choose who lies and steals from me! He kept going, "Why, now when they were about to vote for our membership in the EU, and they are watching the crime situation here like hawks, and Britain is the one supporting us and helping us to solve our problems, and right at this moment, you decided to kidnap, not just anyone, but a Brit? Idiot!

What an idiot!" I looked at him, fuming. How could he take this so personally, and I remembered that chief – the one who was on duty when I had run away from the police station, and how he beat me afterward. What was the big deal? As if I had something against him in particular... I was after my money, my man, that was all, MY MONEY! Then the media began with these stories about Fanos – what a great investor he was, how he wanted to invest into real estate in Bulgaria – absolute rubbish and complete lies! Fanos was a hustler from Cyprus, a dealer just like us. The only difference was that he was a British citizen, and that was why they were standing up for him. If he were from Albania, no one would have lifted a finger for him! But the guy in the uniform was right. I was the idiot. Ali the Immortal. "It's your stupidity that's immortal, Ali. You have always been at the wrong place with the wrong people. That's what you are an immortal fool! So now they're showing you off like a bear in a cage". This was what I was saying to myself as they took me into custody, and then again, they showed me to the next angry chief in the office who swore at me, wondering why I had to kidnap a Brit. Why? Why? Don't you get it? I did it for the money! Of course, for the money, what else? And since Fanos still owes me the money, when I get out of here, I'll find him and get my money back. This is what I'll do first, and then, relaxed, I'll go back to my child. Because you have to know this about Ali – he never gives gifts, and he always gets his money back.

Well and fine, I got a prison cell for a Christmas gift, and yet another charge for kidnapping and partaking in an organized crime.

Nevertheless, if there was anything I regretted, it was that this arrest was separating me from my son, and that I had no idea how long this separation would last...

The Happiest Arrest

If a woman wants you to do something, she'll get you to do it. She'll beat around the bush; she'll pretend she's withdrawing just to get a chance to advance with stronger force. I knew this well, although no woman had had it easy with me. Hell, even I never had it easy with myself, let alone a woman who tried to deal with me. Nevertheless, from my own experience, I know that whatever a woman decides, she'll achieve it. Even if a man is stronger, it doesn't usually tend to work out according to his ways.

I remember the way Gabriella tried to stop me from going back to the villa with the kidnapped Fanos. If I had just listened to her then, I wouldn't have been where I was but rather with her and my son – bathing him, taking him out for walks... I should have done what she had asked me to. Sometimes, you should just do what a woman asks you to do – now I knew it. I also knew how the things would end up with my supervisor. She was trying to get me transferred to Kazichene.

Everyone wanted to go there, everyone but me. It was much easier, much better there. There was a vast difference between Kazichene and the Sophia Central Prison. So why didn't I want to go there? Well, I liked it where I was held. I had the perfect set-up for selling drugs.Business was going great, and I was making money every single day. Nobody else could do what I was doing, nobody else had the connections for good-quality drugs at the competitive prices I offered, and nobody had a strong enough name to establish a system of dealers inside the prison. I had over a hundred clients! Why should I move, and start all over? I would lose everything if I were to go elsewhere and start from scratch. And so, I started with the supervisor – "I'm not like the other prisoners, my leg has been cut off, I need special facilities for disabled people. Look at my cell, I've made it convenient for me, I have a night lamp for reading, and a handle to support myself when lying down or getting up. Why would I want to change all of this?" Quite honestly, the only thing that was inconvenient for me was the spot where I kept the drugs hidden – it was in a hole underneath the floor, right underneath a tile. It was hard to kneel down with the prosthesis to get to it, but there was no other way so it would have to stay there because that was the only place they hadn't searched. They'd checked everywhere else – the walls, the ceiling, my bed. Why should I move when everything there was going so well? My business was booming, and money was coming in. Most importantly, the warden had taken pity on me, and always considered my request when I requested not to be bothered. If it had just been up to him, I wouldn't have had a problem. But it wasn't up to him, it was up to that woman! She was the supervisor, after all. It was the third month in the prison already, and she was still bugging the warden about my case, insisting that I should be transferred, a secure source told me. I did not know what the warden told her, but I was still in the Sofia Central Prison. Finally, the supervisor left for a holiday to the Black Sea. Good. Let her go swimming and sunbathing and relax a little bit, let her clear her mind and leave me alone. After all, I was not bothering her, so maybe she could stop bothering me. Carried away in my business, I forgot about her. Running back-and-forth, I could not let my clients wait. Then I got a new client – that one was quite a character. They brought him into our cell. He was a huge man, about 120–130 kg, all muscle. In prison, strong folks look at people straight into their eyes. When I looked at this new guy in his eyes, I could tell he was a strong man, ready to fight, or defend himself if necessary, and also win if he could. If a person avoids eye contact, it shows they are either weak or afraid, or sneaky, and that they are up to something. Those mischievous ones can attack when least expected, and they always do so from behind. So, in any case, it was just best to give the guy a beating as soon as possible. That way, he would surely be aware of who's in charge – he would surely learn his place from the very beginning.

You'd have been dead!

But that new guy and I kept our eyes fixed on one another from the moment he walked in. "How're you doing? I'm Ali." "How're you doing? I'm Emo." As we said that, we both had the same question in our look. "Emo?Mad Emo?" I asked him. He got close, tilted his head to the side and grinned, replying with a question, "Ali? Ali the Immortal?" We both laughed. I assume that anyone looking at us must have thought we looked terrifying – grinning and laughing like mad men. When people like us smile, and in that case, both of us were smiling, everyone else's mood was typically ruined. Amused, he said, "If I had found you then, you'd have been dead." "If I had found you then, you'd have been dead too," I replied with a smirk. And we burst into laughter because of this old joke that was going between us.

Many years ago, when I was released from prison, they had told me that Mad Emo was looking for me – asking about my address, the guys I hung out with, and how he could find me. Mad Emo was the right hand of a widely known crime boss who controlled the drug market in Sofia and part of the Black Sea area. A man like him wasn't looking for me for anything good, that was for sure. At that time, I was a drug dealer working for myself. A few guys and I had taken over part of the drug market in one of the neighborhoods in Sofia. We were making good money, working honestly for it, and risking our lives. We offered great deals, and clients looked for us, which was a very good thing. But to have someone like Mad Emo looking for us was not good. I knew the guy Emo was working for – I knew everything. All the drug dealers in Sofia worked for his boss. Those who had the balls to work for themselves, dealers like me, knew what they were risking by going about their own businesses. Warning number one was torture and beating – to have your ears cut off or your knees broken, to be thrown on the road, dragging and wailing like an animal until somebody found you and had the mercy to take you to a hospital. Warning number two was the last warning – a one-way ticket to the Vitosha Mountain,[7] where you would be buried two meters underground. The other guys were afraid but not me. I didn't care. After all I'd been through – the war, Mehdi and Mansur's death – I knew I had power in my hands when I held a gun. The faster one always wins, and I had no doubts about my speed. So, whenever they tried to threaten me, I didn't take it lightly, but it still made me laugh whenever I heard that these tough guys were coming for me. Let them come. I would smirk to myself, because they had no idea how heartless I was. They didn't know I wasn't afraid of anything – only of myself, and the monster that I, as a person, had become… So it didn't worry me that Mad Emo was a 120-kg (some 250pounds) building of smolderingmuscles. Big deal! Mansur was huge too but that hadn't scared me. "Mad Emo? Oh, let him come! I am not scared. Let's see which one of us is madder. And which one is indeed immortal?" I was confident that nothing could touch me by then, but our paths never ended up crossing. I went to England, and I forgot about that name altogether. Now, fate had brought us together, and we could joke about it – knowing that our missed encounter had been good for both of us. Now we were real friends, with mutual respect for one another, joking with the ongoing remark that we had been born under a lucky star. Joking and teasing with one another, time flew faster that way. We worked out together till we dropped, and all was good.

Until one day, I went to the warden's office, and who do I see in there? That woman, the supervisor! The moment I saw her, I could tell what was going on in her head. She thought I had already been transferred. She looked at the warden, saying, "I thought you had him transferred already." I felt sick. Here we go again, the same old story. Hopefully, the warden could withstand the pressure and stand his ground. He was a tough man; he had stood his ground for so long already without

[7] Vitosha is one of the mountains surrounding Sofia

giving in. Hopefully he'd continue this way… Needless to say, he caved in. That evil woman won, and I had to pack my bags. I wondered how she could have had that cruel attitude toward a suffering disabled person such as myself… I wanted to stay here; I was comfortable there! Such a mean woman! The warden had all the pity for me, but there was no more he could do for me. By law, these were the requirements in cases like mine; a softer prison regime was more suitable for me… it was even more suitable since she was the one in charge. Whatever regime she chose, that would be it. Realizing I would not be able to get away that time, I tried to sell as much dope as possible; made some quick sales, got the money from the clients, and packed my bags. I glanced back at my cell once again, looking at my hiding place with sadness – that was such a good hiding place, very comfortable… "Well… I hope I'll be back here soon, and hopefully, they can put me in the same cell." I was sure that with my lifestyle, I'd be back there eventually. I didn't know how to do anything butcrime. So, under the pressure of the supervisor, I got transferred to Kazichene. Sure enough, I quickly set up a scheme for bringing stock in there as well. Some people were allowed to go to work, others had to stay in. I wasn't allowed to go out, thanks to my overtly loaded file. So I had to come up with a scheme, and there were many ways to do it.

One of them was using shoes, delivered in a parcel. A new pair of shoes with a thick sole. The inside part of the sole would be cut to make a hole. Then, pre-packed in plastic, the narcotics were placed inside and soles were re-glued. This had to be done very precisely so that the shoes would still appear as being intact. The parcel would be filled with some food, and, along with the shoes, it would be mailed to a prisoner. The prisoner received some food and shoes, all essential necessities. Inside the shoes, the prisoner would find the drugs – also an essential necessity. If you've ever seen an addict in withdrawal, you know what I'm talking about. Shortage of food? No problem, we would get by fine. But no drugs… now that was a serious issue! "Having no money is a problem," Gabriela told me when she came to see me. How was she doing it with two children and no financial support? It was all very hard on her; she was barely making it… She was doing as much as she could, working, running around from sunrise to sunset. Even then, she was hardly making ends meet. "I can't wait any longer," she told me. "I'd rather tell you myself. I met someone. We'll move in together soon." She was acting tough, speaking to me straightforwardly, like a man. She was one of those tough girls, with a terrible knack for screwing up her life with the bad boys. Just like me!

Church in prison

"I understand," I replied after a pause, "This is your life, it's your decision. I'm not mad at you, I thank you for everything. I'll always help you with the child with whatever I can." And we parted. As I looked at my son's photo, bitterness rose up within me toward the prison. This stupid prison where my whole life was passing me by. Once I got out, they would never see me again, I thought. I knew that, due to my condition, they would have to let me go out for treatment at some point.

As I thought about it, buzzing around, doing my chores, I saw Michael Kapustin[ⁿ] in the hallway one day – striding, looking important, on his head there was a kippah (the traditional Jewish cap), and he was carrying a book under his arm. "Where are you headed to?" I was curious. Michael was quite entertaining, and it was always fun being with him. We used to be together in the same cell, and we'd done lots of talking. "If they hadn't hit me and put me in jail, I was going to return all the money to the people," Michael would tell me, and I believed him. Again I asked him, "Where are you headed?" "To the church," he replied, looking at me. Church?! This answer sort of blew me away, and I thought, "Church in prison? This guy must be up to something." But he stopped and explained patiently about this protestant pastor who visited the prison on a weekly basis – preaching, talking about God and the Bible, and praying for the people who wanted a prayer. "It's nice," said Michael, "He's a decent man, and time passes faster this way." "How nice it is when time flies faster," I thought and asked, "How come you haven't told me about it before? Can I come too?" "Why not," Michael nodded, "Please do come, everyone's welcome." I remembered during my childhood in Iran, during the rule of the Shah, we watched American movies about Christmas. We liked those Christmas movies. We loved watching the glistening lights, the fireworks, the festive atmosphere... Actually, as a child, all I connected Christianity to was the Christmas holiday. As an adult, my idea about Christmas hadn't changed much since I'd never cared much. So I went along with Michael to see this thing – a church in prison. "It must be a crazy thing, obviously, but if time flies faster, why not. It's at least worth seeing".

A big, burly looking man, calm and polite, was standing at the entrance of the hall. That was how and where I met Ivodor. "Hello," he said, "It's your first time here, right? Nice to meet you." "Yes, it's my first time here. My name is Ali." "Ali? Are you a Muslim?" he asked. "Yes, I am, but we also respect Jesus, he is our prophet too," I replied, trying to make a good impression. The man smiled and said, "My name is Ivodor.Please, come on in." I went inside and listened to him talk. I didn't understand a lot of the things, and generally speaking, I forgot everything he said. But I would always remember the peace that came over me. There was calmness, ease, rest. I'd never felt anything like that before. Ivodor asked if anyone needed a prayer. I and a few other blokes raised our hands. He prayed for us, and I got dizzy. Bewildered and stunned! I felt this amazing, soothing, bright peace come over me. Peace, security, ease – it was the way I would feel when my father would hug me as a child. The following Wednesday, I went again. I wanted that same experience. Then, each Wednesday that followed, something compelled me to go. Meanwhile, I was still doing what I knew best – I was the source of all narcotics in the prison, and the inmates were buying from me. So the whole week, I was selling drugs. Then, on Wednesday, I would go to the church service. Sometimes, the drug addicts could see me inside through the window and would start whistling, "Ali, Ali…" They would urge me to come out; they wanted their dose. You see, the customer is always right, and so I knew. This sort of business attitude was the reason I always had their respect. I told Ivodor, "I'll be right back." As if I needed his permission. I did not need his permission, but I still asked him out of respect. So I would go out, everyone got their dose, and I was back in to listenabout the Bible. During the rest of the time, I was doing my business, exactly as it should have been done, getting ready for my freedom.Because of my leg, I was entitled to one month leave for medical reasons. My sentence was four years and nine months, and I had already served three years and seven months.

It's time for the big bucks

I would be crazy to go back after my leave to finish my sentence. I'd made up my mind to go to London without wasting any time. My plan was clear, and everything was falling into place. I had the network set up there, I knew people in Turkey, and I had stuff there, and I had contacts and connections in Bulgaria. It was high time I made some big money. So when they let me go, I was ready in no time and left for Ruse right away. I'd made arrangements with a smuggler to help me cross the Romanian border. I already had a fake passport made – it was, once again, of top quality. I had drugs hidden in the car – also top quality.It would prove to be a great sample for the English market. All was going well, and it was going to get even better once I got to London. Of course, first I planned to get my money back from Fanos. He owed me a large enough amount to make that journey worth the trouble. "Wait till he finds out that I'm in London," and my former partner, the British citizen and the prominent real estate investor in Bulgaria, would gladly give it back to me. Fanos, Fanos, you lied to me and stole my money, because of you, the Kurds almost cut my head off, and you, Fanos, gave me up to the cops who almost shot me like a dog. I'm coming, dear *friend*, to take what you owe me.

"You know me, so you know you'd better hurry up. Money is nothing to you, I know this. Let me just cross that border..."

The smuggler was recommended to me by some serious guys. They told me he was tested, and that I could trust him. So I did. Well, he did turn out to be very serious, and, indeed, he was tested ... by the cops, who had made a deal with him beforehand to betray me. They had him cornered about something, and the tested smuggler decided to bail himself out in exchange for me. So... he betrayed me, of course, because Ali was naive and stupid. Ali was always the perfect ransom; no better man to betray than Ali... There I was, at the border control, alljolly, on my way to England. I passed my passport, and right then, they pulled me into a room on one side and hand-cuffed me. A sigh; my trip to England was temporarily postponed, and I was getting really fed up with this betrayal stuff! I'd been hand-cuffed enough times, and I was sick of hearing the usual, "Get down on the ground!" Thankfully, there was no "get down on the ground" this time, but everything else was the same. The patrol car, the cops, the swing-swings along the streets, the prison gate – the same old rubbish. The moment I went in, it seemed like the problems had begun right away. When they saw me, the cops looked at each other, whispering something in each other's ears. Ok, here we go again, the hassle with the cops and problems all around – who had I offendedthis time? But as I got close, they got up on their feet, being very polite and careful. They asked me kindly what cell I wanted to be in and which one I liked the most. Okay... That ordeal was getting on my nerves – I could see that they were trying to pick on me. At the same time, I could see they were actually being sincere and kind, which was really confusing. I had always gotten confused when faced with kindness and politeness. Kindness was not my lingo, and I didn't know how to reply or react to it. I felt a bit ashamed, like a little child. Someone being kind to me was a very rare thing in my life, so I didn't know how to handle it. "What do I want? I want to be in a shared cell, time flies faster this way," I replied. They placed me in a shared cell so that I could talk to people. Yet, it was really bugging me – why were these cops being so nice to me? After some time, one of the detainees asked me, "Is it true, you're Ali the Immortal?" "Yes, that's what people call me. Is that an issue?" "Hang on, I'm not picking on you. There were piles of newspapers full of stories about you – various journalistic investigations of a murder, and the kidnapping of a British citizen, and the joint operation of Scotland Yard and the Bulgarian counter-terrorists..." All detainees had read those articles, as had the cops, even more thoroughly than the detainees. So I had arrived like an international celebrity, without suspecting anything. That was why the cops had welcomed me so kindly, I think I was even gaining their respect. "Do you have something to read?" I asked him. "Well, this is what I'm trying to tell you, the cops have lots of newspapers... with all the stories about you." "Newspapers don't always tell the truth," I replied, "Is there anything else I can read?" "Nope," he said, and two days later,that man was released. A day later, the other prisoners from that cell were released too. I was left all alone, doing push-ups, killing time. Up-down. Inhale-exhale.A series of 50. After 20 series with long breaks inbetween, I wouldmanaged to kill a few hours. To some extent, that helped, but what could I do through the rest of the time? There was nothing to read. The next day they brought a new detainee into the cell. Good! At least I was not alone and there was someone I could talk to. Luckily, he was from Iran. They had caught him crossing the Bulgarian-Romanian border. We started talking – who he was and how he had gottenthere. Then I asked him, "By any chance, do you have a book I can read? Time passes by faster when I read, that's all." It was not important what I read. What was important that reading kept my mind away from overthinking. That was, and still is, the most dreadful thing to get tangled in when in prison – too much thinking – thinking about this and that. In my case, it was about that beautiful child, and why I was not there with him; about the meaning of life in general, and about the meaning of my life in particular. And it all felt very weird. So I asked my fellow countryman, "Do you have a book I can borrow?" He looked at me, paused for a second, and then he answered, "No." But I saw right through his "no" and knew it was really a "yes." Ok, so he did have something to read. Maybe it was a porn magazine, and that was the reason he was trying to cover it up? It is shameful for Iranians to have porn magazines; it's not something to boast about. "I want to read, give me what you have," I told him, hoping it would not be a porn magazine – those had nothing to read, only photos inside. "You don't want to read this book," he replied, a bit nervous. "What's the book?" I enquired as my curiosity built up. Then he pulled out a book in Farsi. It said Bible on the cover. He held it in his hands, looking at me guiltily.

To read the book of the infidels

I understood now why he was looking at me like that – it's a major shame for a Muslim to read the Bible. A Muslim could not read the Bible – that was the book of the infidels! A complete disgrace! We have the Quran, which held the truth that was given to us by Prophet Mohammed, and we needed nothing else. There is no way that we will read the Bible! We are the followers of the one true faith – the Quran is all we need. However, I'd heard so many good things about the Bible from Ivodor, and I'd felt that deep inner peace within my soul during those church meetings – peace I'd never experienced in my entire life... So when I saw the book, I actually got excited. I'd never read it before, because it was hard to understand even the simple things in Bulgarian and English, let alone the deep stuff, the parables, and the metaphors... For the first time ever, I'd come across the Bible in my mother tongue. I grabbed the book out of his hands, exclaiming, "How come you have this book? Why didn't you want to show it to me?" He started explaining how he had gotten it, and how he had carried it with him to be able to show it, pretending to be a Christian. How he had to learn the most important things out of the Bible, so he had to read it... just in case if he was caught, and they tested him. He was hoping to obtain refugee status more easily if he convinced the authorities that he was a Christian... I was no longer listening to him. I lay down in my bed and began to read. Of course, I was reading it respectfully out of everything I'd heard and felt when I had been around Ivodor, but I was reading it as a Muslim too, with the insurmountable disregard and arrogance I had toward it. As a Muslim, we believe we are the latest model of believers, and we have the latest model of religion. We know our faith is the most perfect religion of all, because Mohammed gave us this religion after the rest had already come into the world. We are like the latest edition in terms of religion. We have all the extra things, and the perfected rules. This was how I was brought up, and that is what I thought until I turned 20. Everybody said Christianity was a delusion, and that we had to stay away from the Christian books. So whether I really sincerely believed in Allah or just followed the Islamic tradition as a Muslim, I still had to perceive the world from a Muslim perspective.

I started reading from the beginning – how Christ was born, how the three wise men from the East came to worship him, how Herod the Great sent a word to kill all the children in Bethlehem, how little Jesus talked to the teachers at the Temple of Solomon, and how they were amazed by the knowledge of that little boy... Okay... so far so good. It sounded like a fairy tale, and time passed by so much quicker. I continued on, and it got even more interesting – amusing and funny, to say the least. So funny that I would sometimes begin to laugh out loud, not paying any attention to the new cell mate from Romania and my fellow countryman, who were all looking at me, wondering what it was in that book that was making me laugh so hard. But, what's not to laugh about? "Man, this is absurd! Can anyone turn water into wine? ...and not just any wine, but good, old wine? Yeah! Right! Can anyone feed five thousand people with five loaves of bread and two fish!? How big were those loaves? Were those fish whales or what?" These Christians had to be so gullible to believe in that kind of nonsense. There are no such things in the Quran – every Muslim knows that miracles don't exist; miracles have never happened in Islam and never will. "This is complete nonsense," I thought to myself, cracking up at the words on the page. Then I found some discrepancies in the Gospels – Jesus' genealogy varied in the different Gospels. There was something fishy going on over there, ah?! Didn't they check these books when they wrote them?

I went on reading how Jesus Christ and his disciples walked around Galilee, got to a cemetery and came across a demon-possessed guy. "What's your name?" Jesus asked the man. One of the evil spirits in the man answered, "Legion, for we are many." Then, Jesus commanded the demons in the man to leave him, to get out and go into a herd of pigs. Then the pigs drowned themselves in a nearby lake. At that point in the book, I was having a really good time. Pigs and hogwash! Oh man! This was a good book! Entertained, I kept going, and one-by-one, I read all thefour Gospels. The words of Jesus about giving His life for those who believe in Him struck me. I did think the Gospels were way over my head, ok, well said, but waaaay over my head. Then I went on to the Book of Acts and got to the story about Apostle Paul. Here, my attention perked up at how Saul persecuted the Christians before becoming Paul, an apostle for Christ. He watched and guarded the clothes of those who had stoned Stephen to death, a martyr for Christ. I understood that thing about martyrdom very well. I went on reading. It said, "Meanwhile, Saul was still breathing out murderous threats against the Lord's disciples. He went to the High Priest and asked him for letters to the synagogues in Damascus, so that if he found any there who belonged to the Way, whether men or women, he might take them as prisoners to Jerusalem." Look at this guy, Saul, in big opposition against the Christians. Surely, they cut his head off afterward. He killed so many of them; he's got to deserve it! I turned the page, but I couldn't believe it! Christ himself appeared to him, bathed in light from heaven, and told Saul that he would be His servant despite everything he'd done. I did not understand... What the hell was that? How could someone forgive such a person?! Allah doesn't forgive! What kind of person was this Jesus who forgave all these kinds of people? It really blew me away; I had never heard such a story before – supposedly a real one at that. Such a vicious man, strongly opposing Christ and the Christians, then he became His faithful servant, ready to suffer for His name? For the first time, I took the words in the book seriously. I'd never persecuted or killed any Christians. That meant at least I was better off than Paul. Therefore, there was hope for me too. I was about to like this Christianity. Now I was reading more attentively, thinking, "If God was so merciful to a man like Saul, that He even placed him among His first apostles, why wouldn't He show mercy to me?" With bated breath, I went on reading, taking every word seriously now.

If you believe you will be saved

I read the Epistle of Apostle Paul to the Romans, chapter 10. I got to verse 8, "'The word is near you; it is in your mouth and in your heart,' that is, the message concerning faith that we proclaim". "What comes near me?" I wondered what the word of faith was... And then verses 9 and 10 clarified that for me, "If you declare with your mouth, 'Jesus is Lord,' and believe in your heart that God raised him from the dead, you will be saved. For it is with your heart that you believe and are justified, and it is with your mouth that you profess your faith and are saved." My heart stopped. Hang on here... This was for me! So if I believed that Jesus Christ is Lord and that God had indeed raised him from the dead... my soul would be saved?! I read those words over and over again – Yes, thatwas indeed what the Bible said. Was that all I had to do? That's it? To believe? And there would be salvation for me? But I was a convict, a killer, a burglar, a drug dealer, a robber, and an oppressor... Even the deadliest of criminals feared me! Wait a minute... As a Muslim, I knew very well that, for every sin, one needed a ransom, a sacrifice. For a murder, even if it had been committed involuntarily, one had to kill many big, fat cows, still not sure about what Allah's verdict would be. How could my sins be erased? What kind of salvation was this? Was there truly forgiveness for a man who'd shed human blood and taken lives, voluntarily or involuntarily? I'd always believed my place was in the pits of hell. Who could wipe away the blood I'd shed? I thought about it. I'd considered slaughtering many cows as a sacrifice to wipe my sins away, so their blood could cover the blood I'd shed. "How many cows, though, must I slaughter to cover human blood? Who knows? Who can tell me?" And, anyway, in the end Allah was still going to judge me as he pleased. And what was his will for me? Nobody knew – this had made me believe that there was no salvation for me, that there was no forgiveness to be sought. I would die and go to hell for eternity. Islam teaches us about good and bad, about sin and punishment, but it does not provide us a way out. There's no second chance, there's no forgiveness. There's no one who will offer himself as a sacrifice for our sins. "You sin – you go to hell." If that's the case, what choice did I have, but to live my life here on earth the best as I could, since I was going to hell anyway? The best girls, the best cars, the best dope, the best alcohol, the best weapons – nothing could stop me from having it all. But it said here on the pages in front of me that there was salvation still... For me! What? There was salvation for me!? The next verse, verse 11, even added, *"Anyone who believes in him will never be put to shame."* So, I would get not only salvation, but respect and dignity as well. No hell, no shame. No dirty soul. These verses went down, deep down into the pits where I was stuck, into those endless dark tunnels to which I had tumbled, lost, with no way out until then. I didn't even know where my soul was anymore, but I could feel it trapped behind all the darkness – no light, no way out. And there, in the darkness of hell itself, my soul saw light: "*If you believe, you will be saved.*" My God... is that all I had needed to do all along? To believe? I could be saved through my faith in Christ? Christianity was a good thing – I liked it very much, I said to myself, and I read on eagerly. Then, I came to the following verse:

"*If we deliberately keep on sinning after we have received the knowledge of the truth, no sacrifice for sins is left, but only a fearful expectation of judgement and of raging fire that will consume the enemies of God.*" (Hebrews 10:26-27)

That freaked me out, and I went on,

"*Anyone who rejected the Law of Moses died without mercy on the testimony of two or three witnesses. How much more severely do you think someone deserves to be punished who has trampled the Son of God underfoot, who has treated as an unholy thing the blood of the covenant that sanctified them, and who has insulted the Spirit of Grace?*" (Hebrews 10:28–29)

Now I was terrified... I knew the lifestyle that waited for me once I got out... I didn't know anything else! How could I live without crime? That was all I was good at, that was how I knew to survive, that was my profession, my work! However, now I knew that Jesus had given his life for me, and I was relieved of the bag of evils I had been carrying on my back all through my life. But I also knew what I wanted – to get out and get on with the same old story; I didn't know anything different. But there in those verses, it said that there would be no forgiveness for those who sin after they have received the knowledge of truth. What should I do? I could run away... I'd always run away when I'd gotten into trouble. The army in Tehran, then the murder of Mehdi the Butcher, time and again... Even when I didn't have to, I'd run away, looking for something I hadn't found yet. The emptiness inside of me had increased, and running away

had become a part of me now, just like the crimes that had pre-
ceded the constant escaping. I felt within me, that I might find what
I'd been looking for my whole life in that book; but nonetheless, I
wanted to run. Run, somewhere far away. But, there was nowhere
to run to – I had understood then that you can't hide from God, no
matter where you go.

Then I did something else – I threw the Bible aside as if it had
burned me, tossed it under the bed, I didn't even want to see it. It
was better that way – out of sight, out of mind. I would pretend
that no new knowledge had dawned on me, and that I didn't know
where the book was. "What Bible are you talking about, Ali, you
must be dreaming... Were you stoned again? I will figure it out," I
told myself. "Ali always figures it out," and I said to myself, "One day,
I will stand before Him in heaven, and I'll have to give Him an ac-
count for what I've done. He will ask me why I didn't listen to His
Book, and I will reply, 'Lord, do not judge me harshly. I didn't know
about the lake of fire and the eternal judgement. Yes, it's true, I did
read the Bible, and I did get an idea about a few things, but I must
have missed all that. I read a bit from the beginning, but I never
reached the end, so there's no way I would have known about it. It
is true; I am not lying to you.'" Okay, that sounded reasonable, and
I sighed with relief. I stretched myself out on my bed, turned to the
other side, and all I had to do then was to fall asleep.

Don't be afraid, read!

"Just let me fall asleep, get a good night's sleep, and when I wake up,
everything's gonna be alright," I prayed to myself. I closed my eyes,
trying to fall asleep. I was doing my best, but I couldn't. There was a
tiny, still voice whispering in my heart, "Don't be afraid, my boy, take
the book and read. Don't be afraid..." But I pretended that I was sleeping, and that I couldn't hear the voice. And I must have fallen asleep.
The more you try to pretend to be asleep, the more likely you are to

actually fall asleep. I woke up in the morning, opened my eyes, and saw both of my cell mates packing.They were taking them out of custody to be transferred somewhere else. We were saying goodbye, when my fellow countryman told me, without me asking, "I am leaving that Bible to you, I don't need it." What Bible was he talking about? I thought to myself, telling myself I had no idea. As both of them left, and the door was bolted from the outside, the still, small voice appeared again, "Don't be afraid, my son, read." No... I didn't understand why that voice wasn't leaving me alone, why was it bothering me? When I thought about it, and I realized that that voice was actually brining me peace, tranquility, rest, even love... "Snap out of it, do some push-ups," I said to myself, and began. This had always saved me from internal tension. Inhale-exhale. Up-down. And again – inhale-exhale. Up-down. Every set, a series of 100 push-ups. Every day 1,200, working up to 1,300 – I was feeling pressured, and the workouts kept unwanted thoughts at bay, and they helped me fall asleep faster because I was tired. That is what I wanted... right? So I kept going – up, and down. But on the third day, it was just after I had finished with my workout, when suddenly, I said to myself, "Ok, Ali, so far so good. But what about this – why are you making a fool out of yourself before God? Why are you faking? Are you an actor in a movie, or what? You are being silly. God sees everything and knows the truth, doesn't He? You think you can really cheat God? You know He knows. And He knows that you know that He knows. So what are you doing? You are just lying to yourself." And then, I got upset with myself – "Fine, okay, no problem, I'll pull out the Bible again, and I will read it." I peeped under my bed, pulled the Bible out, dusted it off, and continued reading. I decided to read the Letters of Paul, because it felt like we had the same kind of blood. The First Epistle to the Corinthians, the Second Epistle to the Corinthians, the Ephesians, the Galatians... hmm, it was nice reading, encouraging... I reached to the place where the fruit of the Spirit and the works of the flesh weredescribed – the

Epistle to the Galatians 5:22–23. It said that the fruit of the Spirit is love, joy, peace, patience, kindness, goodness, faithfulness, gentleness, and self-control. All good. Then I read about the works of the flesh – sexual immorality, impurity and debauchery, idolatry and witchcraft, hatred, discord, jealousy, fits of rage, selfish ambition, dissensions, factions and envy, drunkenness, orgies, and the like. Again, I read about the Spirit, and then again, read about the flesh. No, no mistake… It became very clear to me – I had none of the fruit of the Spirit, and I had all of the works of the flesh, in abundance, even. This really made me think deep down. I could see that I was messed up, and even the Bible was pointing at it, so I had to do something… I was so deep in thought, I didn't even realize that they were moving me to another cell. It was as if I wasn't even there. I just kept on reading. My new cell mates were from Kenya and Iran – I just greeted them with a "Hello," told them my name, and went back to my reading. The Epistle to Timothy, the Epistle to Titus… When I finished reading the last chapter of the New Testament, the Revelation of John, I closed the book… I knew I had to make a decision. And then, I decided that I do believe! It was a December night when I fell on my knees on the floor before God and said, "God, you're the One who gives me peace inside of my heart! You love me and forgive me! You are the One I lean on to! Through all this time, You have protected me so that You could bring me to Yourself! It is You I have been looking for all of my life, but I have been looking for You in the wrong places. Now I've found You. I repent for my sins. I am Yours, God. I am Yours!" I jumped right up, waking up the other two guys in the cell. It was probably about three o'clock in the morning. "Get up, get up!" I shouted at them, pulling them out of their beds. "What's the time, Ali, what do you want, why are you waking us up?" Both of them murmured, their minds still slathered with sleep. "Get up!" I shouted, "Now! We have to repent for our sins, wake up! God wants us to repent for our sins! Get up quick, and let us repent for everything wrong that we have done!" "To do what...?" rubbing their eyes, they looked at me as if they were looking at an alien. "We have to repent for our sins and be saved," I kept pulling them, "We are sinners, we are in danger, we have to repent!" And right there, that night, we knelt on the floor, and repented for all of our committed sins and crimes. By the Romanian border, in the Ruse Prison, Cell #10, we renounced all of our evils, and asked God to forgive us for everything that we had done. I continued to read avidly, digesting verse-after-verse, chapter-after-chapter. There was never enough time. This same time that had gone so slowly before was then racing, and it was never enough! I would do push-ups, then read again. And up, and down. "Don't be afraid, just believe!" Inhale-exhale. "I am the Alpha and Omega, I am the bright morning star!" Down, Up. "To the thirsty, I will give freely the water of life." Inhale. Exhale. "And behold, I am coming soon! I am the Way, the Truth, and the Life." "The truth, Ali, is that you can't keep living your life like you used to..." I kept thinking while lying in bed, reflecting over the words I had just read. "Now the Lord is the Spirit, and where the Spirit of the Lord is, there is freedom." (II Corinthians 3:17). Well, if there's freedom where the Spirit of the Lord is, then there was freedom in my cell. It did not matter that this was a prison. Freedom was everywhere. So I had to be free and break the chains of my slavery to my addictions. I had to start somewhere, with something. I remembered Apostle Paul's words, "Do you not know that your bodies are temples of the Holy Spirit, who is in you, whom you have received from God? You are not your own; you were bought at a price. Therefore, honor God with your bodies" (I Corinthians 6:19,20). If that was the case, I could not get stoned any more. Thatwas because, when I was stoned, I was not myself, and I turned into someone else. How could I be a temple of the Holy Spirit when I turned into someone else, and that someone was leading me in the wrong direction – indulgence, addiction, wanting more and more... No, I would not play games with God. From now on, I would do whatever He had instructed. I would live up to His expectations and according to His Word: "Be Holy as I am Holy." "I am sanctified through His Word." Well, I had to start cleansing myself, in my desire to get closer and closer to God. Where did I start? I began with the drugs – that was my biggest problem. "Resist the devil and he will flee from you," it says in the New Testament. Well then, I had to start resisting. I was done with the drugs, and I was praying to God. I did not know the correct way to pray, but there was no other way I could have overcome this addiction on my own. I knew what I was about to go through, I'd seen it before. When you are aware of the hardship you are about to face, you want to be well-prepared. So – in the custody of Ruse, the drug delivery was every two weeks. After I had ordered that, I would have my order delivered within the coming two weeks. This meant that if I missed the two-week delivery once, I would be without drugs for a month.

The hellish visions from the withdrawal

Then, I told the supplier that I did not want to make an order that time. I was convinced that it was going to take me a month to get through that major crisis. I had seen plenty of drug addicts in withdrawal to know how bad the scene couldget – squirming, whining, begging, threatening, crying, self-inflicted pain, and so on – it is like you are possessed by demons that torture you from the inside-out, but knowing these things never helps anyway... Knowing what was coming would not help me. But I finally understood that if I could not circumvent something, and if I could not run away from an issue because it was inside of me, then I had no choice but to go through it, or to stay stuck in it forever. Right there, in custody, I had to get through that thing. It was actually a good thing, because when you are out and free, drugs can be delivered to you in a matter of minutes. However, in custody, I was within closed doors, and there was no way I could get them then, as I hadn't placed the order. It was the perfect place for this compulsory experience. I looked around thinking that there was no way out, no slipping away – there was no dope. God had arranged the necessary conditions for me to give it up, all I had to do was to keep my mind set on it, and just do it, just get through it. That was the right place for me to go through that terrible thing. I would read the Bible – it was going to be easier that way. Push-ups and reading the Bible – that was the winning healing combination... And then, I began to feel the pain creeping in. It started simultaneously, everywhere in my body; there was not a single place that didn't hurt. Nothing was alright; everything was hurting and my body was a complete mess. If I was lying down, I had to sit. If I was sitting down, I had to stand up. If I was standing up, I had to lie down. I was doing everything possible, hoping that the pain would seize. But it did not, it kept on hurting. On top of it all, I couldn't even fall asleep. Awake like an owl, I felt like a wet rag. My head was like a broken computer; memories flashed and went, images, events, pictures... Everything was mixed up – sounds, faces, bothdead and alive, were talking, and I was right there among them – I was neither dead nor alive. I saw my childhood friend, Tagi, smoking hashish in front of me, laughing, "Ali, have you gone mad? What addiction? Hashish is not a drug man, try it!" I should've beat him up then and there, and, in this vision, I had to! I reached out to get him, but he swiftly pulled away from me, laughing, disappearing into clouds of cigarette smoke. I could not breathe... the smoke was suffocating my breathing. When you are going through heroin withdrawal, hashish is horrible; it makes the air sting like acid. You breathe it in, and your lungs go convulsing with pain. It paralyzed me, I could not breathe! That was mustard gas – I was in Halabja and I needed some serum... I had to run up, somewhere, to a higher place to escape the gas. The ambulance was across from me, but Daud was inside, torn to pieces. I could not get in; there was no space for me! I ran toward a nearby hill, it was very close, but the gas was suffocating me. I was running, there wasn't much left, I was getting close, and I was soon to start going up the hill. How?! I could not! It was the hill of dolls... corpses of children. "Dolls, these are dolls..." I screamed, and then, I started running back. But this hill started to move, and the dolls slowlybegan to move too – standing up, they were starting to run after me. "Run, Ali, run!" I was running, and they were still there behind me, with their arms outstretched... just dolls. "Forget about the hashish, bro, that's for kids. Have some heroin, this is the real deal." Akbar was after me, following me, handing me a hit. More precisely, I saw him, not walking, but slipping and spinning around me. "I am running away! I am running away!" I was screaming. "There's nowhere to run, man, there's nowhere to go! Didn't I try to run away?" Akbar was motioning with a cigarette in his hand, dressed in a shirt and a rope tied tightly around his neck instead of a tie. "This is where I ended up." He was pointing at the hole in his head, "I ended up in hell, exactly where you are, Ali, in hell..." "You are a liar, Akbar!" I was screaming, as he smiled and took the rope off his neck to put it around mine. I could not escape, he was slipping away quickly, he was spinning around me, and the rope was suffocating me more and more. I fell on the floor, and I rolled and rolled, trying to shake that pain off myself, trying to get away from it. I could not! The pain had taken a grip of me so deeply, I, myself, had become the pain. It would not work; I couldn't get away from myself... And that pain was telling me, "I am in you, and you belong to me. You can escape prison, but you can't escape me," it hissed, gnawing at my insides, deeper, and deeper. It was penetrating, devouring my joints with its agony. "Expect this every time you try to run away, don't pretend you don't know." The pain tore at my muscles, one fiber at a time.

I would come up with something, I would, I always had – I was wailing, dragging myself on the floor. But I could not! I could not come up with anything anymore, I could not! In my anguish, I started calling out, "Oh Lord, my God! Help me! Have mercy on me, have mercy! Jesus, please save me, otherwise I am going mad! I am dying!" "You've gone mad, there's no God, only drugs will save you!" the pain raged inside me as I was rolling there on the floor, crying out. I was trying to reach down into my joints, inside them, so I could get my hands on that bitch and throw it out of me. I wanted to tear, to shoot, if only I could catch it. "You can't catch me, Ali, and you can't get rid of me, because you are trash! You've tried many times, but there's no salvation... oh no, no... no..." my demons howled; I wailed in pain – I was the pain! Time became stuck, that bitch, it had stopped the clock! It was keeping me there, in the very same spot, frozen – stuck into a single minute of bottomless pain. In that endless minute, I was dying in agony, yet not dying – I could feel the pain in every single fiber of my being. That was hell, I knew it – dying in agony, without ever dying at all. "Please, help me, God! Take me to a place where there is no pain... This pain is stealing my sanity! God! It is robbing me of peace and of rest!" Even when the pain slowly withdrew, I was stuck with insomnia. And then, the pain was driving me mad. I needed help, I called for the warden, as I could not stand the pain. "I can get you some painkillers," said the paramedic who examined me. "Don't you have some morphine?" I hoped. "What are you talking about? This is not the emergency room here! Take an aspirin, if you want, and go back to your cell." I went back and tried do to some push-ups. I could hardly do 10 in a set. It hurt when I inhaled. It hurt when I exhaled. Up – it hurt. Down – it hurt. It'd been the third day already – the same story, the same miserable suffering. Then day four... The purer the drug, the longer and more painful the withdrawal, but I was lucky enough to have been taking drugs with lots of impurities in those recent weeks and the withdrawal lasted six days only. I tried to read the Bible. The pain was slowly leaving, and just when I had given up hope, it began slipping away. It was retreating with a snarl, but it was retreating nonetheless, and it went to collapse somewhere in a corner. Picture a mean dog, snarling and claiming its territory, when approached by a bigger, stronger dog. When meeting the bigger dog, the mean dog goes off to a corner, ready to return if the bigger dog leaves. This is what it felt like. Something in me overcame that evil bondage to heroin, and the pain gave way, though it didn't exactly leave my being. My body was becoming relaxed, my mind was starting to think clearly – I had just had to take the first step, and God was there to carry me through it. I breathed calmly and rested with my eyes closed. Some time passed by, and I could understand what I was reading. I read attentively and reflected on it. I had read in one of the books how Apostle Peter was arrested and sent to prison in chains. However, he lay down and slept, waiting for his death sentence to be carried out. How could a man facing such a situation sleep? What kind of peace and calmness did he have his hands on in order to sleep so peacefully? Then they arrested Apostle Paul and sent him to jail as well. I kept reading, and all these people somehow felt relatable. Many of them were imprisoned in the name of Christ. Some of them were found by Christ in the midst of their crimes. There it was, Paul himself said that Christ revealed Himself to all apostles, and at the end,He appeared to him too – the least of the apostles, the monster. He had considered himself a monster when the Lord appeared to him, bathed in light. I was the same when I read that verse about salvation. I considered myself a monster, yet God appeared to me just like He appeared to Paul – just as I was, consumed with inner wounds and pain, fear and emptiness, and darkness. And I realized that had been why I used to hurt the people around me; that was why they were scared of me... unknowingly, I had become a monster! But God saw the man in me and brought me peace. He didn't see the monster; He saw the man in me and reached out for me. Then I said to myself, "I want to please God. I don't want to disappoint Him with what I do. But what else can I do but crimes? Nothing! Just crimes! That's what I have always done and that's what I am good at." So I had to find crimes that were not against the will of God. There should be some, I thought. I knew myself well too well, and I knew that I would find a way. I had always come up with something. I was Ali, I was the one who always found a way. So I continued to read the Bible, trying to find out what it was that I could do, and I got to the story of King David. It was exactly what I needed. The Bible literally mention that he was a man after God's heart. So he was a good example for me. I read on and on. It said King David attacked the Philistines, defeated them, and plundered their camp. Everything that was won in battle became his plunder. I sighed with relief. I knew I would find a way. Now, I only had to figure out who the Philistines of today were, and I would be allowed to attack and plunder. Because there were no Philistines then, I decided there had to be some modern-day alternative at least. It didn't take me long to think my new plan through. I knew from experience that there was no point in thinking too much. That was why I concluded, very quickly, that the dealers and drug traffickers of modern dayswere my Philistines. God would not oppose me attacking and robbing them, just like he had not opposed when King David plundered the Philistines. "Just let me get out of here, and they'll be all scattered." This idea made me smile. I laid down and put my head down on my pillow, "I knew I would come up with something." This had turned out to be my happiest arrest.

Somewhere, deep in my heart, I also knew that this would be my last.

The Death of the Immortal

I was again at the Sofia Central Prison. At the entrance, the guards pulled their hair in disbeliefupon seeing me again, "Ali, what's going on? Didn't you get released just recently?" "Well, it must have been for a short time only," I mumbled. They put me in the notorious cellblock #12, widely known as "the orcs squad," you know, those monsters from The Lord of the Rings. There were three groups in that cellblock – serious drug addicts, serious crime convicts, and serious drug addicts convicted of serious crimes. All my clients jumped with joy when they saw me because my arrival signified good dope to them. Quality dope at a good price. Ali never cheated by selling junk – only pure dope. That's why all the drug addicts welcomed me on their feet; all of them showing me great respect. Whenever they would go through withdrawal and had no money, I would let them buy it on credit. I never let them suffer like the other dealers did. There they were, full of respect and impatience, asking, "Where's the dope?" "I don't have any. I am not in that business anymore. I am a new man." "Yeah! Right!" they nodded their heads, thinking they understood, "We see, you have something in mind. Probably, you'll start selling it tomorrow?" Obviously, they didn't believe a word I said – not that I expected any other reaction from them. They kept orbiting me, "Dope today, right? Tomorrow? Did you say next week? When?" In order for someone to bring in dope, he had to know when and how to do it. When and how ... Ali knew best. They continued to ask, several times a day, pestering me and waiting. "Guys, no use in waiting, stop pestering me, I am not selling dope anymore." They looked at me, laughing and poking each other. Of course, nobody believed me. Ali wouldn't be selling dope any longer? I kept telling this to all the people who knew me well. No matter what I said, they would just laugh – both the inmates and the officers. It wasn't my problem they didn't want to believe me; I would just keep reading my Bible and living peacefully. A few days later, Ivodor came. I saw him through the cell bars. I jumped, grabbed the bars, shouting from inside, "Ivodor, Ivodor, look at me! I have become a Christian!" He looked up, and clearly, he couldn't believe his eyes. First, he couldn't believe he was seeing me again. He couldn't imagine that I was back in since I had just gottenreleased only a few months back. When he came over to me, I started telling him about what I had experienced, and how the Bible had come my way... After listening carefully, excitedly, Ivodor told me, "I can see you are a different man now, Ali, completely different." "Wait, wait, I'm not done yet," I interrupted him, "let me tell you what I came up with. I read the Old Testament carefully, reflecting on how the Creator of Heaven and Earth thinks, what sort of people He loves and hates. So I get it now! I can't sell drugs anymore, but I can plunder those who God hates, right? You know, King David destroyed the Philistines and plundered their whole camp and everything they found in there? So from now on, I have no worries about how to support myself. It was drugs before, now its drug dealers' plunder – they are my Philistines! I know their hangouts, where they live, I even know where they keep their money. I'll smite and plunder them one-by-one because they have lots of money." I recited all of that without pausing to even take a breath, and I waited for Ivodor's approval.

I couldn't understand why Ivodor was laughing while looking at me. I hated it when people laughed at me, but I knew that, if he was laughing, that meant something was wrong. I trusted him. "You can't do robberies if you believe in Christ," Ivodor said. Then he opened the Bible and showed me dozens of verses for exemplification. "Overcome evil with good," "Do not walk in the ways of evil-doers," and so many others. In general, that was all good, but at first, it made me feel quite disappointed – my only option to support myself and make a living had just failed. Selling drugs was out of the question, and I didn't know what else I could do. "We'll pray," Ivodor said, "but no more drugs and robberies! God feeds the little sparrows, and are not you more valuable than the sparrow? He even clothes the flowers on the fields, and not even Solomon, in all his splendor, was dressed like one of them." "Ok, that's fine," I replied, "But I am neither a sparrow, nor a flower. I can't make it on so little. I hope I won't need to borrow money. I've never had to borrow money in my life. On the contrary, I've always been in a position to give to others. Yes, I know it was dirty money, but still, I had been in a position to lend and not to borrow. People can think whatever they want about me, but I have pride, and drug money fed that pride. I guess it looks like my pride is going to be my first challenge... Oh, help me, God." I asked Ivodor, "Pray for me." After that, I began going around the cellblock to invite people to the church meeting. They were all in shock. Ali, the drug dealer, was most kindly inviting them to go to church? Nobody had ever heard or seen anything like that before! Ali the Immortal had renounced evil and reconciled with God? Nobody dared to say to me, "You're crazy, you've gone mad!" On the contrary, they could see the change inside of me, they could feel my kindness and respect for them... That old Ali, the nervous, angry, and quick-tempered, aggressive bully ... that monster... he was no longer there. There was love growing within me. They were all curious and wanted to come and hear the words of the Bible that had performed that miracle for me. All of them wanted to come – all the bros from the cellblock #12 – the orcs. As for me, I really felt for them. I felt like crying just looking at them, how they suffered with anguish, living like slaves, because I knew... I knew it all too well from my own life-long experiences.

You have come to the wrong address

All through that time, all the drug dealers were still thinking that I was a threat to their business. They were wrecked with concern; the hairs on their back stood straight when they found out I was back. Honestly speaking, no one could compete with me. First off, they didn't have direct access to top-quality dope – first-hand dope. Second, they were extremely greedy themselves. They jacked up their prices, greedy for profit, not realizing that they couldn't win clients that way. And third, they didn't have an effective approach. They couldn't win clients and keep them when there was competition in the market. Since I re-appeared on the scene, two of the drug dealers came to me saying, "Don't sell your dope to our clients. Many of them owe us money. They get it on credit from you, and then they'll never pay us our money, either. So if you don't want any trouble, don't deal with our clients..." If I didn't want any trouble...? I looked at these two dealers – they looked like they were looking for trouble themselves. I wondered if I should pound them or just leave them alone. It was a good sign that I took a minute to think about it; it showed that I was indeed changing. I wouldn't have wasted a second if it had been the old me. I would have jumped at them instantly, because that was not how one did business. In addition, I was of the opinion that problems should be taken care of even before they had the chance to become problems. If I had the feeling that someone would be causing problems, I would find them and give them a good beating. No explanation was necessary on my part. Neither before, nor after. If they couldn't figure out for themselves why they were being beaten up, they could ask around. Eventually, someone would explain it to them. That way, they wouldn't consider causing me any more problems. This was how it was done – people would get a beating even if I had the slightest suspicion. I made sure that my name alone would send chills down their spines. Then they would know better than to mess with me, or my gang, or our business. These guys here clearly didn't know how things were supposed to be done, and there they were, acting like smart asses. I didn't think they were cool; I wanted to beat them. I would have definitely done so before, but things were different with me then. I'd promised to God. He had said, "Ali, don't steal!" I would not steal anymore. "Ali, don't kill!" I would not kill anymore, Lord. "Ali, don't lie!" I would not lie anymore, God. I took all of His commands dutifully, like a soldier obeying his officer's commands in war. If I accepted someone as an absolute authority, I would receive their words as absolute authority as well. I had never done things half-heartedly. It was always all or nothing with me. That is how I always was, and that was who I was.

"You have come to the wrong address," I replied to the drug dealers. "I am done with that stuff. The only thing I do now is talk about God." And they went their way; that had gone well. At that moment, I thought, "You were the same monster, Ali, just like them. How can you judge them, Ali, a person like you?" Contrite and humbled, I thought of the heavy burden God had removed from my back. All my sins and shame. "Lord, forgive me for the thought of pounding these dealers crept into my mind... Have mercy on them as well, let their hearts receive the joy and light I have in my heart now." I wished nothing bad on anybody; I only wanted to tell them about God. Anyone who was interested in that new-found belief of mine was welcomed. And there were lots of people interested because they could not believe how my transformation was possible.How come Ali not selling drugs anymore, wasn't beating people up, wasn't getting frustrated or angry, and wasn't provoking the guards? Somehow, the new Ali was taking over the old Ali. They wanted to come and see that change with their own eyes. They would ask me questions – at first, timidly, but once, they saw that I was happy to answer their questions, gently and calmly, they became bolder. The drug addicts were constantly hanging around me too. They asked for dope, but I told them about God. I sowed good words, good seeds, hoping they would fall on good soil. Good, because one day, my words could bear fruit. Well, some soil was good, some – not so good, but God knew. It had taken years for the little seed that Ivodor had planted in my heart to sprout.

Once, I had seen a photo of a little flower that had sprouted through asphalt... and I always wondered how that little tender flower had the power and strength to break through the hard asphalt. Then I considered how God's Word was a small seed, yet when it sprouted, it could break through the hardest of hearts. That's what the Bible said as well – faith is like a mustard seed. Did I believe I would ever have a chance? No. But the seed planted in my heart had sprouted and hadbegun bearing fruit. From that moment onward I would speak about God, and He knew what was ahead of me. Meanwhile, rumorsspread that Ali had come up with a new plan to bring dope into the prison. That's why he was talking about God and the Bible. He might be bringing the dope into the prison hidden in the Bibles! One of the wardens made the following comment, "Ali is driving us crazy! He must have come up with something new; he's giving us a good show." Then, they started sending informants, and I could tell who they were – they asked me about God, the Bible, how I'd become a believer, what was this and what was that... I talked to them and told them everything word-by-word. No longer afraid, I had nothing to hide that time around. I had peace, light shone over me, and I slept peacefully. There was such wisdom in the Word of God! What peace it could bring! Every person has a soul in need of salvation. Hence, I wished for them all listen – informants, drug addicts, "orcs," criminals, smart asses – let them listen. Informants would listen and report to the wardens – that's what they did! It's true!

Ali has become a believer!

"It's hard to believe, but Ali has become a believer!" "Hmm," the wardens were amazed, not knowing what to think – was that good news or bad news? They hadn't seen anything good come out of me and could not imagine how that transformation had come about.

As for me, I began to see the world through different eyes. I would walk, and think, and pray, and my heart ached inside of me – there were so many hurting people around me, so much pain and suffering everywhere around me! One day, I saw a family visiting a drug addict – a woman, very poorly dressed with two little children, and they brought him a bag full of food. That woman had withheld amenities from her children, so that she could save some money to buy him food. She pleaded with him while the children were looking at him with eyes filled with sadness; who knew how they made their living. And he was in a rush to send them off, so he could take that bag and run directly to the dealer's cell. I watched that whole scene, and as he passed by me, I took him by the collar, turned him toward me, and said, "Hey, man, this woman has withheld food from your children. What are you doing? Where are you going to take it? You are taking the food of your own children to the dealer, right?" And the evil look on his face changed. He bowed his head down, tumbled onto the floor with the bag in his hands, and started weeping like a child, "I can't, bro, I can't live without it. What can I do? I know what I'm doing isn't good, but I can't live without the drugs..." He was sobbing and crying. My God, my heart broke as I stood there, looking at him. I knelt down next to him, and I began to pray, "Lord, please help him! Help him the way you have helped me, have mercy on him too!" And that man repeated after me, still crying... Then he took the bag, and off he went. I continued praying for him. People saw the change in me manifest itself more strongly in cases such as the one described. They could see me sitting peacefully, reading the Bible. All day long. Prisoners from other cells started peeking, poking each other, whispering, and spreading the news by word of mouth. Lots of people didn't believe the stories of my transformation, and they came to me personally to check for themselves. I was prepared. Ivodor had brought me some Bibles to give away to people. Being kind and considerate, I invited them to the sermons. I had love in my heart. Nobody from the cellblock had ever been to the prison church, but all of a sudden, 50 newcomers enrolled. The guards were stunned, thinking I was organizing some kind of a conspiracy through the church meetings. They reported to the superiors, returned back, and ordered, "No way 50 of you are going in together! Only 20." "No problem," I said, "the rest will come next week." I passed by the other cells, inviting them, and taking them to church, so they could experience the warmth and light in their souls, so they might also receive the peace and rest that I had access to. Meanwhile, I continued to my workout routines and read the Bible. I read avidly and insatiably, and there was never enough time. "The Bible is so precious, how it enriches your life," I thought to myself, reflecting on every verse. And as I read, one evening, I was approached by this interesting guy. "Are you Ali, the Immortal?" he asked. "That's what they call me," I replied. "Well, I am Lucho, the Zombie," he mumbled. I looked at him, thinking, "I have seen tons of people like you... orcs, zombies, vampires, monsters." Since I'd lived 20 years in hell, I'd seen it all – all kinds of characters and all sorts of tattoos. This guy had covered himself with tattoos, appearing like an alien creature – his whole neck and arms were black with tattoos. "Yesterday, when you stopped by our cell, you mentioned something about ... was it God or ... is it true you've become a believer and have given up drugs?" he asked, bewildered. "It's true, God helped me," I answered, "I can tell you some more, if you're interested." "How did you stop the drugs? This is what I want to know. I have tried so many times, but I can't stop. The pain makes me go crazy, and I lose my mind. Twice, they've stopped me from jumping out of the window, trying to kill myself." "Drugs open the door for the devil to live in you, bro. I speak from experience, God can help you. You want me to pray for you?" I asked him. "Yes, pray for me," he uttered. "Open your heart and believe. Otherwise, it will just be empty words and nothing will happen. Just to let you know – there'll be pain, for sure. God will soften and reduce the pain, but you'll have to do your part of the deal. It's impossible without the mercy of Christ." "Whatever you say, I will do," Lucho, the Zombie said in return. We both got on our knees and started praying. That was right before they had locked the cells, while we were still allowed to move freely cell-to-cell. I prayed; he repeated after me. We prayed with our eyes closed, as if we were not there. Engulfed in complete silence, I experienced something I have never been able to forget. I couldn't tell how much time had passed by, but when I opened my eyes, I was startled and surprised, because we were surrounded by the ringleaders of the cellblock, who were also on their knees!

Every knee shall bow to Christ!

They had never shown respect for anything or anyone; they feared nothing. On the contrary, everybody feared them. They did respect me, though, and didn't bother me. These same people were now kneeling down with their eyes closed, right beside us. I didn't even know when they had joined us. At that moment, I remembered the Bible verse that says, "Every knee shall bow to Christ." "This is true, Lord, since even these tough prisoners have come to bow down before and worship You," I said to God that night. I felt encouraged because I realized that there was hope for absolutely everyone, as long as their hearts were open to God's love. That's how four drug addicts got rid of their addiction. The first one to walk the path of sobriety after me was Lucho. He went through exactly what I had gone through – lots of pain, for days... But he stopped taking drugs and became a free man. The next one was Krassi, the Dwarf – he was quite the devil, but he repented for his crimes and renounced the evil, for God shows mercy to every sinner who repents. The third one was Fasouli – a Gypsy, a very good boy, but a very miserable drug addict. He gave up drugs, as well. Together, we overcame everything – one after another, they wanted it, and they got it – freedom from drugs through Christ.

Day-after-day, my zeal for God increased. I had read that every believer in Christ should have been baptized in water, so even I wanted to be baptized in water. I approached Ivodor about it. "Pastor, I need to be baptized in water, just as how Christ was baptized in the Jordan River. There's no river here in prison, but I don't want to wait. What can we do? Let's just do it in a tub, you can pour the water over me," brimming with energy, I made my suggestion. "No, it doesn't work this way," he explained, "The whole body needs to be immersed in water when a baptism is done. Isn't that how Jesus was baptized?" Then, I remembered what the Bible had said about the Christ's baptism. Then Ivodor added, "Let me think it through. We'll pray together, and then I will speak to the prison warden." And that's what we did – we prayed, and then he went to the warden. "We have permission to put a big inflatable pool in the prison yard," he announced, "and whoever wants to be baptized, can do it." We all got so happy! About 20 of us signed up for the baptism. Krassi, the Dwarf was beyond himself, jumping joyfully, wondering why we had to wait for even two weeks, and why we couldn't do it earlier. "Well, we have to bring the inflatable pool and set up everything," I replied to him. However, when Ivodor came, I started hinting at the possibility of having the baptism sooner, since there really was no point in waiting for that long! Time passed slowly during those two weeks of waiting – we were counting down the days. When the awaited day finally arrived, we were like little kids, overwhelmed and excited! We lined up, and one after another, we stepped into the pool. Ivodor was standing there; he put his hand on our head, and declared, "I baptize you in the name of the Father, the Son, and the Holy Spirit!" and every single one of us was immersed in the water, our entire body.Wow! That was new, that was amazing! It felt blissful, to be baptized! To be submerged in the water and be washed from all dirt we had all accumulated over time! Cleansed, washed, from all I'd done, from everything that tainted me – my hands, my soul... inside and out. All the dirt from the filthy swamp I had previously made my home was washed from my soul! I had emergedas a brand new person, in the name of Jesus. Those who hadn't experienced it would never have been able to fathom the weight that He had lifted from my shoulders. I felt lighter – new. We were so overjoyed and euphoric, and the rest couldn't understand it, and they were puzzled – some were plainly jealous of what we had experienced, and they admitted, "If we knew, we would have signed up too." "Repent," I challenged them, "confess your sins and deny all evil, and we'll have another baptism soon again." That was the arrangement with Ivodor – we would have the baptisms periodically, and we had also managed to secure the permission of the warden. He had admitted to Ivodor that he could no longer recognize me; I was like a new man who had nothing to do with the old one! This made me so happy because the warden was a genuine man toward whom I had meted out monstrous treatment. His comment filled me with delight and contentment. He wasn't the only one who felt that way about me. Gradually, everyone in the prison began to take notice of the new Ali – Ali who didn't sell drugs or create troubles. They got their head around this new person, but couldn't believe it even then. Then, I realized that for most people sense-making always felt more comfortable than just believing. But I didn't stop working. I began meetings in cellblock #12 every single day. I read to them and shared the words of God, persuading and pleading... Of course, occasionally, some old friends would still come running to me, by mistake, "Hey, bro, there's this deal, we'll make some big money, only if you join us." I would look at them and smile. They would get confused and angry for a moment, thinking that I was making fun of them. Then, they would slap themselves on the forehead, "Oh sorry, man, I forgot that you have become a believer..." Then and there, they would turn around and run to find someone else to help them crack their deal. That was their business; I had my business to attend to. Anyway, I didn't care what people thought of me. Their opinion had always been the least I could care for. In jail, we were all either smart asses, or fools. The old drug dealer, Ali, was a smart ass, but just because I had become a Christian, didn't mean that I had become a fool, and so, I did not let anyone trample on me by asking me to clean cells or do the dishes. In the beginning, some guys thought that I had gone mad, and they tried to play games with me, coming intentionally to provoke me, but they gave up quickly and settled down. Things with me were happening step-by-step, the old Ali wasn't completely gone – sometimes, I even smoked some weed. I thought weed wasn't harmful, at least, compared to heroin, it was nothing. I used to tell myself, "I've overcome my heroin addiction, so I can smoke weed, I'm not addicted to it." I needed some time to come to the understanding that any reliance on a substance is a form of slavery. It was a hard, long journey, but after some time, I was done with the weed too. And I just kept going in that same direction – getting free from all my addictions. People around me were watching me more and more, and they were already making comments, "Maybe it's true, but let's see how long it will last." Frankly, those words didn't bother me. They would have bothered me if I had just counted on my own strength, but I hadn't. Previously, I used to count on myself, and we know by now how far that got me. Now, I relied on God's strength, and with His help, I was able to do what I did. I would gather people together, talk to them, give out Bibles; I would encourage and empower them, help with everything – I lived for them. Even the officers became convinced that Ali had changed, and that he was not the one they used to know. They treated me differently. They started trusting me a great deal... So much so, that they decided to move me to a softer prison.From the Sofia Central Prison, where it was really strict, I was transferred to Kazichene. All because of my good behavior. Well... I didn't like that at all. Again, this Kazichene was there in my way, and again I was going to be forced to go there against my will. I didn't want to go. Not at all. Before I didn't want to leave because of the drugs, this time, I didn't want to leave because of the people. We had just started praying together, going to the church service together, sharing, and supporting each other; people were asking me questions about this and that. Who would look after them when I was gone? How could I leave them? Well, Ivodor was there, but he only came once a week, and I was there every day with them, helping them, offering them support, and praying for them.

Obviously, I would have to talk to Ivodor about what I should do. I didn't want to be transferred; I had just begun my work in that prison. "What do you think?" I asked him. He looked at me and replied, "I think you should go." "Why?" I was surprised… "Why should I move to Kazichene – the warden there hates me. He won't believe that I've changed, and he won't ever forgive me for some of the things I've done. Don't you know that he will never believe that I am no longer the old Ali?!" I asked him angrily. "Listen," he explained calmly, "if you want to step up to a higher level, don't run away from the challenges. Christ did not run away from anything, but instead, he practiced endurance through everything, including the crucifixion." "But didn't Christ die on the cross for us and took all our sins, so there's nothing left for us to carry," I wondered. "Yes, He did die for us. No one wants you to die, but you just have to carry your cross," he shared that pearl of wisdom. "You have changed, and it's obvious." "Go and tell that to the warden in Kazichene," I interrupted him, "all that waits for me there is trouble!" However, Ivodor continued to insist, "Trouble for the old Ali. Aren't you saying you are a new man now?" "Yes, but how can I show this to the warden?" "With your actions, Ali. Kazichene is your crucifix." "Well," I agreed after giving the matter some thought, "but promise me one thing – I will be able to do what I do here." "What is that?" he asked. "Praying for people, giving away Bibles, gathering prisoners together to talk about God – all of this I want to do there too." Ivodor nodded in return, and gave me his promise.

The crucifixion of the immortal

Well, there we were, a whole group of inmates from the Sofia Central Prison being transferred to Kazichene on grounds of good behavior. They took us there in a convoy with armed guards. One-by-one, we got out of the vehicle. At the entrance, the officer on duty greeted us. They used to call him Saddam because of the physical resemblance to him and the distinctive moustache. Otherwise, he was a very good and easy-going man. When he saw me, he was shocked, shaking his head in amazement, "Ali, what are you doing here? You know what awaits you here, don't you? Are you crazy? Where do you come from? Why didn't you stay in the Central Prison?" "As an incentive for good behavior, I am being transferred here," I explained. "I don't know what incentive they sent you here on, but you're looking for trouble, and you know it. The warden will make your life miserable." I smiled. I really liked Saddam; he was kind and compassionate, but he was right about what he's said. During my previous stay, I had tried to outsmart the warden who had no idea at that time that I had become a Christian. He wouldn't be able to comprehend my transformation and neither was he going to believe me. There was nothing that could change that – neither me, because of our bad relationship, nor Ivodor, despite his good reputation. I knew I had a tough battle ahead of me. These thoughts jostled in my head, as I walked alongside the rest of the inmates in the familiar hallway to the warden's office. We used to call him Pali-Motora[8](Short-Fuse), as he was arrogant, harsh, and neurotic. "Get lost!" was his favorite line, and it didn't take him a long time to end a conversation that way. That meant the other person had to disappear and be gone as soon as possible. I was recalling some of my incidents with him, as I stood there in line with the other newcomers in the narrow corridor outside the door of his office. I had waited there before. One time, I had grown so impatient waiting for him that I had broken down the door and was taken out in handcuffs, and then off into custody straightaway. "All the old Ali caused was annoyance and trouble," I thought to myself, with a sigh. At that moment, he opened the door and appeared with his typical arrogance, without even looking around. Casting a single glance our direction, he mumbled with disdain, "Alright, come in…" After that, he went in, sat behind his desk, and turned his face to the computer screen. We all entered and lined up; he looked up toward us, checking us out one-by-one, squinting his eyes. When he got to me, heopened his eye

---

[8] Pali-Motorain Bulgarian literally means: "Fire up the engine"

wide, and his face turned red. Pali-Motora (Short-Fuse) jumped suddenly from his chair, and panting with rage, he yelled, "Why did they bring you here? Who brought you here?"

"I am no longer under strict conditions, now I am on soft…" "What?" he screamed, interrupting me mid-sentence."As an incentive for good behavior?In the Sofia Central Prison? Is that where you showed good behavior?" "Well …" "You can never behave well, you don't know the meaning of the word 'good'! Out! All out!"

Quickly, we all went out into the corridor and stood there, waiting.What else could we have done? Looking at me as if I were an alien, the newbies asked me what I'd done to that guy. "Nothing major," I answered. No one believed me. Inside, Pali-Motora(Short-Fuse) was already on the phone talking to someone. We could hear him outside. "How can you send him here? Are you crazy? What good behavior are you talking about? Don't give me that crap! He can't show good behavior! No, I won't calm down! No, I won't stop shouting! He will never, ever behave!" Apparently, at that moment, he must have hung up because he came out screaming and shouting, "Get out! Get out of my sight! Get back here in the afternoon!" In the afternoon, he had his temper under control, looking calm, and he began to ask everyone, "What room do you want to sleep in? If you know someone here or if you have friends, I'll take that into consideration and will put you in their room." Some people did state their preferencesand he noted them down. "I know someone too," I raised my hand. "No, not you," he growled, "you put your hand down. I'll decide where you'll be." And he did. All inmates were settled, and I was still waiting. At some point, I was finally taken to a cell with two guys whom I had never met before. I could immediately tell that they were his spies. A few days later, they admitted to my suspicion themselves – how he had told them to watch me, follow me, and constantly be on guard. We became friends very quickly though, because they expected to see the old Ali, Ali the Immortal, the monster who Pali-Motorahad known and had told them about. They were amazed, because they saw a completely different man – kind, friendly, smiling, and calm. How could they have known that the old Ali had died a year ago in the Ruse Prison? At that time, when all was going well with the old Ali – the drugs were ready in Turkey, the route from Turkey to England via Bulgaria was paved, and the clients in London were waiting. And right then and there, when he was about to get the big bucks, the old Ali passed away – the Ali who had come into the world with no luck had gone from that world with no luck. Wasn't that all he'd been after all those years? Collecting commissions from drug deals and living his life like a real smartass while others worked for him… I didn't feel sorry for the old Ali at all. On the contrary, it was good that he was gone; now there was room for the new Ali. The latter was completely different from the Ali that the cellmates had learned about from the warden's description. They could tell that I was sincere about being a new man, and I quickly gained their trust… Pali-Motora, who had no intention of even giving me a chance, was a different story, however, and I knew that. That is why a few months later, I just laughed when Ivodor decided to talk to the warden about letting me go out on leave. "Look," I noted to him, "I don't want to tell you what to do, but it won't happen easily, if it happens at all." "Why?" Ivodor was taken aback, "You are a completely new man, and the change has been apparent in all your actions for months now… He might help you out, you never know!" I shook my head, hoping that Pali-Motora would think that way as well. "That's why I have come," Ivodor spoke enthusiastically, "I'm meeting him shortly, and I want you to come with me and wait until I finish talking to him. He might want to see you. He surely must have heard about the positive change that's taken place in you." I nodded in agreement, and off we went together. "This man has such faith!" I thought as we walked together, "I have to follow his example." I sat down, waiting in the hallway, while he went in. I couldn't hear what Ivodor was saying, but after a while, I clearly heard Pali-Motora shouting:

"One more good word about Ali, just one more, and you will lose your access to my office. Do you know what he did the previous time he was here? Do you? He kicked down my door, and he stormed into my office to beat me up! The guards pulled him out after they had hand-cuffed him, and they could hardly hold him! For what he did, he could have gotten an internal sentence! Do you know why, Mr. Kovachev? Because this friend of yours considers himself above these things and has no regard for consequences! Do you understand what I'm saying?"

Ivodor tried to utter something, but, immediately, Pali-Motora interrupted him, shouting:

"I will not let you talk to me about this criminal! If there's a person who is definitely supposed to spend his life in prison, that's him! A dangerous, hardened animal like him doesn't deserve anything else! His incarceration is the best thing that can happen to him, and to the rest of society!"

At this point, Ivodor also raised his voice again,

"Mr. Gaitandjiev, I'm absolutely shocked by your words! How can you say that?! There is a tremendous, positive change in Ali! And no matter what he was in the past, everyone deserves a second chance! We cannot pre-determine his fate like that!"

Pali-Motora went furious, and added,

"Oh, come on! Stop with this show! Just because he pretends to be something, playing, deceiving, and lying, I am not buying it! You might be, but I am not buying this! I warned you – one more word, and you're done here, as long as I am the warden here."

Apparently, that was the end of the conversation. Ivodor came out, moving slowly, I felt uncomfortable looking at him – not because of me, but because of him. I looked up at him, and he stared down at me. As our eyes met, his head went down. He seemed completely discouraged. Obviously, he had sincerely believed that Pali-Motora would extend some understanding. After that meeting, things went downhill. No matter what good deed I did, he refused to see any of that in the right light. The more I tried, the more he provoked me, deliberately. "It's hypocrisy! That's all it is – hypocrisy, nothing good comes from Ali!" he would tell the guards who tried to put in a good word in my favor, not because I had asked them to do so or anything, but because they wanted to. I'd never asked anybody to vouch for me. I didn't want people to praise me or stand up for me. I wanted people to see my goodness through my actions, not through my words. That deliberate denial on Pali-Motora's part was weighing down on me. He was mocking everything I did. Okay, so I get it, I was reaping what I had planted many years ago – the seeds that my previous attitude and my actions towardPali-Motora were, but the situation got more and more difficult as time went on. He found pleasure in bullying me for everything good that I did. "It's a show! What a performance! A great actor!" – those were the only kind of comments he would make about me. I decided that I'd had enough when he forbade me to have my Bible meetings in the club. "Why?' I asked the guard. "Sorry, Ali, this is Pali-Motora's order." "Why?" I was still puzzled. "He said everything you do is just your hypocrisy and a show, and that we should not fall for it. I know that's not the case, and I see how you've changed, but I must follow his order." At that moment, Ivodor showed up, just in time for the meeting we were no longer allowed to have, because the club was locked. "I can't take it anymore; I can't take his attitude toward me!" I burst out, "I can't do this anymore! I might do something stupid; I'll go into his office again…" "Listen, brother, you've got to pass this test," Ivodor tried to convince me tactfully after I had calmed down a bit. "I can go to the Sofia Central Prison and talk to the guys there to have you transferred back, and they will. However, you'll have to pass this test. Otherwise, you won't reach the next level, which I'm confident God is preparing you for through this difficult time." I liked that Ivodor didn't give up easily. I was the same, and that's why we liked each other. "Ok, then," I agreed reluctantly, taking deep breaths, trying to calm down, "I'll stay here, but I'll need God's help!" "Great!" replied Ivodor, "Then I'll keep vouching for your leave from here, so help me God." We looked at each other, and we burst into laughter. What else could we do in that situation – but say "help us God." "Let's pray," I told him before he departed.

To put 15 years on the line for 12 hours

It was a few days later when I saw him next. I handed Ivodor the medical report for my prosthesis. He browsed through it – it was the final medical assessment. Based on that, prosthetic adjustments had been prescribed. He looked at me, "So, we are going to Pali-Motora. I have just received a recommendation letter for you from the warden in the Central Prison." "Go alone. Why do you need me there?" I asked him. "For courage and support," Ivodor smiled, but I couldn't understand if he was joking, or if he really needed my support. Anyway, I decided to go with him – Ali was never afraid of difficult situations.

"If you're here for Ali, you'd better leave now!" Pali-Motora growled the moment he saw Ivodor.

"You see, Mr. Gaitandjiev, I have his medical assessment that clearly says that he needs a prosthesis adjustment, and I have come here to ask you for your kind consideration…"

"Mr. Kovachev, what is it with you and Ali? Is this some kind of obsession or something? Or you think your persistence will change my mind? Is that it? We will bring some doctors in here. They'll do what needs to be done on the prosthesis…"

"It's a 12-hour leave we're talking about. Just 12 hours!"

"I'll let anybody else out for 12 hours, and even more, but not Ali! He is still the same and will never change! Never! Anyone else but him!"

"I'll be with him the whole time. You can hold me accountable!"

Ivodor was quite brave; he had such great trust in a man like me…

"How many years have you been working as a prison pastor, Mr. Kovachev?"

"15."

"And you're ready to put those 15 years on the line for 12 hours for this man?"

"You see, Mr. Gaitandjiev…"

"I asked you a question! Are you ready to sacrifice those 15 years spent building your reputation and good name for Ali's 12-hour leave?"

"He'll be back."

"No, he won't! Are you sure he hasn't made arrangements to escape the moment he gets out? Ali has serious connections in the criminal world; they can organize everything necessary for an escape. Remember, he's done it before, and I can confidently say that he will do it again."

"Ali deserves to be trusted!"

"He deserves nothing! There's no way you can believe an extremely dangerous criminal! It takes one call from him to have several SUVs full of criminals arrive, have them beat the crap out of you, and off he will go!Ali is the missing piece in the drug trafficking puzzle, I tell you!"

"I vouch for Ali, and I'm ready to sacrifice these 15 years that you talk about!"

"Great! It's your own problem that something is wrong with you, Mr. Kovachev! I will personally see to it that your access to the prison is denied. You'll be an accomplice in the escape of a dangerous and incorrigible repeat offender who fooled you by pretending to be a believer, as if wings have appeared on his back like a cherub!... Absolute rubbish! And you'll pay for it! You will pay, not him!"

"I take full responsibility, you just let him go..."

"I can and will let him go, just to see how bad you'll sink in this bog. He'll escape, you'll finish your work here, and this whole farce will be over. You can go now, I'll have his papers ready. On Sunday night, I'll personally wait for you at the gate to see you enter through the prison gates without him. And that will be the end of your reputation and the beginning of some very serious problems for you!"

Red in the face, Ivodor came out and looked at me with a sigh:

"Hey, this man is tough!"

He sighed with relief; I stood up and gave him a big, long hug.

There were three days to go till Sunday. I was very excited. I had cut down the push-ups to 900 a day, but now I was doing 1,000 again. I was a little too tense. During the remainder of the time, I read and prayed...

And there we were on the awaited Sunday, Ivodor and I were standing in front of Gabriella's apartment building. He rang her and said, "We're here, in front of the building." I could not believe she would come out and bring Alik, my son, with her. She'd been living with another man, and they had had a child together, and as for us – our relationship wasn't going very well. Contrary to my fears, she wasn't alone when she came down – Alik was there too, wearing a yellow t-shirt, brown shorts, and brown sandals. I exclaimed at how much he had grown up.He looked so much more handsome than he did in the photo I had of him. I leaned forward gently, I couldn't kneel because of the prosthesis, and I opened my arms wide open for a hug, "Alik, I'm your father!"

The child runs to the father – that's how it goes in the movies. But my movie was different. My son walked toward me, slowly and reluctantly... he didn't smile, didn't look at me... his eyes stared at the ground in front of him. I got up, and ran toward him, I embraced him tightly, and squeezed him, but it felt as if I was hugging a tree.

The trampoline is the most wonderful thing in the world

I looked into his eyes; he looked at me as if I were an unfamiliar, distant, stranger he could only feel indifference for. Questions started darting through my head. "Is this what I am? A stranger?After all these years... Is this what I truly am? A stranger to my only child...? Can I even want anything more since I've been gone for all this time? I couldn't, and I didn't have the right." I so badly wished then that it had been different! Even for someone like me, accustomed to pain, his indifference toward me was practically unbearable.

"Alik," I uttered with sadness, as my heart churned in my chest. "I'm sorry it took me so long to come see you, after all these years. Look!" and I pulled his photo out of my pocket. "You see, Alik, I have looked at you every day all these years, and I have thought of you so much – how we would meet, how we would spend time together, how we could talk, and play... Come, I'll take you wherever you want – McDonald's? Patilanci?[9] Or wherever you say... Where do you want to go?"

He was silent....

"Do you want to go to Patilanci first, and then we can go to McDonald's?"

"Yes," he answered mechanically, without any emotion.

We both sat in the back seat, since Ivodor was driving. I was looking at Alik, and I kept talking... asking him many questions – what he liked to eat, what kind of ice cream he preferred, what his favorite sport was, which girl he likedthe most in his class... I talked to him, and asked him questions, wanting, somehow, to make up for all that time I had been absent from his life and for the coming time when I would be away again. When we got to Patilanci, the ice between us started to break. The moment we entered, I looked at him carefully to see what caught his eyes. The trampoline!

"You want to get on the trampoline, right?" I asked him.

He looked at me in surprise, and asked in wonderment, "Yes, how do you know?"

"Who doesn't like the trampoline?! Every boy loves it! When I was little, I used to like it very much." I just blurted out the first answer that came to my mind. There were no trampolines when I was a child! We had no such things...

Alik got on the trampoline and started jumping. He was jumping so high that I got scared he might bounce off to the side and hurt himself! Anyway, he was fine, and boy, he was tireless too. About 10 min-

---

[9] Patilanci is a famous children's amusement park in Sofia with big trampolines, pony rides, canoe rides, face painting, etc.

utes passed by, then 15… How long could a boy bounce without getting tired?

When I noticed he was getting tired, I asked him, "Can you jump high so I can catch you?"

"I can!" he exclaimed, bouncing off from the trampoline directly into my arms.

"Did you like the trampoline, my son?"

"I did, Daddy! I liked it very much!"

That was the first time he'd called me Daddy!

"I liked it too, my son," I said, my eyes full of tears, as I held him tightly in my arms. "The trampoline is the most wonderful thing in the world!"

Holding him, I savored the scent of his hair, then I let him down carefully, and most reluctantly – I didn't want to let go of him. But he was six years old – a big boy! I knew I couldn't hold him as if he were still a baby! Besides, such big boys get hungry really fast, so we had to get a snack before we went to McDonald's to get some food. Meanwhile, Ivodor was sitting in a corner, taking photos of us, unnoticed by Alik. Then he joined us, and the three of us took the only available table. Nobody else had taken it, because the sun was beating down on it. "I'm going to the restroom," Ivodor said, getting up, "I'm leaving my bag with my personal documents and the car keys with you. Can you order me some cold water, please?" Unattended, he left me all alone with Alik to order for us. A minute later, the table next to ours became available, so we decided to move into the shade. Shortly after, Ivodor came, hurried and concerned, looking, struck with panic, at the table where we were before. The sun was shining in his eyes, so he couldn't see that we were sitting in the shade. I called him, he looked at me, and let out a sigh of relief, "That's where you are! When I came out and looked at the table, I saw no one there…" Then he pulled up a chair and sat down next to us. "This water is for you," I told him, changing the topic. He took a sip, and, going back, he replied, "I'm ashamed of myself, I doubted you for a moment there." "We all have our tests," I said, delightfully, watching Alik taking a spoonful of ice cream into his mouth.

Unfortunately, my test wasn't over even then. The tough part was still to come – taking Alik home and parting with him.

"Are you coming back soon to see me, Daddy?"

"Soon, my son, soon!"

"Ok, I'll be waiting for you next Sunday, and we can go to Patilanci again!"

I didn't say anything. I knew I wouldn't be able to comethe following Sunday. I hugged him goodbye, and watched him run back to his mother. He had so much to tell her about his day. I stood still, my eyes fixed on him. I was so happy – he turned back to wave goodbye! I waved back... Then I went to Ivodor's car, walking slowly, reluctantly... I walked as if I had just been sentenced to the most terrible punishment. That was my punishment – being sentenced to separation from my son, and it had all been nobody else's fault but mine... And that was the hardest thing for me to swallow. So hard that I didn't even have the courage to ask God for help, support, or strength. That was the worst day in my life... it was far worse than the day they had cut my leg off!

When we went through the prison gate, I saw Pali-Motora standing, waiting there. He was convinced Ivodor was returning alone, without me. I could see he couldn't believe his eyes. However, I wasn't entirely happy that I had turned out right. I wasn't happy that I had won this, because I had outgrown this. I was happy that the new "me" had overtaken the old criminal inside of me. I was happy for that one jump from the trampoline into my arms and for the word, Daddy, uttered by my own son. My son! My big boy, Alik!

"Ali, I feel bad for bringing you back here. I'm sorry... Forgive me for this." Ivodor's voice came from afar;he sounded heartbroken. I looked at him, not being able to understand his dismay. "Forgive me for bringing you back to jail," he explained. He seemed confused by my bewilderment. "Ivodor," I put my hands on his shoulders, "You don't understand, do you?! I am free! Otherwise I would not have come back ..."

I was a free man! I was free indeed!

And You Shall Know the Truth

The rumor about the whole thing – my return from the leave, and the bet between Pali-Motora and Ivodor had spread among the prisoners and the guards. That was all everyone could talk about for the next couple of days. I guess my return after my leave had actually impressed Pali-Motora. This new Ali, a man hitherto unknown to him, had returned before his very eyes, and that had completely shattered his recent notions about me. Of course, he was not the one to easily admit to having made a mistake or ill-judgement. Especially now, when everybody's eyes were on him, waiting for his reaction. It wasn't likely he would comment on it, but at least his actions were going to reveal that he had realized then that he was wrong. However, most likely because he wanted to keep his dignity intact in front of his subordinates, things between us stayed the way they were. So, there were jobs for the others, but no jobs for me. The others could go on leave, but I couldn't. I understood, though. How could he believe someone like me with my kind of record? Why would he allow me to work out of prison? What if I escaped? How could he believe so easily that I was a believer and a changed person, just like that? How many times had I lied to him? How could he be sure I was truly a new man, a new creation, with the fear of God in me, and with sincere faith in my heart? That's why I waited in my cell patiently, praying. My words to Ivodor about being a free man had not been empty. The time of empty words, shows, and pretense, like Pali-Motora used to say, was gone. I used all of my time to read the Bible and study the character of God. Due to everything I'd experienced up to that point, there was one thing I was finally certain about – things *were* personal. I had been through borders, prisons, loop holes in the law, and holes in the fences too. I'd managed to escape from the most difficult situations, and I found out that someone had always been there to help me, and someone had always been there to stop me. Back then, I evaluated all the crazy situations I'd been stuck in, all the bad things I'd done, and I had decided that God was not involved.But now, I could clearly see God's protection in all my mess. Every time my life had been threatened, His hand had stood between me and the danger – like an ultimate, invincible barrier of protection. He kept me alive to lead me to salvation. He knew I would come. I read the Bible and saw God as a good father.

The good father loves his silly children

For the good father loves his silly children just the same –even the ones who are temporarily deranged,such as myself. I read, admired, and wanted that one thing only: to live out the words of my Father. As long as I lived byHis Word, my responsibility was toward God – He led me by the hand. That's exactly what He says even in the Bible, and, you see, He always keeps His Word. No matter how thin the ice beneath my feet was, He held me tight and didn't let me fall. The same way that I had held Alik by the hand – I would've never let him fall or stumble, not as long as he held onto me. I would rather fall for him, I would rather hurt myself than allow my child to be hurt... and I was a mortal man with limited power. What about God, who is limitless?

I had lots of time for pondering as I read, as I would wait for the others to return from their respective jobs, so I could share with them what I'd discovered that day. There were guys who wanted to listen, and I told them about God, repentance, forgiveness, and the importance of being cleansed from all evil. I felt that my understanding and hunger for God was growing every day. It was the same with the other fellows. Ivodor provided us with a video Bible course, we organized everyone who wanted to get involved, and we started a group. We would watch the lectures, discuss them, and sometimes, we would even argue about this and that. There were a couple of times that I had to apologize to people if the discussions turned into disputes. I shared everything with Ivodor – he was an amazing source of support with all his knowledge and spiritual maturity. I liked his approach toward things – he stood by me and helped me every day, rejoicing in my growth and protecting me from deception. He did not intrude, bother me, or demand anything from me. He'd chosen the best way to approach me, and he was growing on me. One day, I decided that it was time for me to tell him everything, "Listen, pastor, I must tell you everything." I caught him by surprise with these words. I realized what he might be thinking, and I smiled and said, "No, I haven't done anything dumb today. I just want to tell you about everything I've ever done." He paused for a second and replied, "Confession is your right as a Christian believer and to keep your secret is my duty as your spiritual mentor. However, please do it only if you're convinced that you really want to, and you feel that it's your spiritual need." I agreed. So we sat down, and I told him everything. I don't know how much time it took, but I know I cried several times through my retelling of my life. I felt the heaviness of guilt inside of me still, as I recalled each event. It was hard to believe that I had been capable of all of that... all those evil things I had done. "Come on, brother, move on," Ivodor would gently urge me, "Let go of these things, they don't belong to you anymore, you are a new man." I re-lived everything as I confessed and thanked God thatHe took it away. Like they show in a movie, all the memories came to me, flashing before my eyes – memories filled with filth and abomination, pain, darkness, deception... I so wished then that I had never done those things. All my guilt was pouring out of me, and I felt relieved. Those dark and heavy places within me were all unwinding, giving way to freedom. The burden of shame was becoming lighter.

The new creation has come

In the Bible, it says, "Therefore, if anyone is in Christ, the new creation has come: The old has gone, the new is here!" (2 Corinthians

5:17). I was becoming renewed. It hadn't just been enough for the old Ali to die, now that new life in me needed room to grow. As the old things were being cleared away, room was opening up for new things. I saw a lot of interesting reactions from people who knew me from my old life. One of them was my friend Mad Emo. He had come to Kazichene and had gotten placed in my cell. He had found out that I was there, and when Pali-Motora had asked him about which cell he wanted to be placed in, he had chosen mine. I was beyond myself when I saw him. Of course, immediately, I told him about my faith in Christ. I told him I was a new man, and I had insisted that we pray before the cellmates went to work. If he was going to stay in my cell, he needed to know the routine.

"Yeah, we all go through hard times, brother," Emo said after I finished talking. "I've also been to the church to light a candle or two. You know, when you feel like crap, or you've messed up, go ahead, and light a candle. Why not? After we'd finished some of the best deals, I would even slaughter some lambs to offer to the saints, man. I've done it a few times now. I made a donation to an orthodox church once – they came to ask for money for the reconstruction of their monastery, and I gave them money and asked them to say a prayer for me, for my business and prosperity."

"I am done with that business, Emo…"

"Bro, you must be going through some really crappy time. I've been there too, man. Don't be too hard on yourself, it will pass away. You were born under a lucky star," he smiled, "if I had found you back then, you wouldn't have been alive."

I smiled too. That old joke was still there. But it was obvious that we were speaking in different languages – that didn't mean that I couldn't still love him like a friend. We would do our work-outs together – he had stopped taking drugs and was in great shape. Besides, he regularly received food parcels, so his daily routine of working out and eating was solid. Since I had quit sending inside information to my guys, making connections or recommending them to others, no one sent me food parcels any longer. I had no pocket money, because I was not selling dope either. I worked out, and the prison food wasn't enough, so I started struggling with food, but I wasn't worried. I had seen much worse situations than that one. I prayed as I knelt down on the cement floor. That was a privilege of mine – I could pray any time I wanted, without needing anyone's permission. Anyone could join me, if they wanted. Sometimes Emo knelt down by myside and humbled himself, and this rejoiced my heart. He was a huge man with a huge muscular body covered in tattoos. When he prayed, he became smaller even smaller than I was... I loved him like a brother. I saw a good man behind his fearsome appearance. I deeply believed that God had the desire of performing what He had already performed on meon him as well. The endless mercy and love of the heavens were reaching out for Emo, and deep within, I knew it was flowing through me too. Changes could slowly be observed in Emo's nature, because hebegan sharing his parcels with us regularly, the rest of the guys in the cell, and this was a blessing. Emo was the most welloff amongst us, and he had a generous heart as well. Once a month, on a Sunday, all the Christians would gather together, and we would cook for ourselves – there was a kitchen on every floor in the KazichenePrison. Emo also came to these gatherings, and he ordered food parcels especially for those occasions. Sometimes, he brought a whole bag full of minced meat for the meatballs, "Look, brother, take this and cook it for the guys." We gladly took the bag. We had a Christian meeting too – we had lunch together, talked, and shared.

Tell him that I love him

On one of these Sundays, that quiet, still voice came to me, the same voice I had heard when I was in the Ruse Prison, "Tell him about Me. Tell him that I love him. Tell him to repent of his sins!" I went to Emo's bed, and I touched him on the shoulder. He turned to me. "Brother," I told him, with warmth flowing from my heart, "I used to carry a huge load of heavy sins, but God took it all away and threw it into the sea, and now I'm not burdened anymore. Even though I am here in prison, I'm free. I don't know how heavy your load is, it might be heavier than mine, but God is reaching out for you – give your burden to Him. Let Him take it, and throw it into the sea. Let Him take it, and be free!"

Emo's face became stiff, he squinted his eyes, they were filled with hatred, and I froze. "Never talk to me about God," he muttered, clenching his teeth. "I'm not a cheater, and I will not lie to God promising that I won't sin anymore! I know who I am, I know what I do! Those who have sinned against me, their heads will be cut off once I am out of here! And if you want to remain my friend, never speak to me about God again!"

I bowed down my head and stepped back, almost like he had slapped me across the face. My heart ached for him, he was my friend. The next two months, we never talked about God and the Bible. It was hard for me, but what else could I have done then? He was released, and I was still in. After a while, a guy I knew came into the cell. We hadn't seen each other for a long time. I started asking him about our possible mutual friends – what about this guy and what about that guy. The first person I asked him about was Mad Emo. "Don't you know what happened to him?" he looked at me, surprised, "His case has been all over the media. Ten days ago, they found his body in a ditch near the Serbian border. They say it was a car accident... But nobody believes it because his head was cut off. They identified him through his tattoos and fingerprints.How could it be an accident when his head was cut off with a knife?"

My heart sank. We exchanged info about a few other people, but I had lost my appetite for conversation. I went back to my cell and prayed for a long time. Why had that happened? Why had Emo rejectedthe chance I had come to him with? That was his last chance to repent for all the evil he'd committed and to make peace with God! Having been in his position, I knew quite intimately how a man like him felt – how empty he would have felt inside, the kind of hell that his life was... Death was his constant companion, and he was always expecting it. I felt bad for Emo. At the same time, I realized that my salvation could have been my last chance too, and I was so grateful that I wasn't late,unlike so many of my friends who had gone down. I meditated that day for many long hours. That was also when I found out about my fellow countryman, who had given me the Bible in Ruse – just a week after he had left, he had been deported back to Iran. I said to myself, "God has a plan for everyone. He had sent that man from Iran to Bulgaria so that I could find my way to the Bible." The mercy of God shone bright in all its glory – after all I'd done, He gave me a chance for salvation through Ivodor, so that I could hear about Him and believe. As I had continued to go up and down, doing stupid things, He let me to be arrested, and that's how I got that Bible. Stuck inside, I had nowhere to go – all I could do was to sit and read. And God's Word really changed me and answered all those questions my heart had pleaded to understand for years. I had been very upset about my leg, always asking myself,"Why did this have to happen?" Why did they have to cut it off?" I felt hurt and wronged, like it had been stolen from me. Then, I read this verse: "It is better for you to enter life maimed or crippled than to have two hands and two feet and be thrown into eternal fire." Right after that, I relaxed inside. I understood very well what God was trying to tell me through that verse. I knew what I used to do when I had my two legs.

The evening school in the prison

Indeed, I would have continued to run, and I would've never found His forgiveness. So I eventually stopped complaining about my leg, and I was grateful that a leg was all that I had lost, as opposed to having lost my soul forever. I decided to enroll in the evening school in the prison. If any of my childhood friends had been there, they wouldn't have believed their eyes! I was going to school willingly and eagerly. If they saw how hard I was trying and how much effort I put into it, they'd think it wasn't me! I was striving and pushing to get ahead in school, a place I had once despised and had leaped at any opportunity to skip. It wasn't to kill time either. I could have easily spent all my time studying the Bible. Anyway, time was passing quickly then, so it was clear that school wasn't just to occupy myself with something. I had the desire to be able to share the Bible with others. I wanted to learn to communicate freely with other people in Bulgarian. How could I share and explain God's Word to the guys if I, myself, couldn't understand or quote it in Bulgarian? That is how I began to prepare, and I passed all my exams successfully for two consecutive years. It'd been two years since I came to Kazichene. During all that time, I had been granted just one 12-hour leave – that Sunday, whichIvodor had arranged for me, the Sunday I had seen my son. According to Pali-Motora, I didn't deserve anything more than that. Either way, I was grateful that he had stopped pestering me and had allowed us to conduct our meetings. The guys and I had started a group where we would study the Bible together, pray, and enjoy fellowship. I encouraged every prisoner who was inducted, "There is a chance for you; you just have to repent for your sins. God is reaching out to you through His Word." Meanwhile, Ivodor had organized an Alpha Bible Course – a series of 15 sessions that we had to cover over 10 weeks. Many of the topics were quite interesting, such as,"Is Christianity boring and irrelevant?""Who is Christ?""Who is the Holy Spirit?""How can I be sure in my faith?""Why and how to pray?""How to resist evil?""How to share my faith with others?" And there were many such topics. We listened, discussed, and argued; sometimes we were quite loud and excited. Sometimes,Pali-Motora would send cops to listen in to what was going on, just to make sure that we were only doing what Ivodor had granted permission from him for us to do. It was awesome when the cops would be there with us – I had nothing to hide. We prayed for them too. Every soul needs salvation. Those of them who couldn't handle the praying would storm out. Generally speaking, I was constantly busy running errands. Some days, I even forgot that I was in jail. I was doing things that were important to me, and everything meant something to me. Investing time in meaningless things is more tiring and discouraging than anything else. Previously, my days had been empty and time had passed slowly. I would be faced with uncomfortable questions."Why was my life so meaningless?""What am I living for?""Who am I living for?" Now, I had all these answers, and I used my time accordingly. The Bible says that we must redeem time. I couldn't get that bit out of my head. I was redeeming all the time I had lost – redeeming it throughthe good works, because I had lots to catch up on due to all the time I had wasted. That's why I wasn't even thinking about applying for early release, neither did I expect to see my name on the parole list. It was one thing to have the right to file an appeal after serving two-third of my sentence, and it was another thing to have my appeal actually taken into consideration. For an appeal, I had to have the support of the warden. Pali-Motora had to write aevaluationfor every prisoner who applied for early release. Thereafter, the judge would read that and arrive at a decision. I could only imagine what kind of a recommendation Pali-Motora would have written for me – I did not even want to get into that. I only had one more year to go, and it was going to be a piece of cake. I read, prayed, studied at the evening school, and did my workouts. Most importantly, there was peace within me. That's why I was taken aback when, one day, Ivodor came to me and said that Pali-Motora wanted to see me. I wasn't sure if I had heard him right. "Are you having me on, pastor?" I asked him. "No, I'm serious. He wants to see you." "Are you coming with me?" I didn't know where that was going. "He wants to see you alone," he replied, "You're not in trouble. It's for something good." What? He wanted to see me for something good? The whole prison would be laughing if they had heard that. "Pastor, what are you talking about?!" "Just go," Ivodor smiled. Where was this coming from? Everything had been going well; what was this good thing the warden wanted to see me about?

Pali-Motora has gone mad!

I felt peace as all these questions ran through my head on my way to his office. I knocked, waited to hear a "Yes," and went in. Pali-Motora asked me to take a seat in the chair opposite his desk, and he threw a folder at me, instructing,

"Take it and read!"

"What's this?" I looked him in the eyes.

"Read!" he repeated.

I opened the folder, and then I closed it back.It was my evaluation from my previous stay. I did not need to read that.

"All this is true," I stated, "but it is true for the old Ali, and he's dead."

Pali-Motora nodded, handing me another folder.

"This is your new evaluation. I am putting you on the list for early release."

One of us had to have gone mad, because I couldn't believe what I had just heard. Pali-Motora looked at me with a frown, he cleared his throat, and, with a slightly altered voice, devoid of his typical superciliousness, he added, "I've no idea what came over me, but I almost compared you to Jesus Christ! Take it and read!"I did not budge. I looked him in the eyes again and uttered, "I believe you! I don't need to read it!"I got up, and I was just about to leave the room when I heard, "Ali," I turned around, "you proved me wrong. A man *can* change if he really wants to – even you."I nodded and left. I didn't understand what had just happened. Pali-Motorahad written a positive reference for me! He had also admitted to being wrong about me! I couldn't believe this... Ivodor was waiting for me outside, so as soon as I left the room, I exclaimed,

"Do you know what happened?! He is putting me on the list for early release! And he has written a positive evaluation about me!"

"I know!" Ivodor smiled. "He showed it to me, but he wanted to show it to you himself."

"How is this possible? I can't believe it!"

"God has taken this man's heart in His hands," the pastor explained with all the confidence in the world.

That day, my plans and my everyday life turned upside down. I had just gotten everything going so well – we had formed a group of dedicated guys who were a great example for and a positive influence on others. New people were joining us. I would give them a Bible, encourage them, and pray for them. And right then... They put me on the list for early release. What if they released me? I doubted that the itcould actually happen to a man with my kind of track record.But in case I was granted an early release, who would look after the guys? From morning till evening, I thought about them, I waited for them to return from work, so that we could talk. I would prepare topics for our Bible discussions, and we talked about them and prayed together. These guys had become my family! And then, my mind was being distracted because time was flying, and two committees from the Central Prisonhad begun discussing my early release. They had assessed my application and were on their way to approving it. I didn't know whether to rejoice or cry? The prison had become a home to me. I prayed for peace to remain in my soul, and that God's will would be done for my life.

The third committee was getting ready to meet soon. The day for their meeting was drawing near. The meeting was to be held in the Sofia Central Prison, where Ivodor and I, and the accompanying guards were already waiting. It was just like a courtroom. The prison warden was the prisoner's attorney, the prosecutor was also present, performing their job as the accuser, and the judge announced the decision. While I was waiting for my turn to come, several applications were getting processed for people with much shorter sentences and fewer troubles than I had. In comparison to me, they seemed as innocent as lambs. They came out. All of their applications were rejected, and all of them were heading back to prison. If their applications got rejected, there was no way they were going to accept mine. I knew the things I'd done, and all the charges that had been pressed against me. I didn't know what to expect, but at that moment, I realized that I did want to be released. I wanted to see my son. I wanted us to go to Patilanci again so that he could go up on the trampoline. I would just watch and be happy for him. Then, he could jump in my arms again, and then, I wouldn't let go of him as fast as I had the last time. I always regretted that I hadn't hold onto him longer. As I was thinking about all of that, my turn came.

Ali, you are free!

The judge, a strict middle-aged woman, opened a big folder on the table in front of her, and began to read out my long list of convictions:

"......

- Convicted of murder
- Convicted of being part of an organized criminal group
- Convicted of the kidnapping of a foreigner
- Convicted of organizing drug trafficking
- Convicted of armed assault
- Convicted of physical abuse
- Convicted of illegal possession of firearms
- Convicted of inflicting bodily injury
- Convicted of forging identity documents

- Convicted of illegally crossing the border

Convicted, convicted, convicted...

He has spent 14 of the last 20 years in prison; 4 of those 14 in solitary confinement.During the short period that he was out, he continued his criminal activities and has found himself behind bars again."

I'd done it all... I had... Nobody would grant me a release after onelook at all the things that I was guilty of.There wasn't a person in the world who would be crazy enough to let me go early. The applications of those before me had been rejected for crimes much smaller than mine... The judge finished with the list of the charges and convictions against my name and added, "Request: Early re-lease".

I bowed my head. If I had been a spectator, and it had been somebody else's case, I would have been confused at how they even considered processing an application such as mine. Why did they have to take me all the way back like that, back to the bottomless bog of the old Ali and his crimes? It made me feel bitter. I was doing so well until then, and I liked staying in Kazichene. On the inside, I was free regardless of where I was. The guys and I were studying the Bible together, praying... We were a family and we liked being together.

"Early release: Granted!"

The voice of the judge was coming from afar, and I ignored it. I was thinking about the boys and my plans with them – the following day was Wednesday, and we had a church service every Wednesday. I needed to prepare for the service...

"Ali, you are free!" I could hear a voice, one that was closer.

... I'd decided what topic I would talk about... It was on one of the Epistles of Paul – 1 Corinthians 3:16, "Don't you knowthat you are the temple of God and God's Spirit lives in you."

"Come on, Ali, you're free," the voice sounded a bit upset.

I got up from the chair, turned around, and headed for the exit of the room. Ivodor was standing at the door, with his eyes full of tears... So it was true, I thought to myself, I was not dreaming. There, at that moment, I realized what had just happened.

I left Kazichene at the end of November. That morning, Ivodor came to see me and instructed me, "Call me when you have your papers ready, and you're already out. I'll send a friend to pick you up. You don't have to stand in front of the prison, you can come straight to my place. Today, we have a Christian conference, I'd like for you to come."

I was released in the afternoon. Alone. Free. Freedom is a funny thing, it can be scary. It brought forth scary questions such as, "Where to now?" "What do I do?" The moment you are free, you have the right to choose! If you're exercising the right to choose, then it must mean that you're free! That afternoon, I could do whatever I wanted. I could call anybody I wanted. Not just Ivodor. I could hear a voice inside me whispering, "Do you have to ask for help? You are free; you can choose your own fate. You can do everything by yourself. You are strong. You are a man of position. You have had everything you've ever wanted. You can have everything you want again. Are you going to ask them for help?! Are they going to tell you who to call, where to go, and what to do? One call and you're back in the game!" All of those questions made sense... I knew that voice very well. The question then was whether or not I would listen to the voice. Then, I took out my mobile phone and dialed a number. "I am out, in front of the prison, waiting for you," I said and hung up. The car came very quickly. I got in, and twenty minutes later, I found myself in front of a building I'd never seen before. "Welcome to the 'Mission,' brother," said the driver who jumped out of the car to open the door for me, and I took out my small duffel bag with my few belongings.

We went inside, he opened the door in front of me, and I found myself in a small room full of people. I did not expect to see that many people inside. I bowed my head and hunched over, feeling a little uncomfortable, even ashamed. Shame was a new emotion for me, it made me feel vulnerable and defenseless. I didn't know what to do, but I wished to go invisible in that moment. Fortunately, the speaker at the front was teaching on a topic, and so, I could sneakily curl up in a corner, unnoticed. Then I heard the speaker say, "Hello, Ali, we welcome you here among us!" Oh, come on, not that! I wished I could just vanish then. I just wanted them let me be… but, instead of letting me be, a hundred heads turned around to look at me. Through my peripheral vision, I could see a hundred smiles, full of warmth and acceptance. An elderly woman and her husband reached out to me, "Welcome, Ali!" I looked at them in wonder. "We know you," the lady added when she saw my amazement. They knew me…? "Yeah, right! What do you know about me? You don't know anything!" I wished I could tell them that, but I kept silent. "We know you, we prayed for you today," her husband added with respect in his voice. Then I moved to the nearest available chair, I sat, leaning forward, cupped my face in my hands, and sighed. My palms became wet from the tears that were streaming down from my eyes. These strangers had already prayed for the new Ali, and they seemed to know him better than I did. I, on the other hand, still needed time to get to know my new, unfamiliar self.

Tell us! We know everything!

However, neither my old "buddies," nor the cops had any intentions of leaving me alone easily. I was walking down the street when an SUV pulled over, and some huskies pushed me inside. I thought they were cops because that's how the cops caught criminals – without a warning. So there we were; they were driving, and we were talking.

"Come on, tell us what you're up to these days. How's drug business going?"

"No, I am out of the drug business now."

"What is it then? Smuggling people or robberies?"

"Nope, none of that. God doesn't want me to do such things."

"What then? Frauds? Come on, spill the beans already! You know you can't hide from us, we find out everything anyway."

"Look, you can follow me, and you tap my phone calls as well. You know I used to break several SIM cards a week, and that was just because I didn't want you guys to track me down or listen in to my conversations. For the last three years, I've had the same SIM card. I've got nothing to hide. You will know it if you listen in to my Skypeconversations,or if you read my emails – I've got nothing to hide. I believe in Jesus Christ, I am a born-again Christian, and I have the fear of God in me. Illegal things and I don't go together anymore."

They looked at each other and asked me a few more questions – they had to do their duties, you see. Then, they dropped me off at the traffic lights of an intersection somewhere. They did their job, made me acknowledge them – as they liked to say – and left me alone. Until the next time, of course. They were just doing their job;that did not bother me. I knew what the old Ali used to do – they had the right to check on me. I understood them – from the outside, they saw the old Ali, but what they failed to see was how different I was on the inside. They needed some extra time to process of all of that, and time confirmed to them that I was telling the truth. That's why their visits became rare, and they did not have to make me acknowledge them any longer. Every now and then, they would call me to go visit them in their office, and we did our talking there. It was totally fine with me, because I wanted them to see my new lifestyle – see that I was a new man. Mere talk was not enough, they had to see it in my life. Therefore, I continued to do good deed every day without wasting any time. Whenever they called me, I went. Only if the calls were from the services, that is, not just any calls. Apostle Paul says in his Epistle to the Romans, Chapter 13: "Everyone should be loyal to the authorities..." So I had no problem with that – all authority was contained in God. The old Ali was not at peace with God, and therefore, he kept fleeing from the authorities. I had nothing to hide, nothing to be afraid of. In fact, I wanted them to know more about me so that they could know, for sure, that I was indeed a changed man. Those who have things to hide are the ones that have things to fear. The Bible says that whoever is of an upright standing has nothing to fear.

In the beginning, life was difficult. I had to find a job... a normal, legal job. I'd never worked in a regular job since I'd been a welder in Tehran before I had become a volunteer in the army. Since then, in the 25 years that had passed by, I'd dealt only in illegal business. It was time for me to pass my next test – working in a legal job. I had to find out what was it that I could even do legally, and I had to find someone would be willing to hire a man with a past like mine. The offers for illegal jobs kept pouring in.

It's raining gold

One guy I knew gave me a call, asking me tomeethim over coffee, adding that it was urgent... I told him he would be disappointed upon meeting me. I decided to go anyway because just like he had something to tell me, and I had a few ideas about what thatsomething might be, I supposed, I had something to tell him too. So we met and he started:

"Listen, bro, I heard you were just released, and I am not sure if you know what's going on, but I'll tell you – it's raining gold in Bulgaria these days, man. It's raining Euros, bro. Smuggling is a goldmine! It's the best business! I know you know lots of people, I know you have many open doors. I know you. Take over, bro, I know people too.They have sent me to you, man, we'll bathe in money."

"Even if you gave me sacks of money, count me out of this. I'm not taking over anything."

"Right, you're not taking over anything, bro. I've heard that now you're into the Bible or something. I'm a believer too, brother, we're all believers. You don't have to do anything, just... help us connect with the guys on the other side. One word from you, and all the Iranians and Afghans will start to go through us. Just make the connection for us! That's it! Whatever we get, we'll help churches, brother, we're believers too."

How was I to explain my new reality to that man?

"Since you say you're a believer, can I pray for you?"

He looked at me sadly.

"Oh, bro, how come you got yourself into this Bible stuff now, it's messed up your brain... It's raining gold, man!"

He left a bit upset;he didn't even pay for his coffee even though he had been the one to invite me. Anyway, I wasn't upset. There's a time for salvation for everyone, as long as they answered the call for it. So I paid the bill and rushed home. A new friend from the Mission, whose name was also Ali, had opened his home for me to stay with him and his wife. They lived in a one-bedroom apartment. It was a tiny little place, even for them, but their hearts were big – so they let me sleep in the kitchen. Ok, so far, so good, but what was I going to do next? What was I going to do for a living? "You can't do anything; you can't do any work," a voice whispered into my ears. "What will you do? You're a criminal, all you can partake in is crime and nothing else." I just prayed to God, prayed and prayed... And then, that voice of discouragement disappeared, and peace came in. Thousands of questions flooded my mind, and still, I had no answers for them. So I continued to pray, "God, please, just give me a job, any job, I don't want to be in need of money, I don't want to borrow money or rely on people. I don't want that, Lord! I'll live a simple life, and I'll work. I just don't want to beg!" Right then, my host and friend, Ali offered me a job with him. "I wash windows, there's work for you too, if you want." Immediately that voice started talking, "Ha! Ali the Immortal is going to clean windows now! Shame and disgrace! The whole city knows you, man! What will people say?!" That voice was depressing – it was the same exact voice that had sent me to prison time and again. The same voice I had heard while I went through withdrawal; the voice that had told me that there was no salvation for me. Then, the still small voice from within whispered too, "What else is greater proof that you're a new man, that you aren't the old Ali? You wanted a job, right? Any job? Well, you have one!"

When did you get a butcher shop?

"Oh, Lord, my God, I will clean windows then, and I won't complain!" We got up at five o'clock in the morning and went off to work. It was -18°C(zero degrees Fahrenheit) – it was a cold winter! I walked with my prosthesis on the icy streets, careful not to fall. I had prayed before we had left, and so, I was on my way with great joy, humming "Pour Your Spirit over Me." I felt so cheerful, cleaning windows – using mostly anti-freeze because the water froze so fast that the rubber of the brush would get stuck to the window. I cleaned the windows outside, and, on the inside, I cleaned myself too. I was working; I was humbled. One of those days, as I was cleaning the windows of a butcher shop, I heard someone on the street calling my name.

"Ali!" I turned around to see a black Audi Q7 pull over. One of the guys I'd known rolled down the window and said, "Didn't you just get out, and you already have a butcher shop?"

"It's not my shop."

"Why are you cleaning the windows then?"

"That's what I do for a living now."

"What are you doing?" It was good that he was sitting down when he got my reply, otherwise he would have fallen on the ground.

"Yea, I am working in a legal job now."

He was dumbfounded.

"Ali, you're crazy or what? Cleaning windows? Come on, get in the car, and let's go! There are plenty of jobs for you, man!"

"I have a job. I clean windows..."

"Ok, give me your new number, 'cause I've only got your old one... I'll call you, and then we can talk."

I gave him my number.

"What do you want to talk about? I'm no longer interested in what you do."

He never called. It's not like I expected him to – it would have been a waste of time for him. We did not speak the same lingo any longer, neither did we have the same interests. He probably deleted my number right after taking it, if he had even bothered saving it to begin with. There were some, however, who were a lot more persistent and determined than he had been. "Let's go out for coffee and talk." "What coffee and what talk?" I asked, "I am no longer interested in what you do. How about going to church with me?" Two of them even came to church! But they ran away – they could not stand the Word of God, they could simply not take it, it was way too hard for them. People have their day and time for salvation, one can't force it on anyone. I used to run away from God before... I told Ivodor about those guys, and he smiled:

"Do you know that saying about the skeletons in your closet?"

"What closet?" I took everything quite literally.

"Doesn't matter, it's just what people say."

"No, I don't know it."

"Well, it's about your memories and secrets from your past, the place where they are hidden."

I got it. Now I understood what he was saying. He continued slowly, which meant he was going to say something important, "The point is, you've changed your address, and that closet belongs to your old address. You've already moved to a new home. Your spiritual address is new!"

Oh man, I liked how that sounded! I had truly moved to a new address, and I did not care about old skeletons any longer. I felt so good at that time in my life. Ivodor was such a great support to me, a precious brother and mentor. That saying about the skeletons had come at a very timely moment, because a few days later, I got a call from a guy who wanted to see me "urgently." That guy was a man of opportunities, with many high-profileconnections, and he wasa big deal – an intelligent and elegant man. That's what I had called him – The Elegant.

You got the wrong man

We met in one of the parks downtown, a place with an orthodox church right in the middle of the park. We walked and talked, and he got straight to the point, "Look, brother, there's this problem. One guy is getting in my way quite often now..."

He said that and looked at me. I understood clearly what he was saying. If someone was getting in his way, it meant that person had to disappear. If someone had been getting in his way a lot, it meant that that person should've already been gone. I understood that, along with the reason why he wanted to see me that urgently.

"He messed up some really great deals, and he's not being a good help to his partner. His partner happens to be my friend, a wonderful man who thinks that he might be able to reach an agreement with the partner's son, who, in turn, seems to be more reasonable than his father... So, he might retire and sell his shares. Then I'll partner in a business that enjoys monopoly in an entire industry field. I'll have huge influence..."

"You already have huge influence... You are on TV all the time among some of the VIPs in the country."

"It's one thing to be on TV, it's another to have a say in who will be shown on TV," The Elegant replied, smiling. "And if I get into this format with your help, of course, then I'll have the power to control who, will be on TV and when."

He had always known how to come up with these ideas, knowing how to spin a great web with his cunning ways. Before, I had liked him – such a smart and polished man. Now, however, I felt that his spirit was a different spirit than that of mine.

"We're talking about lots of money and high positions. This is why I need this job done quickly," he looked at me again. "We'll talk about money, everything will be taken care of... We just need to make the connection with the Serbs."

"Look, I don't do this anymore..."

The Elegant interrupted me, and gave me the example of this one businessman who had become very well-known just recently, telling me about the amount of money, power, and influence he enjoyed. "If we do the job, I will become just like that guy," he explained to me. Man, he was persistent!

I had had enough, and I blurted out, "This guy you are giving for an example, his wife and children were blown up in their SUV, right before his own eyes. That's the one you're talking about, right?"

"Yes, but then he..."

"He what? Is this why you are so impressed? What is his money good for now? Don't you get it? Whatever you sow is what you'll reap. Can you become rich with blood on your hands? That blood will call for your blood tomorrow, won't it?"

"Hold on, don't go there..." he waved his hand.

"It's true! If we shed blood, we'll pay with blood, right here on earth. And then, it gets even more frightening up there."

"Oh, come on, now you'll tell me about this Jesus stuff... I heard you've become a believer..."

"Yes, I'll tell you about Christ. The blood of Christ calls for better things than the blood of the victims. That's because the blood of the victims calls for more blood, butthe blood of Christ calls for forgiveness."

"Listen, Ali," the Elegant smiled, but there was arrogance in his grin, which was very annoying. "Okay, okay. You know best ... If you've decided to play this way, so be it. Everyone plays their own game in their lives."

"The question is not about this life only, but also about the life after this one..."

"That's what I mean – everyone plays their own game. But I'll tell you one thing – a leopard can't change its spots. I've seen many people play their games, some even began believing in their games... But everything comes to an end fast. A leopard can't change its spots..."

"Who's the leopard?"

"It's just how the saying goes... it could be any leopard."

"Look, I don't know who that leopard is, but if that leopard believes in Jesus Christ, just like I did, I'm telling you, that it can change its spots..."

Speaking with passion, I looked him directly in the eyes. He just listened...

"Are you happy?" I asked him suddenly.

"No!" after pausing for a second, he replied, looking a bit dazed.

"Well, I am! Can I say a prayer for you?"

"Yes," the Elegant answered, looking at me. "Here?"

"No," I said after I thought about it for a second. "Let's go inside the church."

There, he knelt in the corner, and I prayed for him – it was a long prayer I said with all my heart and soul. The priest in the church watched me pray and didn't interrupt me. He was a good priest. After I finished praying, the Elegant stood up, his eyes were full of tears... I asked him to hold on to the good inside of him and not harm anyone. Then, we went our ways. I was so happy.

The next day, I got a phone call from him – seeing his name on my mobile screen made me happy. His words took me by surprise, though: "What did you do with me yesterday? You did something to me... It was as if I was stoned..."

"Do not offend the Holy Spirit," I interrupted him. "Every sin, and every blasphemy will be forgiven,except for the blasphemy against the Holy Spirit!"

"Listen, stop with this nonsense, I have a serious offer for you..."

"Delete my number from your phone. I am hanging up, and I will do the same with your number."

I hung up and deleted his number, along with that "elegant" chapter of my life.

Ali, the Believer

There were many chapters in my life that I had to close, and there were chapters I knew nothing about yet. One of these chapters had to do with my legal papers – quite a complicated issue like most things about me. Since I had learned that complex issues sometimes had very simple solutions, I went directly to the Immigration Office. As they say, grab the bull by its horns. It was a Tuesday, the day of the Head Officer's visiting hours. I waited in a long queue until my turn came.

"What do you need?" the officer asked.

"I just recently got out of prison, so I'd like to be issued identity papers."

"How many years have you served in jail?"

"Fourteen from the last twenty."

The Chief Officer jumped up, caught himself by the head, and called for the officer dealing with Iranian immigrants.

"Where did you catch this one?" he exclaimed.

"We didn't catch him."

"Where did he come from?"

"He came by himself."

The Chief Officer became angry:

"You think I am stupid or what? How did he come by himself, since he's served 14 years in jail, and now, after just three and a half years he's fallen into a completely different category... Who in his situation would willfully come here?"

"He did," the 'Iranian' officer noted, pointing at me.

The Chief Officer stared at me, not understanding how I had come – it didn't make sense to him that a criminal would march up in there and ask for identification papers.

"What do you want?" he repeated his question, but his mind was elsewhere.

"Documents," I responded.

"Fine," he replied after a pause.It seemed as if he had already come up with a solution. "Come back next week, your documents will be ready then."

I left the office, full of joy and happiness. Like any normal Bulgarian citizen, I would receive documents to establish my identity legally! It was a done deal! So, here I was, the following week, running back with great anticipation. All I wanted was to be completely legal, nothing else. I waited for my turn, went in to see the Chief Officer, and got my papers. I looked at them, and... What did I see?

Deportation to Iran

It was an order for revoking the right of permanent residence, a five-year ban on entering the territory of Bulgaria, and orders for deportation to Iran! There were 14 days until the order would be executed with an option to make an appeal. For the coming two weeks, I was to go to the Third District Police Station and sign in every day at nine o'clock in the morning. What a nightmare! I took the papers, signed them, and left. I was confused. I didn't understand what was happening or why. Nightmares flooded my mind! I recalled the mother of my precious childhood friend,Shiravan, crying, telling me about the last time she saw him before they hung him. His last wish, before the execution, had been to see his mother. When she walked in to see him, he unbuttoned his shirt and cried, "Mother, look what they did to your son in the name of Allah!" When they tortured him, they had cut his belly and messed up his insides. Then they closed him with a few stitches just before his mother's visitation. His terrified mother told me how she was able to see Shiravan's intestines through the crooked and poorly done stitches. That's what the Islamic Security Services were like; that's what they did to those who proved inconvenient to the regime. How could I know what to expect if they got hold of me? It might turn out that they would be doing me a favor if they simply hung me, like what they did to Akbar, my crime partner from the past. Why was all of that happening to me? After all that I'd gone through to get to that point?

"Calm down, please! That's all I'm asking you to do, calm down!" Ivodor instructed me when I called him to tell him everything. "I know lawyers who can help you. And we will pray to God, and do everything we can."

As he was telling me this, I could pick up on the uneasiness and worry in his voice. I hung up, feeling alone. Completely alone. Abandoned. No hope, no way out. Darkness surrounded me... darkness crept inside of me. "Eli, Eli, lama sabachthani?" I remembered the words of Christ on the cross, "My God, my God, why have you forsaken me?" At that moment, the phone rang.

"Ali? It's Diana Radoslavova, I am a lawyer. Ivodor contacted me about your situation. Right now, I am on maternity leave, but tomorrow morning I'll meet you in my office. I'm taking over your case. Everything will be ok. Don't worry."

Apparently, Ivodor had told her that I was worried. How else was I to feel in that situation? By the end of the conversation, I thanked her for being that kind to me. I went home; however, that phone call had done little to calm my worries. I felt absolutely no calm. I closed myself in my small room. I just wanted to hide somewhere. I took off the prosthesis, so I could kneel down. I knelt right by my bed and turned to God, praying, "Why, God, why? Why now, when I'm full of strength and passion to run the race you've set before me?"

I felt heavy, as if I was filled with rocks. I tried to pray, but the question, "WHY?" kept bothering me... WHY? Then suddenly, a thought began to settle down in my mind. This deportation might be God's plan for my future life – deported back to Iran to share the Good News about Christ in the jail that I would be put in. The worst scenario would be that I would sit in jail for some six-to-twelve months before they would resume the murder case for the death of Mehdi, the Butcher and hang me. Until then, I would talk to the prisoners about Christ, so that some of them could be saved. There was nobody who could really stop me! One way or the other, I was already on a death row. "God, if that's what you want, let it be Your will! Just give me the strength and the confidence to do it!"

Now is not the time!

I began to pray and that same small voice inside of me started speaking to me again. I could recognize it by then. It said, "Now is not the time to go back to Iran." It was such a soothing, gentle voice that it made me feel alive and exuberant again! Lying down on the bed, I tried to relaxed and put my head on the pillow. I felt relaxed. At the same time, I was so exhausted that I fell asleep immediately.

The next day, I was already waiting outside Diana's office before the appointed time. I couldn't believe the energy she had even in her advanced stage of pregnancy! She came and started comforting me, "Don't worry, Ali! We'll fight. It is truly a delicate situation, and it won't be easy, but we'll do everything possible. We'll appeal the decision in the Supreme Court." I could tell by her voice how concerned she was, and I was so grateful that she cared. I replied, "I heard God's voice last night, and I know everything's going to be alright." Diana looked at me, amazed. "Ivodor told me you are a believer in Christ as well, and that's why I feel comfortable speaking like this... Otherwise, anyone would think I'vegone crazy."

"I'm a Christian," she replied, nodding her head in agreement.

"Then, I want you to know that everything will be alright. Prepare yourself, but don't worry. The moment you open your mouth, God will already have the words prepared for you to speak in Court."

I was trying to calm her down now instead of the other way around, "Tell me about yourself and what you've done from the very beginning." After her original surprise, she continued as a real professional...

I took a deep breath and began to tell her about all the adventures of my life one-by-one...

"Wait," she said. "I'll get a copy of your criminal record, because it will take a long time for you to tell me everything. Now let's ask God to guide us..."

In that way, with God's guidance, Diana took over and began to prepare the appeal against the order of the Immigration Office. I left, and I was not scared, instead, I was fired up! God was with me; not anybody else, but God Himself. Christ said, "All the authority in heaven and on earth has been given to Me, and this authority I give to those who believe in Meto tread upon serpents and upon the power of theirenemy!" It was clear that the devil may have power, but through faith in Christ, I had authority beyond the one of the enemy! So no problem then! I did not wonder or doubt; I did not ask what God wanted to tell me. He had already said to me all that he had to, and it had all been clear enough for me to believe in.At that point, there was nothing that could have held me back from having faith. Nobody could stop me in my previous life when gangsters and cops had tried to puncture my influence and my control over the drug market in various neighborhoods. Nothing could stop me from becoming the boss then, let alone now, when God, the Almighty, the greatest boss of the entire universe, had empowered me to work for Him, and on His behalf! Who could have possibly stopped me then? NO ONE! Therefore, I went left and right, full of peace and great confidence, performing good deeds. One of those days, a man called me, speaking with an authoritative voice, and he told me, "I need to talk to you. It's for your good," he said. Ok, since it's for my good, why not?

This pen will sign the paper!

We met in a cafe downtown.

"I know you're having difficultiesobtaining resident status in Bulgaria," the man said.

"God is in control of every difficult situation. He has already provided me with a solution for this problem," I commented.

"This can be easily arranged," the man went on, playing with a pen in his hands.

"There's nothing difficult for God."

"But it will cost you," he added, clicking his pen.

"Jesus Christ has already paid whatever price there was to pay on the cross."

"I mean, you'll have to pay," he repeated, rubbing his thumb into the index finger of his right hand.

"Let God's will be done," I replied, "We are to do things in accordance to the law, not against it."

"You don't understand," annoyed, he raised his voice, "It's up to this pen," and he showed me the pen, as if I'd never seen one before, "whether you'll be living here in Sofia and drinking your coffee at the cafes downtown, or you'll be deported back to Iran, where you'll be hung in the gallows?"

"Look," I replied calmly, "I have fear, of course, but it's the fear of God. Whereas death... I'm not afraid to die, and it's been like this for a long time. But let me tell you a story, do you have a minute to spare?"

"Go ahead," he looked at me, inspecting me.

"Well, there was a woman who had strong faith in God, but she worked for an evil and godless master. Once, she asked him if he could lend her some money. "I will work it off, master; you can deduct it from my salary. Please help me, because I am in a great need." "Why don't you pray to your God?" the master asked sternly. "You're right," the woman answered joyfully. "You're right, master, I will pray to my God. He is good and strong; He's always helped me, and I am sure He'll do it again. The woman entered her room and started praying. Then, the evil master called one of his servants, gave him twice as much as the woman had asked for, and commanded him to go and give it to the woman, but he instructed the servant to tell the woman that the devil had sent it to her. "Let's see what she'll do," the master gloated. The servant took the money and did as he was ordered to do. He gave the money to the woman; she took it joyfully. "My God is so good!" she exclaimed, "He's provided twice as much of what I'd asked for." "Don't you want to know who's sending you the money?" asked the messenger. "Oh, that doesn't matter," replied the woman, "My God is so strong, he can make even the devil send it to me. There are no limits for my God."

I looked this man straight in the eyes and told him, "My God is so powerful, that if it's His will, those documents to be signed with this very pen in your hand, it will happen! Everything shall bow down before God's will!"

His eyes opened wide, the pen slipped from his hand and rolled on the table.

"You really have become a believer," he muttered. "I didn't believe it at first, but now I'm convinced you are."

And that is how we parted ways. To get home, I had to use the subway those days. Often times there were police officers checking for documents, and I'd been pulled aside time and time again. Every single time, I patiently explained my case, and the cops would check with the Third District Police Station, where my words would be confirmed, and only after that repeated procedure would they let me go. Several times in one trip, I would waste between 30 min to one hour that way, but what else was I to do? I just got used to the ordeal, and that was all. However, I could tell that time that things were different. It was full of cops, and, of course, they were checking people's papers. Of course, I had no papers. They pulled me into a room at the Serdika subway station. I could tell that the whole procedure was going to be different that time, more complicated than it had been during any of the previous times. It turned out that there had been a bomb threat, and so the room began to fill up with detained Iranians and Afghans – apparently that was the profile of the suspects. Some guys from the SNSA (State National Security Agency) came and began interrogating, which was a common thing in such cases. Me, however, they pulledover to the side, and every time I tried to ask or say something, they told me, "Stay there and keep quiet!" I did not like what was going on. I called Diana. I could hear some children's voices in the background; they were celebrating her older child's birthday... I felt terrible about disturbing her during her family time, but I told her what was happening and that things didn't seem good to me. Diana immediately responded, "Tell them your lawyer's coming right away! I'm leaving immediately!" I told them, but the cops did not seem impressed. Diana indeedarrived within minutes, quite literally, walking inside with a big folder under her arm, there were no small folders when it came to my case, and then, she began talking to them. "Wait outside, please!" they told her. On her way out, she looked at me, making a sign with her hand, asking me to calm down. I was already calm – her presence itself was giving me peace. During that time, they were talking on the phone, having discussions about me... After just five minutes, they let me go! When Diana saw me walking out, she heaved a sigh of relief. Whenever I received help and support from Christians who weren't obliged to do anything for me, I always told myself, "This is your sister, this is your brother, and this is your family." It's amazing to have a family and to have their support! Diana was preparing all the papers for the hearing, and she was asking people to sign a petition for me. After two days, 96 people from the Mission church had signed it. What could I say? How was I to thank each one of them? That was not all... These people were asking if they should talk to their friends to sign it as well, and asking how many people's signatures were needed for the petition. "No, this is good, we don't need any more," Diana replied, "This is sufficient evidence that Ali has changed and that people trust him." She attached the evaluation from Pali-Motora as well as some other papers. She also explained to me, "Ali, we do the best we can and, in my opinion, our position is well-grounded. However, I want you to know it won't be easy because the current practice of the Supreme Administrative Court is to confirm the acts of the Immigration Office. However, we do have a chance, and we're going to fight. I just want you to be prepared for various options. If it's necessary, we'll appeal with the European Court of Human Rights in Strasbourg." "Diana," I answered calmly, "You get ready for the hearing, and we'll pray. God will give you the words to speak." "Yes, let's pray," she confirmed, smiling, and then added, "I have to admit something to you. Your faith truly amazes me sometimes." My faith did not amaze me, however. Faith is the natural state of the human spirit. What amazed me was when people started trying to reason about the Bible, which book is canonical and which is not; and which version of a verse is the more accurate translation, and which is not, because of this and that. It was craziness. It's like your father tells you something, and you ask him which version his words are in, and if it's not the one you like, you won't do what he's asked you to do. This was offensive to Him, and should have been even to the followers! Just have respect, and do what He says. He's your father, your Creator, after all! Nevertheless, whenever I came across these kinds of cases, I just kept quiet, simply because I had respect. I was born a Muslim, and I had and still have respect for those who were born Christians. That's why I even felt sorry for them because they had no idea what kind of power and might there was in the name of Jesus Christ! Why couldn't they understand how much they were missing by not knowing that? But who was I to judge anyone? Neither the dark past of the old Ali, nor the faith of the new Ali had given me the right to judge people.

In fact, I was about to go to court and meet the judge... yet again. That day came, and Diana and I were outside the court room. Ivodor was there with me too. I felt tense. Despite the peace in my heart, my mind was like a beehive of hundreds of buzzing thoughts, full of anxiety, uncertainty, and ambiguity...

What is this prosecutor saying?!

The session began. It was the prosecutor's turn. From my experience, I knew I could not expect any good words from a prosecutor. However, the more he talked, the more I got confused... That prosecutor was not like the others; it seemed like he was saying some good things about me. "The corrective work has given positive result. Ali can recognize and solve his problems, realizes the consequences of his actions..." I wondered if I was hearing right, or if a twist would come in his speech any moment. But he kept going in the same direction... I started fidgeting inmy chair, asking Diana if I was understanding everything properly. I whispered to her, "Something is not right." I wanted to find out if she was hearing the same things as I was, that the prosecutor was indeed saying good things about me. Diana, however, gave me a sign to sit still and be quiet. Then I leaned over to her and asked, "Are you hearing the same thing? The prosecutor is saying good things about me?" "Shhh!" she whispered, but I could tell she was also perplexed by his words. The prosecutor went on, "He sees his son regularly and takes care of him as much as he's able; he connects to the values of our society; he seeks employment opportunities; he displays positive attitude in his behavior and conduct as a result of accepting the Christian faith and values..."

I could not believe that the prosecutor was actually speaking in my favor; that had never happened to me. I listened and looked around; I was still bewildered. I leaned over to Diana to ask her again; she still made a sign for me to keep quiet. The prosecutor kept going, "... he has a positive attitude towards the legal system and has ramified his mistakes... due to good behavior in prison, he was released early from serving his full sentence... He doesn't use drugs or alcohol."

For a good 45 minutes, that's what I heard. I looked at Ivodor occasionally, but he was sitting far away, and I couldn't ask him. Everything seemed very strange, but it was finally over. The court withdrew for a meeting, and then announced, "The act of the Executive Body was stipulated in violation of the administrative and procedural rules; the reasons given do not match the facts of the case. Led by all of this, the Supreme Administrative Court overrules the order of the Director of the Migration Directorate with the Department of Internal Affairs to impose compulsory administrative measure, i.e. deportation."

I gave Ivodor a tight hug, and I embraced Diana gently because she was so far along in her pregnancy and her belly was quite big. I was trying to contain my joy, at least while still in the corridor of the court house, but I found that very difficult to do... They were not going to deport me back to Iran! I began to jump and shouted on the street; I was beyond myself! Having a family is an amazing thing! Ninety-six people had believed in me and had put their names on my petition! How had that happened!? Thank you, God! To have a sister and friend like Diana, a brother like Ivodor, and so many friends who supported me... That was absolutely incredible! Some friends celebrated with me in the evening while the phone kept ringing; friends from the Mission kept calling and rejoicing with us. Iran was postponed. It was not time yet. Who knew? Maybe one day, the time would come when I would go to Iran as a missionary. Only God knows! Who can stop a person determined to speak about his faith in Christ? Whoever they were...

Ali, you've become a Christian?!

Soon after, one evening, when I was on Facebook, a woman who seemed unfamiliar sent me a friend request. Her name was Nelly, a

Bulgarian name. After taking a careful look at her profile picture, I realized that the woman was Neriman! She was an old friend of mine who came from a Turkish background. I hadn't seen her in ages. I accepted her friend request, and she messaged me right away. "Hi, Ali, it's Neriman. I am using my Bulgarian name on Facebook." Neriman was wild at the time we had dated. The meaning of her name, "tenderness," always seemed funny to me, because she really was a wild one. This one time, she had beaten up a girl just because the girl had been flirting with me. In fact, I had to convince Neriman that the girl had just looked at me, or she wouldn't have left her alone. If she had known the truth, the poor girl would have probably suffered a lot more than she had... But those were some old stories of the old Ali's past. Now I had other things to talk about.

"Where are you, Ali?"

"In Sofia."

"How come you have internet in jail? You! You always come up with a solution..."

"What are you talking about? I'm at home."

"Wait a minute! So you're out, not in jail anymore?"

"No, not in jail. I'm free. Where are you?"

"In Ruse. I'm coming to see you."

"If you want, you can come, but isn't it quite late to leave tonight? It's a long trip."

"No, it's all good. There's a night bus."

Neriman was clearly still impulsive, a tough girl. I'd always liked her. Indeed, early in the morning, she arrived in Sofia and came straight to see me. As soon as I opened the door, she jumped on me with a huge embrace and held me tight... "Wait, hold on," I said, holding her hands gently, taking a step back. "But I want to hug you," she looked at me, puzzled. Before, we would not waste time talking. Then, it was different, and she was absolutely stunned. "We will hug each other later if need to," I added, "Now let's sit down and talk, you can sit over there." She continued to stare at me, not understanding why I would not let her hug me and kiss me! I began telling her what had happened through the years after we had lost touch, all that had happened to me... She interrupted, "Listen, Ali, I know you too well! You've always been like this; you like that life-style! Inside and out, that's you. You get out of jail just to go back to it all. You'll do something again, and they'll catch you."

"This time I won't do anything because I believe in God."

"You used to believe before too. I remember you used to tell me that there is a God."

"It's one thing to say that there is God, it's another thing to believe in Him. Before I did not know who God was."

"Who is God?" Neriman looked at me, wondering what had happened to me.

"Jesus Christ is God! I believe in Jesus Christ!"

She sat in complete disbelief.

"Ali, you've become a Christian!? I can't believe it... I can't believe it!"

I nodded, without saying anything, looking her right in the eyes. Then, I continued. She listened and listened with her eyes wide open. I paused at this one moment, expecting her to say something, when she thoughtfully, and somehow, still with doubts uttered,

"Ali, I do remember the old times when you had whole bags full of money, but I have never seen you talk like this – so peacefully, joyfully, and lovingly. You have changed. I know you, Ali, and I see a completely different person sitting in front of me.

"It's because of Christ."

Then I pulled a Bible out. "Take this book, Neriman, and read it. That's all I want from you! Just read this book!"

Before she left, I asked her if I could pray for her. "Yes," she agreed. We both knelt down, closed our eyes, I put my hand on her head, and we prayed.

"Ali, I've never heard such a prayer, I'm mesmerized," she said after I'd finished praying. "I've prayed many times, but I've never felt such peace and so much love!"

A few hours later, she called me while she was still on the bus to ask me about this verse and that verse, and what they meant. She started reading the Bible and was already bombarding me with questions the very same day. On the next day, the same things happened. Three weeks later, she called me and said:

"Ali, I am coming to Sofia. I want to confess my sins, to renounce my old way of life, and I want to be baptized and become a Christian."

I'll be waiting for you, Neriman – I responded with excitement.

And she did what she said she would. She came, got baptized in the water in the Mission and accepted Christ. Shortly after that, she left for Germany. (She lives there now, regularly goes to church, and lives as a Christian. Sometimes, we talk to each other briefly on Facebook).

I hardly had any spare time. I was getting more and more occupied working with the refugees who were coming to Bulgaria from the Middle East. Mondays, I was in the camp Busmantsi, and Thursdays, I was in the camp of Harmanli. I got up early to rush to the camps to deliver aids to the people who were taking refuge there. Humanitarian organizations relied on me, and the number of my tasks was constantly increasing. I carried packages for men, women, and children; for the women we put some sanitary items, and for the children, something sweet, whenever was possible. I wanted nothing in return. I had no hidden agenda. I knew that the refugees will start feeling the selfless love of Christ after my second and third visit, and that love would bear fruit. I knew them; these were people of dignity who lived in a very harsh situation and in almost unbearable conditions. And they themselves began to ask me,

"Ali, is there anything we can do for you, to make it up to you?"

"No, you don't have to do anything. I don't do it to get something in return."

"No, no, come on," they insisted, "we want to do something for you."

"Are you sure?" I asked.

"Yes!" They were so certain about it.

Then, I gave them a Bible in their native languages, Arabic, Farsi, or Urdu and told them, "If you want to do something for me, take this book and read it. This is the Bible. But if you do not want to read it, it's ok. Next week, I will be back here, with you, no matter whether you read it or not."

I meant it, and I visited them again. And again, I brought something for them because that was and is the unconditional love of God. I believed that it was through showing His unconditional love that I had gotten some of these people to read the Bible. They read it earnestly, passionately, thoroughly, as it was meant to be read– the simple Word of God. Some of them came to church after they were released from the camp, and before they continued their journey onto Western Europe. Of course not all of them had legal rights to stay in the country, but that was not my business or responsibility. It was theirs. My job was to help those people in need and reach them with the Truth. That's why, for a while, I used to go to this house where some illegal immigrants were hiding. Every time, before I went, I prayed to God to protect me, so that the cops wouldn't catch me while I was in there. I knew my papers were legal and met all the requirements, but for a man with a past like mine, it would have been hard to explain why I was there. Yes, more and more people could put in good words about me, support me, and stand for me, but it was still best to avoid getting into trouble. I was going there to do God's work, that's why I asked Him to keep me safe and to protect me. If it were His work, He was in charge. When an officer calls a soldier to fight, then the former should provide everything for the latter – weapons, food, clothes, and a bed. The soldier's only duty is to fight. So I prayed and followed His ways. The Lord took care of everything, and I had nothing to fear. Praise God, no cop came to this house whenever I would visit there, sharing stories about Christ and praying for them. Not even once when I was there! The cops had surrounded and raided the house more than 20 times, arresting everyone inside. At a certain point, the owner gave up renting the house out to foreigners because it was too much trouble. However, I did not give up, although, it was an on-going adventure to help and work with refugees. Like the ones I worked with.

Where is Sofia? Where is Athens?

One day my phone rang, and I could tell from the number that it was a call from another country. I answered; it was an Iranian calling me from Athens, trying to explain something to me. "Please, listen to me," he said, "I know these people you know. They gave me your number." It turned out the guy was a smuggler. He tried to explain the situation about this boy who was an Iranian Kurd. They had to take him from Turkey to Athens, Greece. That was the arrangement he had been paid for and was no longer responsible for what was to happen thereafter.

"What's the problem?" I asked him.

"The problem is they took him to Sofiainstead to Athens. They made a little mistake."

"A little mistake?" I shook my head. "What's a bigger mistake?Taking him to Egypt or what?"

"Listen, brother," the man started pleading. "Can you please help?"

"I can't," I replied. "Didn't the people who gave you my number tell you I don't do illegal things anymore?"

"Yes, they did tell me," he interrupted me. "That's why I'm looking for you. Can you, please, let him stay with you just for one night?

So he's not out on the streets. The relatives have already paid me, and they know me. If he gets arrested, his relatives will find me, and I will be in trouble. You can't joke with those people, man. And this young man is lost right now."

"Do you know of his whereabouts?"

"I know roughly," the guy answered, giving me details about where the young man should be, what he looked like, what he was wearing.

I left right away and went looking for him in downtown. I found him nestled in the corner of a hotel, a young boy, scared to death, looking like a lost puppy, literally trembling with fear. I approached him quickly, speaking in Farsi, "Start walking beside me; don't ask anything." I went down the street, throwing a look behind me to check if he was following. I saw him, walking, like my shadow. I brought him home, showed him the bathroom, and began to cook dinner. I'd just done my shopping that morning. I was getting ready for the guys to come over for our home group meeting, to fellowship, pray and read the Bible. We had dinner quickly, and while we waited for them, I told him:

"Listen to me now. I'm a Christian, and I'm helping you because you're in need right now. If you get caught, it will be very bad for you. Whether you are a Muslim or a Christian, it's your business. To me, you're a person in need, and that's why I'm helping you in the name of Christ. Don't even tell me your name, just don't worry, nobody will hurt you. You're safe here with me."

He sat in the corner of the bed in my little room, and I gave him a Bible in case he wanted to read it. Nearly 20 people crowded in my little room, literally on top of one another. We prayed, read, discussed the Bible, and we even argued, raising our voices a bit. Finally, we reached an agreement and then had tea. That's how our meetings ended. Afterward, my friends started introducing themselves to the young boy. "He's my friend," I said, "He's staying with me for a couple of days. Don't bother asking his name." That was enough for them to stop with the questions. The next day, some people called me to let me know that they were coming to take him to Athens, to fix the mistake of that crazy smuggler who had messed up Athens with Sofia. The boy called me afterward to let me know that he was fine; he was in a house; everything was okay and that I did not need to worry about him. He spoke to me with great respect, which was normal because he had only seen love from my heart and nothing else. Everybody respects genuine love and generally admires it too. Every other day, he began to call me for small talk. I must have grown on him. We did not talk about the Bible, or about God – he did not bring that up and I did not want to push the same on him... One time, during one of our small talks, he said:

"Uncle Ali, I'll be leaving for Germany shortly."

"I hope they do take you there," I replied. "Can I pray for you?"

"I'll be very grateful if you do," he uttered and I felt the gratitude in his voice.

He called me a week later.

"I'm in a town close to the Danube River. Tomorrow they'll take me across the border. This number won't be working any longer, but I want to thank you for your kindness and goodness, Uncle Ali."

"God is good, my boy. I'll continue to pray for you."

This was our last conversation. After that, he disappeared – I hoped his trip to Germany was safe. During the next couple of weeks, my daily errands occupied my life. It was not until a whole month later when I got a phone call from an unknown number. Upon answering, I heard:

"Uncle Ali, glory to Jesus Christ!"

I recognized his voice instantly, as goose bumps rose on my skin in response to the passion in his voice. I hadn't even said a word to him about Christ!

"You didn't have to tell me anything. Your goodness was enough – to let me stay with you that night, and the way you treated me, a complete stranger. And then, the meeting you had, everyone was that way too – that love that was among you all!"

"How was your trip to Germany?" I asked him, and I was so happy!

"In the secret compartment in the cabin of a truck, the Bible you gave me was in my hands the entire time. 'Please', I prayed to Jesus 'let me get safely to Germany and I will surrender my life and soul into your hands forever!' And God opened the borders right before the truck; they never stopped us! They just looked at the papers and waved at us to go."

This young man had become a fiery Christian, and I was amazed by it! When did the seed fall into his soul? How had it grown into a tree that fast?

"Uncle Ali, I'm forever indebted to you. I owe you my life," he added, his voice trembling.

"God bless you, brother," I finished, and my voice trembled too. It was as if this boy had been a son to me, my spiritual son.

I wanna be like you, Dad!

I thought of my own child. I was grateful to Gabriella for the way she cared for Alik – my son was always with clean clothes; he'd never been hungry, thirsty, or neglected. I knew that could not have come easy. I'd never stopped being grateful, no matter what my relationship with Gabriella had been over the years. It hadn't always been good. The worst had come when she hadn't let me see Alik on one of his birthdays. I had tried calling her, but she never answered. Then I called my son – to congratulate him, and to check if he wanted to see me for a while, but I told him that he needed his mom's permission, otherwise we couldn't see each other. I was hoping we would get her permission, but a minute later, he called me and snapped angrily, "Mom said No! I want to, but she said No!" And then he hung up. Oh, it hurt so much; my heart was aching. Then I heard a voice whispering, "Who can stop you from seeing your son? How can they tell you when to see him and when not to see him? Or how many hours you can see him for? How come?! He is your son! You have rights over him too! Go and take him now! You are Ali, the Immortal! Nobody can stop you – it will take only a couple of minutes!" It's true it would take only a couple of minutes to get my son. I knew that voice, and I had chosen not to follow it anymore. And it hurt! I was about to go... But then, I decided to call one of the sisters, Mariana. She was always there for me, and we used to pray together. She was my mother's age and had the same approach as my mother did. She'd always been concerned and could always find something to scold me about. She had helped me so much, with no hidden motives, without ever wanting anything in return, so much so that I call her "mother."

"Mother, I feel heaviness inside," I told her over the phone, "Can you please come over to pray together?"

"I'm coming, Ali, I'll be there," there was so much goodness in her stern voice; it was enough to calm me down. I went home and started cleaning my room. I knew the first thing Mariana would do was to check around, examining everything carefully, and eventually, find a flaw to scold me about. Sometimes, she even put her glasses on, and examined the floor, all the way down the hallways, around the bed, everywhere. Now she did the same – the moment she entered, she looked for her glasses, so she could start with the quality check. "Mother, please don't put your glasses on. I have just finished cleaning; I have mopped the floorsonly yesterday... I have also cleaned the bathroom carefully..."

She looked at me and decided to have mercy on me. She could tell how burdened I was. We prayed for peace in my soul, asking God to keep me in His love and give me rest. Then I saw a picture in my heart – it was of Christ, when he was praying for the Romans while they were hammering nails through his hands and ankles to put him on the cross... and His words, "Father, forgive them for they don't know what they are doing." And suddenly, the whole pain in my heart was gone, and I started praying for Gabriella, "Father, forgive her. She doesn't know how much she's hurting me, forgive her!" My soul filled with peace, peace flowed through me like a calm river... I took in a deep breath. I am blessed when I bless others. I turned to Mariana:

"Mother, would you like some tea, if you have time?"

"I have to go. I had something else to do when you called me, but I came here," she explained. As she left, she reminded me, "Remember to clean your room every day!""I clean it every day, mother," I assured her while seeing her off at the doorway.

Mariana was and is truly like my mother; she could relax only after she was done with the scolding. As for me, I really cleaned and aired my home regularly. When in prison I had gotten used to taking care of myself; I liked cleanliness and fresh air. How could one live otherwise? Lack of those vital elements was not healthy for anyone. I went back to my room. The radio was on, and at that very moment, they played the song that hit me every time I heard it – Cat's in the Cradle. The song's about a father who is always busy with work and always promises his little son that he will find time to play with him soon. That happened time and again, and every time, his son spoke to his father with admiration and told him he wanted to be like him when he grew up – "I wanna be like you, Dad!" Time flew by, the little boy turned into a grown-up man with a family. His father was retired. When he called his son to talk to him, his son was in a rush, explaining he was so busy at work, he did not have any spare time. Then suddenly, the father realized his son had become just like him. So sad! I didn't want that to happen with me and Alik. Indeed, I used every opportunity and occasion I could to meet him. We were now close; we spent time together and talked. It was not as often as I'd like to, but I had to be patient. It was good enough that I could share my faith with him. We even prayed together and read the Bible to-gether. It was enough to be grateful for! I was also glad that my relationship with Gabriella improved. We talked to each other, not like we used to talk when we were together, but we did talk. During one of these conversations, she surprisingly asked me:

"Ali, can't you live in the middle? Like everybody else... Why do you go from one extreme to another? When you were a criminal, you were barely out of prison, now you have become such an extreme Christian that you constantly carry the Bible with you and pray to God. I am a believer too, but you've gone overboard with what you do; it's too much."

"Look, Gabriella," I answered her immediately, "I can't live in the middle, what will I do there? People who haven't made up their minds live in the middle. Some of them refuse to make the choice; others are still considering which path they should choose. I have always made my choice. Formerly, when I was in darkness, and now when I am in the light too. What would I be doing in the middle?"

From complaining into gratitude

I was not sure if she understood me. But that was the truth! I was happy then! I took Bibles to people who had come from Iran and Afghanistan to read and get impacted. They accepted Christ into their hearts, turning from the darkness into the light. Everything happened so quickly, so easily... Sometimes, I thought about everything having happened so easily, and I said to myself, "Why was it so hard with me? Why did it take me so long, and why did I do all those evil deeds while I was still in the kingdom of darkness? Why?" While praying one day, I asked God, "Heavenly Father, why didn't I get saved earlier? How come nobody gave me a Bible before? If I had the Bible 25 years ago, I wouldn't have spent my life in prison, I wouldn't have done all those evil things..." I was praying, but I caught myself murmuring and complaining against God. Suddenly,

I could see my whole life rolling before my very eyes, just like a movie. Then, God spoke right to my heart, "If I had given you the Bible then, you wouldn't have had the experience you have now. If you had had a Bible then, you wouldn't have been able to do even a fraction of what you are doing now to expand My Kingdom." Immediately, I stopped complaining. My mind worked fast, looking back, I pondered over a thousand things... And, then I understood that it was true. God had allowed me to reach the pit of hell, so that, after my salvation, He could turn me into an instrument in His hand. Through me, He could reach the captive souls of lost men, men who are the way I used to be. And then, God was able to reach the pit of hell in others through me, and He could save people from the grip of the devil's hands. As I realized that, slowly, as if nothing had happened, I stopped complaining and began to thank Him for His plan.

This was not the first time my complaining turned into gratitude during prayer. The situation with my leg still weighed me down. Although it was my own fault, and I had said to God, "If I am wrong, please don't let me get there to kill him," it still weighed me down. Once, I was complaining again, "Why did you let this happen to my leg, God?" And then, I remembered the Bible verse, "It's better for you to lose one part of your body than for your whole body to go into hell." I remembered again what I was doing when I had both my legs, and again, I began to thank Him for being real with me, for loving me and providing a way for me. When you are honest with yourself, you are honest before God. There's no point in deceiving yourself or thinking that you can deceive God. He knows everything, and still, His love is unconditional.

Zeal greater than love

In the beginning, my zeal was much greater than my love because I saw how people came to the Mission to be baptized, driven neither by a desire for repentance nor for the love of God. They did not come with that sincere excitement and broken heart, the way Neriman came, for example. These were mainly refugees who needed documents. I found that offensive to Christ's sacrifice. I shared with Ivodor, and his comment was, "I can't see into the human heart and judge who is sincere and who is not. If you can, tell me." Apparently he expected me to say that even I could not. "We can't baptize these guys, they are just pretending to be Christians," I said sternly and made several Afghan young men go back. I stopped them from receiving the baptism because I could recognize the spirit in them. During the sermons, they laughed and talked and that had happened more than once. I asked them to share their joke, so that we could all have a good laugh, but they smirked and kept quiet. They saw that they couldn't play their tricks on me, and I found out that they went to another church to get baptized later on. Afterward, I saw them on the street and they admitted, "We figured out you won't let us get baptized, and we found another way. We needed a baptism certificate. Just in case, if they stopped us on the way to Germany." These guys were not the only ones I took the initiative to stop from being baptized; all because of my zeal. However, God softened my heart and reminded me that I was not completely honest at the start of my walk with Christ either. I could not be the judge… That right was not given to any person, the right to judge another person's relationship with God. That's why I stopped interfering; I stopped intervening, and let God be the judge. My job was different - not to judge but to help.

I liked helping refugees, prisoners, and drug addicts the most. I took the addicts to RETO[10]. I found them to be the best. When I found drug addicts in the dens around the neighborhoods, and I knew where most of them were, I took them right to RETO. Sometimes, they did not want to come and ran away, and since I hada prosthesis, it was hard for me to chase them. However, my great perseverance helped, and I caught them. Some needed more time to be convinced, but at the end, all of them agreed to go. The staff from RETO was and is still great. They

[10] RETO means *Hope*. It is a non-profit organisation similar to Teen Challenge, a Christian Centre to help addicts free of charge

also have stores where the drug addicts undergoing treatment can work. In those stores, they themselves learn how to make a lot of things; they work hard and really help out, and that is why I respected and supported them, although I never quite liked the word, "drug addicts." It's not that it was not correct, it was. Drugs could cause a heavy dependency, no question about that. However, drug addicts are not the only addicts. There are so many addictions. I had been among many people, and I had seen it all. Some people are addicted to soccer games, others are addicted to soap operas – both of these addictions are still very dangerous! Anything that allows you to hide from unfavorable situations cannot produce good fruit! There are so many other addictions that nobody talks about, and that's why those are almost impossible to treat. Besides, not all addictions are bad. For example, I am addicted to God and fitness. I can't fall asleep until I pray and do my push-ups. Even if I am very tired... it is only after I have prayed that I can fall asleep with my body half on the bed and half on the floor. Sometimes, I'll wake up during the night and realize that I'd fallen asleep in that way, so I pulled myself up to my bed and went back to sleep. That was another dependency – whether we wanted it or not, we had to sleep. So it's not about having a dependency or not, because we all have dependencies. The only freedom is to choose what you'll be dependent on. Addictions steal that freedom. That's the freedom of choice, yet it doesn't mean it's easy... Most of the time, living in freedom is a hard thing.

I want to go back tojail!

Once Ivodor called me and said, "Ali, you should go to the Central Prison immediately!"

"What's going on?" I asked.

"After serving his sentence, one of the inmates has been released, but he's in front of the prison and doesn't want to budge. He keeps knocking on the door, asking to be let back in"

"Poor guy!" I could imagine how he felt.

"He doesn't know what to do now that he's out and wants to go back; he's gotten too used to the life in jail, and he likes it in there. Please, go and help. The officers don't know what to do. That's why they called me, but I am out of town, and this is an emergency."

I was off, rushing to the prison. My heart was aching. I knew the kind of fear that man must have been feeling, fear of freedom, of light... Prison was like a magnet; it attracts you once you've heard that evil voice tell you that you are doomed to go back. Prisoners are like blind sparrows, crushed by the darkness. They are all transformed into bats who can't handle light anymore... However, deep down in their hearts, their soul searches for the light. We are not bats; we've been created for the light. I knew this very well because I, myself, was a bat before. That's why I ran to that prison. I could see that man, leaning against the wall, not wanting to budge. It was as if he was glued to the wall. He was not in prison any longer, but the prison was inside of him, keeping him locked in the invisible cell of fear.

"Hello, I am Ali," I came close to him and extended my hand for a handshake. I couldn't remember if I had seen him before.

"I don't know you," he was looking at me with distrust.

"I recently got out. I know what it's like." In a few words, I told him who I was, and why I was coming to see him.

His distrust began to disappear from his eyes, and now he was ready to take my hand.

"I'm scared," he blurted out, helplessly, "It's scary being out."

"I know, brother, I know. Is this your luggage?"

"I am a thief, I can't do anything else. I'll be going in anyway, so what's the point of coming out?" he continued as though he hadn't heard a word of what I had just said.

"I've been there, brother, I have... Is this your luggage?"

"Yes, it is," he looked at his bag, then at me. "How did you deal with it? How have you overcome it?"

"Come, come with me to the cafe across the street and I will tell you everything. Here, let me help you with the suitcase," I was speaking to him gently, trying to yank him away from the magnetic pull of the prison.

"I got this," he replied, still checking me out, and he took his bag in his hand.

We ordered some coffee, and I began to tell him. "In the name of Jesus Christ, the King of peace, come with me. You can stay with me for a while, you will be among friends. Trust me, I have been where you are coming from." He was smoking, staring out right in front of him, as if he was not even hearing me. I was about to lose hope when he got up, picked up the duffel bag, and turning toward me, he said, "Where to?" And together, we headed to the Mission.

Male attention is very dangerous!

I had brought quite a few people there just to spend some time in a safe place until they decided when and where to head off. One could not make them come, and one could not make them stay either. The most unfortunate example was this girl, Ghazal, a 25-year-old Afghan, whose beauty fully matched her name ("deer" in Persian, author's note). Men would drop their conversations and turn their heads in her direction whenever she passed by. It spoke only of impending trouble. I had told her to be careful and to stop flirting, because when the deer is found in a situation like hers, it becomes a very easy prey for the jackals. Instead of being more careful, she did the opposite – she carried herself provocatively and did everything to attract men's attention increasingly. I saw it, and I invited her to come with me to the Mission. That same night, Angel Kovachev, Ivodor's son, and his friends hosted a concert dedicated to the Iranian group in the church. All the way to the concert, she flirted with me. When we reached the meeting place, I turned to her and told her:

"I've listened to you all the way here, now you listen to me very carefully. I want you to end the flirting and to stop hitting on the men around you. I have brought you here because you are not going to be in danger here. Whether you will become a Christian or continue your Muslim faith is your own choice. But here you are safe!"

I could see in her eyes that she understood what I was saying. Later, she came one more time, after which she suddenly disappeared and stopped answering her phone. Some friends told me she had met this smuggler, an Afghan, and had moved in with him. Later, I got some other news – she had gotten transferred to another smuggler in Serbia, under the pretext they would help her get to Germany. Once she got to Subotica, Serbia, she was locked in a room and forced into prostitution – providing services to 10–20 men a day... Whoever used this smuggler, also used her service. My heart dropped – didn't I tell her? I did! How could she be so gullible?! Anyway, I found a way to send information to the Serbian police through some friends of mine there. They rang me later, and let me know that they had arrested the smuggler, and that she had been freed. Since then, I hadn't heard anything about Ghazal. So I decided I needed to be more explicit. That's when this Iranian family contacted me. They had been released from the Lubimec camp and had to leave for Germany right away. Their daughter was still in the camp due to some problems with her papers, but the smugglers had told them that unless the two of them left right then, they would lose the money that they had already paid. They had none left. So they were pleading with me:

"You are the only person we trust! Please look after our daughter and don't let her go to Germany with creeps!"

"Once I find out when the next group made of families and children is leaving, I will send her with them, so they could look after her like their own child," I tried to reassure them.

Their daughter was a sweet and beautiful 18-year-old girl, but she looked even younger. She came to my place a week after she was released from the camp, asking me:

"Uncle Ali, did my parents leave anything for me?"

"Yes, they did – some money, clothes, and a little bag with some make-up."

"Can you please give me the bag with the make-up?" she asked me, impatiently.

I gave it to her, and said:

"Listen, if I had a daughter, she would have been older than you. I want to ask you one thing – do you want me to help you or do you think you can handle this by yourself?"

"I can't do it alone. Please help me!"

"I will help you on one condition – if I am taking the responsibility, I must have authority. No matter what I tell you, I don't want to hear a no in return."

"Okay," she agreed.

Since she agreed, I took the bag with all the make-up from her hands, and threw it away in the bin.

"Wait, uncle Ali, why are you throwing my make-up away?"

"We had an arrangement, right?" I challenged her. "If you want, take your make-up and go, it's your will. If not, forget about it. The less you attract men's attention, the safer it is for you. The refugees travelling to Western Europe are like a flock, and there are lots of wolves lurking along the way, looking to tear apart and eat. Women are the easiest prey for them. I have heard many stories, and I know a lot of things – I don't want you to fall into their hands, because they will take advantage of you and will treat you like dirt."

I didn't mention anything about Ghazal, but I could tell by the look in her eyes that she understood my point, and that I didn't have to explain any further. I hoped that she would listen to me.

"This is my first condition," I continued. "My second condition is that you stay in Sofia until I find a family that is about to leave, and then you can leave with them. I don't do smuggling, and I'm not making anyone leave Bulgaria to go to Germany. However, I do have enough information and know enough people to tell what is safe for you and what is not. You will leave when and with whom I say after I assess the situation. You got this?"

I'll pay you. Just find me a smuggler!

She nodded – that meant we had reached an agreement. A few days later, she left with a group that was safe for her. After arriving in Germany, her family sent me a photo – all of them together, smiling and cuddling. That photo meant so much to me! I had another photo that was quite special as well – of Layla and Sahid. "I'll pay you, just find me a smuggler!" Layla had asked me. Layla was a tall Iranian beauty with big dark eyes and a slender figure; I met her in one of the camps.

I told her about the conditions I had told Terme's parents, "I can help you, but I don't do smuggling, and I don't want money." Then I invited her and her little boy, who was about 10 years old, to come to the meetings of the Iranian Christian group at the Mission.

"But I'm not a Christian," she said, looking at me skeptically.

"It doesn't matter; there's nothing to worry about," I explained, "You'll be safe there, among fellow countrymen. Whether you're a Christian or not, it's your own business and choice."

While I was waiting for a call for another reliable group of serious people, I talked to her brother in Belgium.

"I can't have peace until my dear sister and nephew come here. I'm so worried about them and so scared that they might get hurt along the way..."

"I'll do whatever I can for their safety."

"I'll be forever grateful to you."

"No, it's not me that you should be grateful to, but to Christ. Without my faith in Christ, I would have been in one of these camps right now."

That was it – I didn't say anything else, and he didn't ask. I got the impression that everything was clear to him. A month later, after Layla and her son had arrived and had reunited with her brother's family, I received a photo of them on Facebook. Sahid called me to say thank you:

"I was wrecked with worries until I they were both safe and sound here with us. I'll be forever grateful to you. There's something in you that I thought had long disappeared. You refused to take money from her, and you didn't take advantage of her as a woman… Something that all the rest did."

Some time passed by. Sahid called me again to tell me he'd become a Christian and has been attending a Christian church. Layla was still a Muslim, but their brother-sister relationship was wonderful. "It's great. After all you are related, you have to love each other," I told him.

At the right time, there's salvation for everyone. One can't forever resist the selfless love of God. This love wins people over and opens doors, even those that are unexpected. Through the Mission, I was getting contacted more and more often for help by humanitarian organizations. There was even a club established by the wives of some diplomats that was getting involved and showing great support. Organizations supporting refugees contacted me as well. I told them about Christ too, but they kind of resisted, and were closed up to the good news. I could understand, and I stopped pushing it in their faces – their time hadn't come yet. I needed patience.

The most difficult part of it for me has been when people are impressed by the reflection of Christ's light in my life, but they refuse to open their hearts to the very source of that light, Christ Himself.

Nevertheless, I know what had happened to me in prison once I became a believer. I've seen how light scatters the darkness. I've seen how even the worst criminals – the ringleaders of the most hardened criminals – have knelt down to pray.

I've seen how everything takes its own time, and it's all for the Glory of God.

There is this one thing I believe – every knee shall bow down before Jesus Christ.

Many Eyes are Fixed on You!

Years have passed by since that day when soon after I was released from prison, an old preacher approached me and looked into my eyes. I didn't understand what this stranger wanted from me – why he tried to avoid the spotlight and the hundreds of people gathered in that big auditorium. He found me right there on the last row and slowly said the following words to me:

"There are two roads you can take – the old one or the new one. It's in your hands which one you'll choose. However, remember one thing – no matter which one you choose, there are many eyes fixed on you."

Today my road took me to the prison again. After all these years of freedom, the prison gates opened, and I stepped in. I knew that doorstep so very well. Some of my cell mates were still in, others, who still took drugs and used to buy dope from me. However, today I was about to bring them something else, being armed not with weapons but with love, faith, and compassion. After waiting patiently, today, for the first time, I had permission to stand in front of my fellow brothers and tell them my story – the story of the new Ali and who he is beyond the walls of this building. I stoodin the front, looking at them, and I said:

"Brothers, each one of us has a burden to carry, this is our life. Some of you know me from my old life and can tell the others how big and heavy my burden of sins was. Anyway, I won't talk about the old Ali. I'll tell you about God's love that doesn't know any limits. I'll tell you about God's mercy revealed to a man born in Islam. Christ reached out for me, the Muslim, and pulled me out from the pit where I had fallen. Won't He show even greater mercy to you, who have been born as Christians? Won't Christ's sacrifice be valid for the ones who are born Christians even more than the ones born into Islam?

Brothers, be brave to open your heart for the mighty name of Christ – the mightiest name under the sun – it transforms people's fate, through faith in Him, our souls can get saved from sin. If I was saved through Him, so can you! All you have to do is give Him room in your heart, and He will start changing things around you and within you. Take the first step, which is faith in Christ, and you'll see darkness withdrawing away from you. Then comes the second important step: your works, because people will judge you not according to your words, but according to your works. You'll have to be patient because people won't accept your justification blindly and accept you, even if you have been justified in court. Anyway, you have to be confident you'll surely succeed with Christ. You have no other choice but to succeed! With Christ, you'll always bear good fruit, and that speaks louder than your words. A person's works have a loud voice, brothers! Their voice reaches far, far beyond! If I cry right now, my voice will reach as far as the corridor. If I go out and shout, they'll hear me in the neighborhood. The human voice has a limit, but the voice of the good works can reach the other side of the world! It can even surpass the limits of this world!"

I looked at them as I spoke – each one of them. One of them had his face cupped with his hands and was leaning forward; another one was looking as if his life depended on what I was saying – and he was right, because his life did depend on it. Yet, another was leaning back, squinting his eyes, and the fourth one was scratching himself on the head, wondering if I was talking to him. I could discern the spirit of unbelief and despair hovering around them, but the Spirit of hope and salvation was there as well, waiting. Which spirit would they choose? What road would they take?

253

I called upon people who wished for me to pray for them. I knelt down in prayer, most of them also knelt down and repeated the words after me. I stood up and looked at them again. They reminded me of a National Geographic documentary about caterpillars – they had created a cocoon and lived in it all that while, spinning their own prison and having forgotten about the wide world outside. What a limitless and amazing world they could have had! But they could not see it. All they had to do was tear the cocoon and breakthrough, and they would surely turn into something very beautiful. However, if they never got out of their cocoons, they were sure to rot inside and die. Thatwas how the situation was with the guys in front of me – if only they could tear apart their old world of pain and suffering, criminal intentions, fears, and nightmares they carried for themselves and others – if only they would let the Word of God and Christ change them...

That's why I'll surely keep going back there – to help them tear that cocoon from the outside and encourage them as they try to do the same from the inside. Because in all these ugly, grey cocoon prisons, there are all beautiful, new people on the inside. I know it! I know it so well! And that's why, I, Ali the Believer, have shared my story in this book to bring hope where there's despair, light where there is darkness, and faith where there's doubt.

Of course, the good works keep speaking.
I believe if you haven't heard about them yet, you will soon!
You might even read about them... well, why not?

Where are the people from the book today?

An active member of a church, **Ali Dini** constantly works with refugees and drug addicts as well as looks after prisoners and their social adaptation after they are released from the prison. He also leads the church meetings for the Iranians and Afghans, and that occupies his time almost all of his evenings. During the day, he visits refugee camps and boarding houses in the village of Lubimec and Sofia.

Ali has a dream of establishing a big Christian community center in Sofia, where people in trouble can be provided with warm food and the Word of God. He deeply believes that the establishment of such a center will not take long. He's convinced that the time when he will be taking Christian missionaries to Islamic countries like Turkey and Iran is coming soon.

Pastor **IvodorKovachev** continues his mission to serve in prisons and work with convicts, drug addicts, and other dangerous social groups. The Mission Protestant Church (www.missiata.org) and the Mission Salvation Foundation that he founded are constantly increasing their field of activities and are incorporating more and more community responsibilities within the realm of their services. Their latest big project is the Palace of the Happy People in the Mladost-1 neighborhood in Sofia.

KalinGaitanjiev – Pali-Motora (literally, Fire the Engine) doesn't hold that office anymore and has left the Corrections Department completely.

Diana Radoslavova, together with her family, is currently doing missionary work in Arousha, Tanzania, as a part of the Canadian Mission Pamoja Ministries (www.pamoja.info). Even from a distance, she continues to be involved with her foundation Centre for Legal Aid – Voice in Bulgaria. After spending two years in Africa, she'll be returning to her home country, Bulgaria.

Afsaneh has been living in Australia with her family for a long time now.

Neriman (Nelly Angelova) lives and works in Hamburg and uses most of her spare time to work in collaboration with the Mission, Ali, and IvodorKovachev.

Mahboube, Ali's mother, is still alive and well in Iran and is at peace that her son has long stopped partaking in illegal activities. That's why she doesn't ring him as much as she used to in the past.